Reading Dante

Reading Dante

GIUSEPPE MAZZOTTA

Yale

UNIVERSITY PRESS

New Haven and London

Yale University Press books may be purchased in quantity for educational,
business, or promotional use. For information, please e-mail
sales.press@yale.edu (U.S. office) or sales@yaleup.co.uk (U.K. office).

Excerpts from Dante's *Divine Comedy* are taken from the following
editions, translated and with commentary by Charles S. Singleton:
Divine Comedy: Inferno © 1970 Princeton University Press, 1998
renewed. Reprinted by permission of Princeton University Press.
Divine Comedy: Purgatorio © 1991 Princeton University Press. Reprinted
by permission of Princeton University Press.
Divine Comedy: Paradiso © 1975 Princeton University Press, 2003
renewed, 1991 paperback edition. Reprinted by Princeton University Press.

Set in Minion type by Westchester Book Group.
Printed in the United States of America.

Library of Congress Cataloging-in-Publication Data

Mazzotta, Giuseppe, 1942–
    Reading Dante / Giuseppe Mazzotta.
        pages cm.— (The Open Yale Courses Series)
    Includes bibliographical references and index.
    ISBN 978-0-300-19135-6 (pbk. : alk. paper)   1. Dante Alighieri,
1265–1321—Criticism and interpretation.   2. Dante Alighieri, 1265–1321—
Appreciation.   I. Title.
    PQ4390.M544 2014
    851'.1—dc23

                                                        2013024101

A catalogue record for this book is available from the British Library.

This paper meets the requirements of ANSI/NISO Z39.48-1992
(Permanence of Paper).

10 9 8 7 6 5 4 3 2

I dedicate this book with love to my grandchildren:
Peter, Dasha, Giuseppe Khaleel, and Azura Marie

Contents

Preface

In the fall of 2008 I complied with a request to have my Dante in Translation course videotaped in the Open Yale Courses series. It is a course that I began teaching in 1969, when I was on the faculty of Cornell University, and I have been teaching it ever since, with very few occasional intermissions in between.

Over all these years (as is my wont with all other courses), I have taught without notes. This habit has one definite advantage but also at least one big disadvantage. The disadvantage is clear: my "oral" style does not directly translate into the legible prose it has become in this book thanks to the extraordinary talent for creative writing of Taylor Papallo. Taylor has masterfully transformed the nebulous approximations of the transcripts of my course's twenty-four lectures into faultless English, and I gratefully acknowledge my debt to him. Above all, he and I have decided to keep in this book the skeleton structure, indeed the rhythm (the movement of a sentence, repetition, cadence, the improvisation, and so on), of a spoken talk.

On the other hand, one obvious stylistic advantage in the adoption of the conversational, informal tone of the classroom is that it allowed me to cut to a bare minimum the use of technical, philosophical language and to engage in spur-of-the-moment, extemporaneous, offhand remarks and interpretations. Plainly, in a book the act of improvisation, which we usually link with impromptu musical or poetic performances or the comic theater, typically finishes in mere contrivance or fiction, however desirable it may be for the sense of immediacy it conveys. The qualities associated with oral communication were replaced in this book by what could be called a deliberate artlessness. I have deployed this rhetorical mode not because I meant to write a "popular" book on the *Divine Comedy,* but because I think that Dante did write a poem that would be "sung" in public and would be suitable to all, to the scholars, the philosophers, the friars and the popes, political figures as well as "everyman" in the streets of medieval cities. As is known, the poem represents a wide assortment of characters, styles (the high, the low, the plain, and their mixtures), schools of thought, theological perspectives, and diverse social and political backgrounds.

To represent this variety of experiences, disciplines, and political-theological questions Dante self-consciously invents a new poetic language, which amounts to saying that he shaped a new way of thinking, one that transcends the traditional oppositions between philosophy, poetry, and theology. The premise of the *Divine Comedy*, which was written in the "vulgar tongue," in Italian and not in Latin, so that a simple woman or a man at the lower end of the social ladder would understand, is that, however divergent and contradictory the exchanges and discourses among characters are, however mixed its style (lyrical songs, invectives, moral teachings, dialogues, prayers, and so on), they are all bound in a "conversation" with one another. It is a conversation that is born of familiarity and yet cannot be understood within the horizon of what is familiar. Dante has a way of turning all fixed conceptions about the values of the familiar and the known upside down, as readers discover that they are—that we are—at sea, disoriented or lost, and that the poem challenges and puts into question all that has been taken for granted as final (politics, justice, the illusoriness of limits and of the boundaries of the various worlds that are represented, the senses of history, knowledge as transgression, the failure of political and religious authority, freedom and its values, and so on).

This call to the iconoclastic, critical self-reflection that the poem unfolds suggests that, hermeneutically speaking, the *Divine Comedy* resists popularization. There is always something else, something more, in every line of the poem, and the palimpsests behind the overtness of the literal sense force us readers to launch headlong into the "more" that the poem offers. Beginning with the central canticle of the poem, Dante tries to chart the course for the pilgrim himself; he will do so again for the fewer brave sea-voyagers in Paradise, and, again, eventually for those the poet refers to as the "people of the future": in reality, he wants his poem to become the everyman's *vademecum,* as a way of making possible what we see from the edges, the limits and the limitlessness of the human. The poem guides the reader in acknowledging one's actual place in the world and in wanting to find that place by breaking out of the prison of the self and its mirrors. Individually first, but also as members of the pilgrim Church, he hopes his readers will discover that they all have in common something profound: they all take different routes in a common pursuit, at the end of which it is possible to look into the knot where the human and the divine are bound together.

In short, for Dante there is nothing more fascinating than a conversation, as those waiting for a banquet to start know. It is the time when we see ourselves in another and another in ourselves.

Finally, I would like to express my thanks to the Open Yale Courses for inviting me to participate in this venture.

CHAPTER 1

Lectio Brevis

I'd like to begin with a brief introduction, what was once called a *lectio brevis* in the classroom setting, to the contents of this book and those of Dante's texts and to the context of these contents—the context within which Dante thrives, grows, and writes his poem, a poem that, as you know, is called the *Divine Comedy*. First of all, the well-known title I just mentioned is not actually the title that Dante gives to his poem. Dante calls the poem simply "comedy." "Divine" is the epithet that readers throughout the centuries have assigned to it, to indicate both what struck them as the sublime quality of this text and also the content therein. The poem deals, after all, with the imaginary journey of a pilgrim, an ordinary man living in the thirteenth or fourteenth century, to God—divine content, indeed.

The *Comedy* is the story of nothing less than seeing God face to face and coming back to tell the tale. Seeing God, being overwhelmed and dazzled by God, places the text squarely in a tradition of visionary literature, but here I will emphasize the writing of the poem about this fundamental experience. So, what kind of poem is this? What is its genre? Is it an epic? Is it an autobiography? Is it a romance? I think it's all of the above. Perhaps the best term for it is *encyclopedia,* a word that means a "circle of knowledge," representing a classical idea that derives from Vitruvius, who wrote of the genre. This idea of circularity is crucial, in the sense that to know something you have to have a point of departure, from which you will pass through all the various disciplines of the liberal arts, only to arrive right back where you started. The beginning and the ending in a liberal education must coincide, but you will find out things along the way that allow you to see with a different viewpoint or perspective.

So Dante has written an encyclopedia, taken to ordering a tradition of liberal arts. But what are these liberal arts? The liberal arts are the arts of words (as opposed to the arts of numbers like arithmetic, geometry, music, astronomy), and they include grammar, which also encompasses poetry and history; dialectics, or the art of deciding what the truth of a statement may be; and rhetoric, or the art of persuasion. The aim of these liberal arts is to arrive at ethics, metaphysics, and theology. And why are they called liberal? They are called liberal to distinguish them from the so-called mechanical arts, an old medieval distinction, and they are also called liberal because their aim is to free us. It's as if knowledge contains within itself the power to give us some form of freedom, to free us from various sorts of tyranny: the tyranny of action, above all, the tyranny of having to do things with your hands that will distract you from the great aims of theory, contemplation, and thinking. So, the implication of calling the *Divine Comedy* an encyclopedia is that clearly it deals with education, with the path to knowledge. The aim of any encyclopedia is to educate its readers.

But Dante's poem is also an autobiography, the tale of the poet's own quest for knowledge, for it reveals the process by which he comes to know the world around himself. And what kind of question is Dante asking about the world around him? Dante raises a number of political, philosophical, and ethical questions in a very lucid and probing manner. What is justice in the world? How do the claims of justice go along with the realities of passions and the collision of conflicting desires? Do I know things, and am I all right on account of (or in spite of) what I know? Is my will really weak? If we know what we *should* be doing, then we all know we should be just, but that alone does not really make us just, right?

In order to attempt to answer these and other questions, Dante goes on writing a poem, which is about a literal voyage to Hell, in order to demonstrate that you can get out of Hell (literally or metaphorically) and rearrange your old vision of the world and yourself. Because every time you talk about ethics or politics, the real questions being asked are: "Who am I?" "What am I doing to come to some kind of understanding of the world around me?"

Of course, we can't begin to understand that question from Dante's perspective until we know something about the world around Dante. As a result, I'll now turn briefly to a discussion of the concrete context of Dante's life, the contours of his existence. Dante Alighieri was born in 1265 in Florence, a city inhabited by seventy thousand people by the time that Dante was of school age. He was born into a family that he would claim was nobility, but which actually was quite impoverished, and Dante is known to have been embarrassed by the activities of his father. Dante never mentions his progenitor, but we know from poems that others had written against the poet, attacking Dante and his genealogy, that the father was accused of usury; he loaned money at a very high interest rate. So, we have a possibly unhappy domestic sphere within the wider realm of thirteenth-century Florence, the context of Dante's childhood.

While still a child, Dante experienced two critical private events. The first is that by the time Dante was eight years old, his mother died. The second, slightly connected to the first, is that when he was nine years old, he met a young woman: it is as if he could not but transfer onto the newly found girl the love for the lost mother. He doesn't even know what her name is, or at least that's the fiction he wants us to believe, since he probably knew the name of his neighbor, but at any rate, he calls her Beatrice. These two events can be interpreted as intertwined through a sort of psychological transfer onto this young woman of the love Dante feels toward or wanted from his mother, for he talks about Beatrice as if she were a mother to him. He describes her in the poem using very maternal language, a language of great generosity, the language of the generosity of love.

Dante lives through these two critical events in Florence, and then he goes to school, beginning his education with seven thousand Florentine boys and girls in the public schools that were available to them. Of all the teachers Dante encounters at this school, only one stands out to him, only one gets pointed out in the *Comedy,* a man by the name of Brunetto Latini, whom Dante places in Hell. Many students want to send their teachers to Hell (not my pupils, of course), but Dante actually does it. Who was this man? Why was he important enough for Dante to include in his poem? If you go to Florence and read the memorial stones that are all over the walls of the city, Brunetto Latini is remembered as one of those who civilized the city of Florence. How? Well, he was a rhetorician first and foremost, in the Ciceronian tradition (he actually translated and commented on Cicero's rhetorical works). He was a rhetorician who believed that politics and rhetoric go hand in hand, that political problems are ultimately problems of speech and argument, that rhetoric is the art of persuasion in parliament and in the streets of the city, where large decisions can be made and reached.

This was the essential work of Brunetto Latini, bringing together rhetoric and politics. Dante admires him especially because he is a teacher who gets involved in the political realities of Florence, and Dante wants to follow him in turn.

Brunetto Latini dies while Dante is still young, of course, but in 1290 Dante decides to follow in Latini's footsteps and enter the political life himself. It was his greatest mistake because political life in Florence meant being in the throes of harsh partisan battles between two factions known as the Guelphs and the Ghibellines. The distinctions between these two groups are not so clear-cut: the Guelphs were supposedly those who believed in loyalty to the Church, while the Ghibellines believed in loyalty to the empire, but this sharply separated division of loyalties to the two major institutions of the time is overly simplistic. At any rate, Dante becomes an ambassador for the city of Florence and starts to travel all over the place, much as Latini had done, but he finds himself caught in the middle of this factional war, and when he is sent to the pope in 1302, he is banned from returning to the city. Machinations had taken place, so that Dante's property is confiscated and there is a threat placed on his head, a threat that should he be caught returning to Florence he will be put to death.

So, 1302 marks the beginning of Dante's new education and new experiences. He goes into exile, an exile which was deemed at the time to be the severest possible condemnation of an individual. The medieval idea was that the inherent value of an individual depended on the position that the individual occupied in the city. Thus, to be without a city, to hold no place within the city, is to be nothing. As a result, Dante goes begging from one city to the next, maybe even traveling as far as Paris, but exile, this harshest of punishments, turned out to be a blessing in disguise, as well. A blessing because it removed Dante from any sense of loyalty to partisan viewpoints. He was no longer a Guelph or a Ghibelline, he was no longer caught in these wars, he was now able to occupy a transcendent point of view.

Ultimately, then, this is the true story of the *Divine Comedy*. Dante died in 1321 in Ravenna, where he was buried, so he wrote the entire poem in exile, and the poem came out of his experience of exile. The *Divine Comedy* is the story of how exile allows one to see best what the problems of cities can be. It is the story of how one can go from perceiving the world in a partial, provisional, fragmentary manner to pulling that world together and seeing it in its totality. In exile, he started one project that aimed to find a possibility of unifying all the languages of Italy, he wrote a political text about the necessity of unifying the world with the empire, but the real process of unifying all of his experiences is to be found in the *Divine Comedy*.

But before we get to this poem written in and of exile, we will turn to a discussion of another great work by Dante, a work inspired by another meeting with Beatrice: the *Vita nuova*.

CHAPTER 2
Vita Nuova

Dante's first work was the *Vita nova,* or *nuova.* I could say that it was his first finished work, but in a way it's not finished; it's a deliberately unfinished work. Many of Dante's works remain unfinished. He interrupts them, as he breaks off and decides to move on to other projects. This is the case with the philosophical *Convivio* (Banquet). It is true for his text on language, the *De vulgari eloquentia* (On Eloquence in the Vernacular). And it is also true, in a way, with the *Vita nuova.* The text ends with a vision, but we don't know what will happen after this conclusion. There is a kind of suspension that occurs. At any rate, we cannot call it finished, but we may call this the first full work that Dante writes.

The title means "a new life," which probably refers to Dante's youth, for the work describes the autobiographical account of Dante as a young lover, as the poet who falls in love with Beatrice. You may recall that I referred to their encounter, which occurred in his early life, soon after the death of his mother, as a decisive event for Dante. What is interesting in the text is that Dante describes this love for Beatrice, but he also subsequently describes her death. As a result, Dante the pilgrim, the lover, the poet, goes on to record the confusion and the sense of loss that ensues in the wake of Beatrice's death. His betrayals become an ethical drama, as most lyrical poetry of the Middle Ages does, and then he ends up having his final vision. So, there is youth, there is a new life, but there is also death, and this youthful new life will thus be seen to be a multifaceted signifier, the various meanings of which the narrative will be shown to sustain. Besides "new," the Italian *nuova* means "surprising," "unexpected," even "strange," "novel," "marvelous," and this variety of meanings gives a certain direction to the way in which we should read the story. Primarily, we have to accept that all of these meanings are true as we move forward.

At the same time, the novelty and strangeness are paired with "life," that is to say with autobiography, which literally means "writing about myself." So, I should say a few things about this structure and the questions it raises before we get into the narrative as such. From one point of view, we might all agree easily that the text belongs to a tradition of Provençal poets, if you know that they would often write about what they would call *vida*—life, a word that lingers in modern Spanish. These poets, among them Jaufré Rudel, would write their poems and append a brief account of their lives to their works.

Let's say, then, that in the *Vita nuova* Dante is writing about himself and inserting the poems as part of the texture of his own life. As an autobiography, though, the text also echoes and is modeled on the most important autobiography written in the Middle Ages. In fact, it was written by a man who could be called the founder of the autobiographical genre, St. Augustine, who wrote *The Confessions*. A confession, which is a witnessing, is really, in this case, part of the story of his life, from his childhood in Africa; to his growing up as a gifted young philosopher-turned-rhetorician; to his move to Rome, where he becomes a teacher despised and paid by his students; to another move to Milan, where the narrative's climactic conversion takes place. This particular conversion is achieved in a garden and leads into a discussion of the hermeneutics of the biblical Genesis, as if the new life that he found through the conversion could only issue into a commentary about all beginnings.

Furthermore, the whole idea of autobiography for Augustine is that it coincides with a conversion. I can say that Augustine is fully aware that autobiography is, in effect, the same thing as a conversion because autobiography demands two voices all the time. It is necessarily ambivalent—it demands the voice of the narrator who is outside the narrative and who can look back. The mode of writing autobiographies is always retrospection: I look back at my life and try to figure out what are the stages, what are the events, what is it that makes me the person that I am now. As a result, there's a necessary distance between the voice of the protagonist and that of the narrator, who knows more than what the protagonist knew. You may have the most abbreviated version of an autobiography, that is to say a journal or a diary, and you may go home at night and jot down all the great events of the day, but you may overlook the most important one. You may have had a meeting with someone, you may have caught sight of some

person, who will reenter your life ten years from now and give an altogether different direction to your life. All autobiographical experiments,
like all diary entries, are uncertain and fundamentally false because you
can only write about what you know at that point and you can never really
write about the whole structure of your life. To be able to write about the
structure of your life, you have to die, which is Augustine's ultimate idea of
conversion here. It's a symbolic death by means of which you come back
into existence, you come back into life as a new man with a new life, and
only from that standpoint can you have all the necessary detachment to
look at your past and decipher that which was previously in a haze.

The other reason you need this double voice in autobiographies is obvious. Because if I go on writing about my life without any sense of what my
life is about, can you imagine what happens? I end up writing down every
single thing that I do, which means that I would need another life to be able
to say, "Well, I got up in the morning, then I brushed my teeth . . ." and so
on. It becomes a random, senseless accumulation of facts without any particular meaning or direction. Not to say that this is what we see in the autobiographical writings that precede Augustine, the most powerful of which
for Augustine are the Psalms of King David, which display a kind of reflection, a turning inward, while they try to pinpoint his shifts in mood, moral
judgments, temptations, the idea of his own system. But even this method
is really only an internalization of one's life. Augustine will go into the interiority of his self, into the interiority of his consciousness, but he will also
describe what has happened to him in the public space. Thus, the dual voice
persists as he goes inside and outside all the time.

Dante's *Vita nuova* is a really complicated text from this point of
view: while it is an autobiography, it is amazing how little he actually tells
us about his own life. There is nothing concrete about this text. We know
that it takes place in Florence, but Florence is not even mentioned. We only
infer that it's Florence because at one point there's a description of a river
that crosses by it. And in fact, Dante uses this image primarily because he
has had an inspiration, and his words come to him with the same kind of
strength and naturalness with which the waters of the river flow.

So, what is Dante really doing here? It's a little abstract. It's kind of an
enigmatic account, unlike that of Augustine, beginning with a reference to
the book of memory: "In my book of memory, in the early part where there
is little to be read, there comes a chapter with the rubric: *Incipit vita nova.*
It is my intention to copy into this little book the words I find written under
that heading—if not all of them, at least the essence of their meaning."[1]

First of all, it's a *book* of memory, not necessarily an act of retrospection, and memory has a number of other implications and dangers. What are the implications? Well, Dante is writing this when he's twenty-four or twenty-five years old; it's a provisional retrospection of his growth as a poet. He certainly knows the famous Greek myth that memory, Mnemosyne, lay with Jupiter for nine successive nights and from their copulations the nine muses came into being, so Memory is the mother of the Muses, which means that art is always an act of remembrance. There are also some dangers on which Dante will reflect at length, such as the fact that if you get caught up in the activity of memory, you run a serious risk, namely that of changing your sense of life and reality into phantasms. The Greeks used to place memory in the heart, and as you may know, in Italian we still say *ricordarsi*, "to remember," which contains the etymology of the heart—*cor/cordis*. But in the Middle Ages memory is already part of the imagination; it's called the eye of the imagination, which means that it has a visionary component to it. Still, with memory it's like you're always looking backward, and you're not Janus-like, you don't look in all directions, you don't look ahead. As a result, Dante will ultimately turn against memory.

The second thing that we get from that little exordium at the outset of the text is that Dante finds words that have been the inscriptions of memory, and he's not going to repeat them all, only some of them. We know that Dante has cast himself as the editor of his own book; that's the double structure of this little text of his. The text is full of doubles: it's a book of poetry, and it's a book of prose. It's not an unusual structure: Boethius' *Consolation of Philosophy* is written like that. Dante also writes other texts like that, but what are the implications of this form? Well, there's a lyrical self who has been in the throes of a great passion for Beatrice, who struggles sometimes with his inspiration, who waits. And that's the crisis he has: he's always waiting for words to come to him, always waiting for Beatrice to say hello to him. There is a way in which he casts himself as a passive protagonist, weak-willed, unable, believing that the will can direct him wherever the will wants. But he finally understands that he had better get out of that mode, and in effect, just talking about the formal structure now, the whole text is written in the past mode, a commemoration of a great event in the private life of Dante, the love that he cannot even define, the woman he did not even know. He doesn't even know what passion is, and part of the tension of this text is his attempt to understand what passion means and what it is that it's doing to him and to his mind.

By the end of the text, chapter 41, we read a sonnet about the famous vision of Beatrice sitting at the foot of God's throne, and Dante decides he has to go there to meet her. He says, "After I wrote this sonnet there came to me a miraculous vision in which I saw things"—a visionary burden of the narrative is maintained throughout—"that made me resolve to say no more about this blessed one until I would be capable of writing about her in a nobler way." It should be noted here that "blessed" in Italian, *beata,* is a pun on the name of Beatrice, the one who is blessed, the one who is the bearer of the good. He can't write more about her now, since he needs to do more work first. So, he will stop. That's what I call an inevitably unfinished narrative. "To achieve this I am striving as hard as I can, and this she truly knows. Accordingly, if it be the pleasure of Him through whom all things live that my life continue for a few more years, I hope to write of her that which has never been written before of any other woman. And then it may please the One who is the Lord of graciousness that my soul ascend to behold the glory of its lady, that is, of that blessed Beatrice, who in glory contemplates the countenance of the One *qui est per omnia secula benedictus"*—that is to say "and to all times blessed," so that the work ends with another pun on the name of Beatrice.[2]

To me the most important point of this paragraph is the intrusion of the verb of the future, the only time you find it in the narrative: "I hope." The whole text is contained within an exercise of memory, an idea of something which is past, and that tempts him greatly because if something is past and you think that you can control it, you can certainly decipher it, you can hope to extract from it some particular meaning, complacently or not. But then he ends with a projection of the self into the future, another work of his that is to come. This is the preamble to something more that he cannot really contain, so memory is abandoned and the work ends with an image within the horizon of the future. This is a crucial moment. The limitations of memory can be understood only from this point of view of the future, signaled by hope, which is grammatically tied to the future. He says, "I hope to write," there's no future there; "I hope" is in the present. But *to hope* is a verb that in Latin, for example, always take the future participle. One says in English, "I hope that I will do this"; "I hope I would have done this" doesn't work. "Hope" is a verb of the future. It is also, in substantial terms, a virtue. To say "I hope" is a theological virtue, and hope here too always implies the future. It says that the past is not really over and done with because once you enter into the category of hope, you really believe you can change the meaning of the past. The fact that things may happen whereby all your past errors can and will be seen in terms of a new life means that there is the possibility of change instead of destruction.

To summarize, we have prose and poetry, we have the voice of the lover and the voice of the editor, we have a text of memory that at the same time turns against itself, points out the limitations of memory, and opens to the future through hope, and you have this idea that something amazing is going to happen, something that, though no concrete sign of this is given, will take place within the self. It's the moment where Dante abandons Augustine. I began by saying that the rhetorical mode that Dante really follows is Augustine's *Confessions,* which is a text of retrospection and ends with a commentary of Genesis. Dante, instead, ends with what we call a prolepsis, which means a projection to the future. Autobiography has this kind of future dimension and cannot be contained. In other words, it's not over and done with.

Just to make this even more intelligible, a text that is most like what Dante has written in the *Vita nuova* is really *The Portrait of the Artist as a Young Man* by James Joyce. If you cannot have a conversion, if you cannot die as Augustine says you have to do when you write an autobiography, then what you can do is write about yourself with a kind of temporal distance that is brought by time. You can say, "I'm no longer the young man I used to be, but I do know those passions." You can remove yourself from them in exactly the same way that Joyce does in *The Portrait of the Artist as a Young Man,* which ends with the projection of descending into the smithy and writing, forging the epic of the future. It ends with a project for the future, a mode of autobiographical writing that Dante clearly put forth first.

All right, that's the mode of the text, but what actually happens in it? It's a love story. It's the love story of a young man who meets, at the age of nine, a young woman who is roughly the same age. He doesn't even know who she is, but he feels a kind of bliss in her presence. Then he sees her again nine years later, so we know that there is a kind of numerical symbolism running through the text, where the number for Beatrice is nine, a multiple of three, a Trinitarian number. Anyway, she reappears, and Dante is convinced that this is going to be the love of his life, but he doesn't even know what love is. At the beginning he knows only that he does not know what love is, and thus the economy of this narrative generally focuses on trying to ponder what love may be.

The culture of the Middle Ages is filled with the literature of love. The *Vita nuova* could be viewed as one of the many love books of the Middle Ages, but what are the other famous love books of the Middle Ages, which are completely different from the love books that preceded them? One example is *The Art of Courtly Love* of Andreas Capellanus, which is a codification of what love is: the idea that love is an art, the "art of courtly love," that it's obviously natural instinct or thrust or passion and yet has to be changed through a sentimental education. One has to learn how to contain, how to hold off excesses, how to hold off the potential disruptions and violence that love will commute. There are the romances of Chrétien de Troyes, which are all about love at the court, the place of pleasure within the unfolding of responsible life. There are so many other texts from this period, many of the Provençal poets come to mind, that Dante evokes when he writes about love. And of course, the Middle Ages are not the first time that people reflect upon love. The Greeks tried to do that, and you may remember that Socrates always wonders what love is. Is it a figure of speech, a manner of feeling, or is there such a thing as love? Is it a god that possesses me? Is this a natural instinct that we call love? This variety of passions, this variety of ways of understanding love, all figure within Dante's text.

The main thing is that Dante meets Beatrice, and his love for her comes over him suddenly and powerfully. The whole point of this narrative is that things seem to be happening to him. He is a passive figure, and even love comes to him. He doesn't will it, he doesn't look for it, and in many ways, it gives itself to him, as indicated by this passage from chapter 2:

> Nine times already since my birth the heaven of light had circled back to almost the same point, when there appeared before my eyes the now glorious lady of my mind, who was called Beatrice even by those who did not know what her name was. She had been in this life long enough for the heaven of fixed stars to be able to move a twelfth of a degree to the East in her time; that is, she appeared to me at about the beginning of her ninth year, and I first saw her near the end of my ninth year. She appeared dressed in the most patrician of colors, a subdued and decorous crimson. . . . At that very moment, and I speak the truth, the vital spirit, the one that dwells in the most secret chamber of the heart, began to tremble so violently that even the most minute veins of my body were strangely affected; and trembling, it spoke

these words: "Here is a god stronger than I who is coming to rule over me."[3]

These are set descriptions of what love is. The point is that Dante doesn't will it. Why does he present himself as unwilling this passion? Because passions that are unwilled seem to be more important then the things that we will. If they are unwilled and they happen to me, then they may have the mark of a secret necessity. There may be a pattern behind them that I cannot comprehend. Dante will find out in time that the will needs to be in turn ruled by reason, but here this figure of love is a god, really a literary conceit. Dante has no real idea who is speaking to him. He takes refuge in the chamber of his mind, and there he is engaged in deliriums, dreams, and so on, which is to say, all the clinical signs of love. He thinks that love is a passion that debilitates him.

This whole problem will come to a head with the first sonnet that he writes. Dante was eighteen years old when he wrote this poem, and it is really a kind of dream. And it begins, "To every captive soul," so you can tell from the outset that it is going to be a horrifying dream:

> To every captive soul and loving heart
> to whom these words I have composed are sent
> for your elucidation in reply,
> greetings I bring for your sweet lord's sake, Love.
> The first three hours, the hours of the time
> of shining stars, were coming to an end,
> when suddenly Love appeared before me
> (to remember how he really was appalls me).
>
> Joyous, Love seemed to me, holding my heart
> within his hand, and in his arms he had
> my lady, loosely wrapped in folds, asleep.
> He woke her then, and gently fed to her
> the burning heart; she ate it, terrified.
> And then I saw him disappear in tears.[4]

So the poem is a nightmare about a lady who is asleep, held in the arms of the lord of love. She wakes and eats the heart that is given to her. It's a story of how the heart nourishes love, that's the sense of it. It's another involuntary experience, since a dream comes to us without our will, and Dante admits that the meaning of this sonnet was unclear for this reason.

At any rate, he writes the sonnet and sends it out to his fellow poets in Florence. He sends one copy to the person who's going to become his best friend and to whom this book is dedicated. His name is Guido Cavalcanti, and we shall see him in Hell, since Dante suggests he will end up in the circle of his father in *Inferno* 10. Guido answers, because it was the fashion of the time to respond to a poem using the other poet's rhyme scheme. And Cavalcanti tells him that he was right, that he really had the vision, which means that he cannot quite trust love, that he has to turn away. It's a kind of admonition to Dante: move away from all of these figments of love and turn to philosophical studies. It's only in the works of the mind that you can find some kind of truth and stability for yourself. A physician of the time, another Dante, Dante da Maiano, also decides to write to him about the sonnet. He says that Dante has humoral problems and that he should take cold baths and then everything will be okay. He just needs to rebalance the equilibrium of his humors. One man, the physician, reduces love to a question of bodies, as if it were just a disease, and the other reduces it to a question of love's danger vis-à-vis the stability of the mind. Dante will listen to neither of them.

The rest of the *Vita nuova* will be an attempt to understand what this love really is. Several crucial chapters will address this question. For instance, in chapter 8 Dante describes going to a funeral, where he sees a dead woman. And the point, I think, of that scene is that there is a body and this body is inert and dead, and there is no possible connection between Dante and this dead body. Thus, love is not tied only to bodies. There must be some kind of animation, some kind of soul or life, that accompanies it. In chapter 12, Dante finally seems to be moving a little bit away from the Provençal way of describing love, in conventional terms that I will describe to you shortly, and he has another dream about the god of love who comes to him and says that it's time for him to put aside all simulacra, all fictions, and all emptiness.

Let me now say a little bit about the history of describing love and the kind of questions that Dante raises in regard to this tradition. Whenever we think about love in modern times, the formulation of love as we understand it today is essentially medieval. The Greeks do not have the romantic idea of love the way we do. They understand love as an intellectual pursuit, as an ascent of the ladder of being. To them, it's the work of philosophers, and minds can go through the various degrees of intellectual reality until one can finally grasp love. There is friendship, of course, but there's not the idea of the love of a man for a woman, which is so crucial to the romantic understanding of love. The Romans had no understanding at all about either of these conceptions, what the Greeks knew, what we know. The most important Latin voice on love is, in my opinion, Catullus, who talks about love as something to be slightly embarrassed about. It's a weakness, and a serious person does not involve himself or herself in this kind of pursuit, because you have to do the serious work of living: attending to political issues, going to the forum, negotiating, and so on.

But along comes the Provençal world in the south of France, the Provençal courts, and suddenly love changes, both its meaning and its contours. Now love is the love of a man for a woman, and it's usually described, as you can see in Andreas Capellanus and *The Art of Courtly Love,* or in the texts of Chrétien de Troyes, as a clandestine, secret relationship. It need not be within marriage because marriages are usually business propositions. It is a kind of emotion that's potentially violent and potentially problematic. What is the sociology of love? Can a nobleman fall in love with a plebeian woman, can a noblewoman fall love with a plebeian man? It's a predicament, this question of what love can be, and yet the poets always describe it as an experience that causes insomnia, that results in a loss of appetite, that renders the lover pale and mute in the presence of the beloved. They constantly describe the physical properties of love.

And after the Provençal idea of love, the next great revolution regarding love is visible in what is contained in this text of Dante's. But Dante is not the only one to shift the perception of love; Dante's not the only one to have brought this revolution about. His teachers and peers, the likes of Cavalcanti and Guido Guinizelli, were headed in the same direction. Namely, they were all considering the notion that love has to be explored for the changes it brings *to the mind.* How can it be? This is the kind of problem that they raise. How can it be that I see a woman and the image of that woman obsesses me? What does this say about my mind? Why do I want to be better than I am? How am I going to be educated in the light of the love that I feel for this woman? In effect, this metaphysical aspect of love is the special burden of this text.

The first time that we see this revolution in the *Vita nuova* occurs in chapter 19. This is the turning point in Dante's understanding of what love is: "Then it happened, that while walking down a path along which ran a very clear stream"—we can assume that it's the Arno River, but Dante's not interested in the outside world, he's only interested in what love does to his inner self—"I suddenly felt a great desire to write a poem and I began to think how I would go about it." What an extraordinary moment! Finally he's not just jotting down words that come to him, but instead he begins to think! He continues, "I began to think how I would go about it. It seemed to me that to speak of my lady would not be becoming unless I were to address my words to ladies"—and not just to any ladies—"but only to those who are worthy, not merely to women. Then I must tell you my tongue"—he hasn't totally abandoned the mask of passivity—"as if moved of its own accord, spoke and said: *Ladies who have intelligence of love.* With great delight I decided to keep these words in mind and to use them at the beginning of my poem. Later, after returning to the aforementioned city and reflecting for several days I began writing a *canzone*"—meaning a song, which for Dante is the noblest rhetorical form—"using this beginning and then constructed it in a way that will appear below in its divisions." It begins:

> Ladies who have intelligence of love
> I wish to speak to you about my lady,
> not thinking to complete her litany,
> but to talk in order to relieve my heart.[5]

It's a poem of praise, close to a certain kind of religious poem called *laude,* which has the same root as "laudatory" in English. To praise is Dante's aim here, one that he would like us to distinguish from flattery. When praising, you really don't expect anything in return because you are just yielding to the allure and the power of what is in front of you. Flattery always implies some kind of circuitousness, a desire to get something. Flattery always implies some degree of manipulation.

But the most important phrase here is "ladies who have intelligence of love," because, finally, intellect and love are no longer two disjointed activities of the mind. It's the opposite view of that of Guido Cavalcanti, who believes in a world in which one is sundered from the other—and we will come to that in *Inferno* 10. Cavalcanti thinks that time is split from itself anyway, that experiences are all fragmentary. He believes that if you have a passion like love, you can never quite come to understand anything. In fact, when you are in the throes of passion your mind ceases its operations. So, this poem is written against Dante's best friend, the same man to whom the text is dedicated.

As a result, we are forced to think about the relationship between friendship and love. Is there anything better than friendship? Is there anything better than love? Dante—this is the radical element of Dante's thinking—brings us to the point where you really have to distinguish between things that seem to be equally powerful virtues. What is friendship? The text is dedicated to Guido Cavalcanti, which means that friendship implies a conversation, a conversation of minds. The word "conversation" comes from the Latin for "things turning together." Therefore, when we are conversing, minds are turning together harmoniously, looking for common agreements, and the condition for friendship is that you've got to like each other even more after you engage in discussion. You disagree, but you do so benevolently. In *The Ethics* Aristotle counts friendship as one of the major virtues, and so does Dante in his own rewriting of *The Ethics,* which is the *Convivio.*

But love is still more important than friendship for Dante because love forces you to think. Something happens to you that mobilizes your mind. You've got to go looking for the signs of love. The mind is engaged in an extended self, in a mode of self-reflection. A great text that I'm sure Dante read is the *Metamorphoses* of Ovid, including the story of Pyramus and Thisbe, lovers who can see the smallest chink in the wall through which to communicate and all the inventiveness that comes with even that minimal possibility. Love makes us think in ways that we could never really imagine because it is tied to the imagination. So, intellect and love are now rolled together, and that's the revolution.

This is the beginning of the so-called "sweet new style," the kind of poetry that Dante and his poet-friends write, which is a rethinking of what the Provençal poets were doing. The Provençal poets wrote their poetry in the mode of "I tremble, and I shake, and the image of the beloved I cannot even describe to others. I have to keep my passion away from the flatterers because they are going to violate my secret and so I have to always protect it." There is a sense of singularity and uniqueness to their passion. These Tuscan poets—Dante, Cavalcanti, Guinizelli—come along and say that what really matters is that love—especially Cavalcanti's sense of philosophy as love of wisdom—can become part of an intellectual ascent. Knowledge only favors love, and love mobilizes the mind to go on thinking.

I'll delve into these concerns again and again as we proceed, but for now I'll say that the great philosophical debates in the thirteenth century are always between the so-called voluntarists and the rationalists. A simple divide: the voluntarists are those who believe that if I want to know something, I have to love first, for love is crucial to my knowledge. The rationalists would say that you have to know first in order that you may love, and it's a fierce debate. Dante is circumventing all of this. For him intellect and love are like the two feet that carry us along, where you move one and then you move the other, and only in this way can you walk without being hobbled. The sweet new style indicates, therefore, a highly philosophical, highly intellectual kind of poetry, a poetry where a woman or the love of a woman can take you up to the divinity, in the understanding that that which rules the world is not just an idea, but a kind of love, and therefore love is the only way of coming to it and pursuing it.

The *Vita nuova* continues in this vein, and then we arrive at a little sonnet immediately after chapter 19. Dante explains that "after the canzone"—that last poem about "ladies who have intelligence of love"—"had become rather well known, one of my friends who had heard it was moved asked me to write about the nature of Love." Dante started like the Provençal poets, but he's not refining their idea and instead wants to think about the philosophical conception of love, without losing sight of the immediacy of his passion for Beatrice. He continues, "Having perhaps from reading my poem acquired more confidence in me than I deserved, so thinking that after my treatment with the previous theme, it would be good to treat the theme of Love and feeling that I owed this to my friend, I decided to compose a poem dealing with Love." This time Dante's poetic impulse produces a sonnet, which begins:

> Love and the gracious heart are a single thing,
> as Guinizelli tells us in his poem:
> one can no more be without the other
> than can the reasoning mind without its reason.
> Nature, when in a loving mood, creates them . . . [6]

Here we see the shift to a full awareness of the need to learn about love.

This means that this whole text really is traversed by two interrelated themes. One is the story of Dante's love for Beatrice and his understanding of what love is. Is it a physical impulse? Is it a demon? Is it a figure of speech? Is it a simulacrum, another fiction that we tell each other? The other thematic strain of this text has to do with learning to be a poet. Dante is also telling us the story of his poetic growth, of how he begins by imitating the Provençal poets, then imitates the poets of the sweet new style, and then finally finds his voice. These two themes also shed light on each other because only Dante can understand these things about love, and if he truly understands things about love that nobody else has understood, he can go on writing poems that nobody else can write, which is actually a famous hope that he expresses in chapter 42.

I could also mention the poem in chapter 21, "The power of Love borne in my lady's eyes," where it's not only about the nature of love but how Dante tries to find love within Beatrice. It's not the god of love that has been abandoned, it's not the conceit of love, it's not the strange and enigmatic words of love that have come to him from oracles and traditions; now love is love for the concreteness of Beatrice herself. The text also contains an impressive sonnet in chapter 26 about the apparition of Beatrice. She wanders through the streets, the world is silent, and she's wrapped in a kind of mystery and an inapproachable light. There's always some kind of distance. This is that poem:

> Such sweet decorum and such gentle grace
> attend my lady's greeting as she moves
> that lips can only tremble into silence,
> and eyes dare not attempt to gaze at her.
> Moving, benignly clothed in humility,
> untouched by all the praise along her way,
> she seems to be a creature come from Heaven
> to earth, to manifest a miracle.[7]

Dante here has love, heaven, and earth mixed up in his head. Beatrice brings heaven down to earth and asks him to rise up to heaven.

How does Dante escape this tangled sense of constant wonder? Beatrice appears, and it's a miracle, a wonder, and as soon as you believe that what you perceive is a wonder that you don't quite understand, you want to try to understand it. So, there's a sense of constant perplexity and great excitement at the idea of Beatrice, and Dante attempts to move past the wonder via poetic reflection.

But then Beatrice dies around chapter 29. How real can she be now that she's dead? How can Dante relate to someone who is dead? Dante will do what perhaps some others would do: he tries to find a replacement. He goes looking for someone who reminds him of her and then finds, in chapters 35–39, this woman who fits the bill and who has so much mercy for him that he can't help but be drawn to her. Yet, he understands that in his attempt to duplicate Beatrice, he renders the love for Beatrice no longer singular, which is problematic. Either he believes in the singularity of the figure he loves, or if he believes in the possibility of duplication, then he is undercutting his own poetic project.

Dante is caught up in all this drama, then, until finally he sees some pilgrims passing through his city, and this sighting offers him an important change in direction. Dante writes a critical poem in response to this vision, beginning by addressing the pilgrims directly. They don't listen to him, they know nothing about him, but he addresses them all the same:

> Ah, pilgrims moving pensively along,
> thinking, perhaps, of things at home you miss,
> could the land you come from be so far away
> (as anyone might guess from your appearance)
> that you show no signs of grief as you pass through
> the middle of the desolated city . . .

This phrase is normally used to refer to Jerusalem, "the desolated city," "the abandoned city," but in this case it refers to Florence.

> . . . like people who seem not to understand,
> the grievous weight of woe it has to bear?
> If you would stop to listen to me speak,
> I know, from what my sighing heart tells me,
> you would be weeping when you leave this place:
> lost is the city's source of blessedness,
> and I know words that could be said of her
> with power to humble any man to tears.[8]

This is truly a great shift in the movement of the *Vita nuova*. Dante realizes that he is not like these pilgrims: he's not going anywhere; he's moving in circles. Now he has been shaken from the circular self-absorption in which he had found himself. The second important occurrence here is that Dante understands that the mythology he has been constructing about Beatrice is an absolutely private mythology. It means nothing to anybody else. These pilgrims come from afar, and they are separated "pensively," a word that implies suspension. The pilgrims are halfway: they are here now going through Florence, heading toward a destination, and nostalgically separated from the world they left behind. And Dante too is not going anywhere, but he doesn't have Beatrice with him, and unlike the pilgrims, he has no idea where to go. The effort he has to make is to transform his private mythology into a public discourse.

This, then, is the transition from the *Vita nuova* to the *Divine Comedy*. The *Divine Comedy* will be the text where Dante will finally literally stage his own passion through the passions of others, involving all others in his discourse and creating what I would call a public mythology. The text ends with a journey of the mind that will allow the next voyage to go

> beyond the sphere that makes the widest round,
> [as it] passes the sigh arisen from my heart;
> a new intelligence that Love in tears
> endowed it with is urging it on high.[9]

In the closing lines of the *Vita nuova* Dante sees Beatrice far away and decides to undertake a new journey, the journey of knowledge, the journey of exploration, the journey of life, the journey at the heart of the *Divine Comedy*.

This is really the kind of poetic experience that Dante needs at the outset of his career. He's still a young man. He's exploring a lot of possibilities; he's gathering all the voices around him, internalizing them. The *Vita nuova* is not the same kind of encyclopedic text that the *Divine Comedy* will necessarily be, but Dante does use it to evolve all discourses, all whispers, all groans, all noises. The whole world has to speak through his poem. This is ultimately an effort to try to find himself as a poet with a project, one that will necessarily be future-oriented.

In fact, there is no poet that I know in the Western tradition who is so given to the idea of the future and who is more of a poet of hope than Dante is. I will call him a lot of things. I'll call him the poet of exile, which he is. I'll call him the poet of love, which he is. I'll call him the poet of peace, which he is. But above all, and especially here, he is the poet of hope, in the knowledge that hope is the most realistic of virtues. Because he tells us that not even the past may be dead, that really despair is the most crucial sin that one could have in this universe. That's the substance of this poem, and in that sense, it's a preamble in preparation for the *Divine Comedy*.

What happens after the *Vita nuova*? Beatrice had died in 1289. Dante has married a woman he will never mention, a woman who belongs to a prominent family in Florence, the Donati, troublemakers that Dante doesn't really like. And Dante will enter public life, until 1302, when he's banned from Florence and forced to go into exile. Once he's in exile, then his production will start again. He writes one of the first treatises on language in the Western world. He writes a text of philosophy and theology. And then he writes his *Divine Comedy*. That is where we will find him in the next chapter: in the middle of life's journey in Canto 1 of *Inferno*.

CHAPTER 3

Inferno 1–4

Before beginning our exploration of *Inferno,* let me say a few things about the poem in general, the structure of the poem, and then we can get into the first four cantos. In my preface, I mentioned the title of the poem. We refer to the poem as the *Divine Comedy,* but it should be just *Comedy.* That's what Dante called it, and he called it *Comedy* for a number of reasons. The first reason is that it ends with happiness. It's a story that begins with disorder, a catastrophe if you wish; the pilgrim is lost in the woods and then works himself out toward the light, toward the truth, toward God. In that sense "comedy" describes the thematic trajectory of the poem. It's going from one condition to another, and from this point of view it's literally the opposite of the tragic movement. In the tragic movement, you always have an initial state of cohesion or initial state of happiness that moves toward fatality or disaster.

The second reason for the title is stylistic. Dante calls it a comedy because he adopts the vernacular, first of all. The other possibility would have been writing it in Latin, in the language of philosophy and great cultural exchanges, but instead he uses the Italian vulgar language. It also means that stylistically he adopts a humble style. According to the ancient Greeks and Romans, there were three levels of styles. First, there is the high tragic style or the sublime style, which describes events involving kings, since style must have some kind of aptness to the situation that the story describes. Then there is a middle style or an elegiac style. And finally there is a low style, the style of comedy, the vernacular style, capable of encompassing all other registers, which Dante will adopt.

However, it is a somewhat peculiar implication for Dante to call a story like his a "comedy," and the implication is that, in effect, he undercuts the idea of a rigid hierarchy of reality. For Dante, there is no neat separation of the high, the middle, and the low. That which is low and humble, such as the experience he is describing, an ordinary human being living around the year 1300 who manages to have this extraordinary experience of going up to see the face of God and coming back to the earth to tell us about it—it's really a sign that the low can become high and the high can become low. Thus, the classical distinctions of which we read in the *Poetics* of Aristotle, which Dante did not know, or in Horace's *Poetic Art,* which Dante did know, are illusory. That system is not the way that Dante wishes to proceed, so Dante has a number of aims that he's pursuing in calling this text "the comedy."

With regard to the formal structure of the poem, it's divided into three parts: Hell, Purgatory, and Paradise. Each of them contains thirty-three cantos, with the exception of *Inferno. Inferno* has thirty-four cantos, which means there's a separate one—Canto 1—plus thirty-three. They are neatly separated in that Canto 1 represents a kind of rehearsal. It's a journey that fails. Dante's real journey will begin with Canto 2.

The poem has one hundred cantos, but the basic unit of his narrative is the number three. In fact, it's written in a metrical form called *terza rima,* a rhyme scheme that goes ABA, BCB, and so on. So, the number three is the fundamental symbolic number of division within this text. What is the reason for this? There is a key aesthetic reason that we find crystallized in a verse from the Book of Wisdom, "You O God, have created everything according to number, measure, and weight." And the *Divine Comedy* has to duplicate the symmetry, the order, and the harmony that Dante thinks he sees in the universe. The poem is presented and introduced as a reflection of that superior, divine order of the universe and wants to be part of it. It's ambivalent, both reflecting and aiming at metonymy: the part that wants to be attached to a larger whole.

These are some general concepts that will help you understand the pattern of parallelisms that we're going to find within the poem. And I'll mention one particularly important parallelism now. You should be aware that the poem has a linear structure from 1 to 100, and yet, within the tri-partition of the poem—Hell, Purgatory, and Paradise—there are cantos that correspond to one another. Canto 6 of *Inferno* prefigures Canto 6 of *Purgatorio,* and both of them will in turn prefigure Canto 6 of *Paradiso.* This is also true of Cantos 10, 10, and 10, and so on; the pattern can be fol-

lowed in a fairly systematic way. The poem is thus structured both verti-
cally and horizontally.

With these general concerns out of the way, we can now begin with
Canto 1, a very well-known canto that contains the general preamble of the
poem. It begins:

> Midway in the journey of our life I found myself in a dark wood,
> for the straight way was lost. Ah, how hard it is to tell what that
> wood was, wild, rugged, harsh; the very thought of it renews the
> fear! It is so bitter that death is hardly more so. But, to treat of
> the good that I found in it, I will tell of the other things I saw
> there. I cannot rightly say how I entered it, I was so full of sleep
> at the moment I left the true way; but when I had reached the
> foot of a hill, there at the end of the valley that had pierced my
> heart with fear, I looked up and saw its shoulders already clad in
> the rays of the planet that leads men aright by every path. Then
> the fear was somewhat quieted that had continued in the lake of
> my heart through the night I had passed so piteously. And as he
> who with laboring breath has escaped from the deep to the
> shore turns to look back on the dangerous waters, so my mind
> which was still fleeing turned back to gaze upon the pass that
> never left anyone alive.[1]

It's a great beginning. It begins in a very extraordinary way, in the
middle, for the beginning is the present reality of the pilgrim who finds
himself lost. There's more in that first line: "Midway in the journey of our
life"—what is he saying? I think it's fairly clear that the first conceit, the
fundamental conceit, of the poem is that life is a journey, which means that
we are always on the way. We just don't know where we are going yet. Dante
will find out soon, which means that we are displaced, and we are going to
have a number of adventures. It means that we are not yet where we want
to be. And in fact, Dante calls it *our* life. That possessive is his way of establishing that this is not yet a unique experience. It's something we all
share and something which might also concern us. We too are on the journey of life.

Then, in contrast to that idea, there is also an autobiographical focus.
There is a stress of "*I* found," "*I* came to myself within a dark wood," and so
on. This is going to be, much as in the *Vita nuova,* an autobiographical story.
It can only be a personal story, but here the self is going to see the world and

is going to see himself through the prism of the world. He will enter a public space.

The great difference between the *Vita nuova,* which we explored in the previous chapter, and the *Divine Comedy* is that the *Vita nuova* was destined to fail as a narrative, precisely because the protagonist is drawing us and drawing himself within the solitude and interiority of his own life, a life which was completely disengaged from the concerns of the outside world. The *Divine Comedy* starts with that kind of shipwreck, the shipwreck of other intellectual activities that he will describe at length, but then it heads in a different direction.

As soon as we read this first line, "I found myself in a dark wood," traditional commentators will tell you that Dante is here in a state of sin, that the dark wood is really the condition of spiritual despair. He's at an impasse; we know he doesn't know where to go. I, however, feel that this allegorizing is a bit too easy, and we have no evidence for this interpretation in the poem yet. What we do know is that Dante is lost in a landscape that is terrifying. He is caught within it, and he's clueless about how he got there. He knows one thing, though: he wants to get out of it.

But then he goes on about how hard it is, "so bitter that death is hardly more so. But, to treat of the good that I found in it, I will tell of the other things I saw there." Suddenly, in a way the poem is already over. He's now shifting from the narrative of events: I was lost in the dense, savage, harsh wood of the night. His gaze rends this night, tries to find a way out. He cannot see anything beyond himself, but then he immediately says that in order to tell the reader about the good he noted in the woods, he will first have to speak of other things.

So, right from the start we can see that the poem has a double narrative focus. The first focus is that Dante is going to tell us the story of a pilgrim who is caught in what we call the diachronic, the time-bound—a number of encounters which he cannot quite understand. As a result, he's led by Virgil, as we're going to find out soon, but he doesn't fully comprehend what's happening to him. Then there is the second focus, the poet who has seen it all and enjoys an omniscient perspective. The whole poem really moves around this double axis: the axis of a synoptic view of the poet who has become a poet because he had this experience as a pilgrim and who then tells us about this experience. That's what I call a synoptic and omniscient narrator, and he is able to examine what the pilgrim did not know. There's a kind of irony in this discrepancy between the diachronic viewpoint of the pilgrim and the synoptic viewpoint of the poet. It goes without saying that the structure is not that neat, that there are moments when one's point of view will encroach upon the other. But this is the general idea.

The second movement of the canto begins, "I cannot rightly say how I entered it, I was so full of sleep at the moment I left the true way." It's a kind of torpid, lethargic lack of consciousness. His faculties are dormant. "But when I had reached the foot of a hill, there at the end of the valley that had pierced my heart with fear," he continues, "I looked up and saw its shoulders already clad in the rays of the planet that leads men aright by every path."[2] Dawn breaks, and he looks up toward the sun, believing that natural sunlight is going to unveil to him the layout of the land so that he may find an escape route from this particular disaster.

If this were a Platonic narrative, the poem would come to an end right here because this is what happens in a Platonic narrative. You are in a cave, as in *The Republic,* you see nothing, only flickers of light, like being at the movies. They are simulations of the truth; they are projected on the side of the cave, and you mistake those shadows for realities. If you are really wise, if you are a philosopher, then you know that you can turn your head around and see where the source of true light is, and then you are saved. The whole experience of the cave is predicated on this premise: that knowledge saves you, that knowledge is virtue. And knowledge does save you to the extent to which it can heal what one could call the wounds of the intellect: ignorance being the wound that knowledge, learning, education, and philosophy can cure. Dante will find out very quickly that this idea is a false promise, that in many ways his own realities are going to be a little bit more complex than what one can find in manuals of philosophy about how we get saved and how we can save ourselves.

So, Dante turns toward the light and then he fears this passion that he feels because it's a passion of the soul, the fear that paralyzes him and his discernment. It literally stops him, and he does not know which way to go. But the overpowering passion at this point of the poem, which "had continued in the lake of my heart through the night I had passed so piteously," has been quieted a little. It's a dark night of the soul, and this is a spiritual experience coming to a head. The text proceeds, "And as he who with laboring breath has escaped from the deep to the shore turns to look back on the dangerous waters, so my mind which was still fleeing turned back to gaze upon the pass that never left anyone alive."[3] The whole passage is replete with Neoplatonic language. He is talking about himself as if this experience were a flight of the soul or the mind. This is the idea that we have experiences that are purely intellectual, the kind of experiences that we can all find when we are reading a book, when we are studying, when we are thinking.

Yet, there is immediately a great shift that I want to focus on briefly. Dante has been talking about the flight of the mind as an experience of a shipwreck, and many epic stories begin in this way. Think of *The Aeneid*, the shipwreck of Aeneas on the shores of Africa as he is about to enter the city that Dido is about to build, an occasion that will bring him to a great revelation and a great love story with Dido. Here there's no such relief for Dante. It's the shipwreck of the mind, a mind that seems to be unable to define both his whereabouts and his destination. However, as soon as he does this, as soon as Dante understands that is what the problem is, he shifts the language from mind to body. He says, "After I had rested my tired body a little, I again took up my way across the desert strand, so that the firm foot was always the lower. And behold, near the beginning of the steep, a leopard light-footed and very fleet, covered with a spotted hide! And it did not depart from before my eyes, but did so impede my way that more than once I turned round to go back."[4]

The intrusion of the body and the questions of what the body is and what it represents are the great difference between Neoplatonic narratives and Dante's kind of experience. The body stands for the limit of purely intellectual journeys. The real journey that he has to undertake is the journey of mind and body, and the body stands for the irreducible historicity of one's self. The body stands for one's own reality, the passions. It stands for one's own will. This is the difference between what the Greeks understand as the great intellectual adventure, which is one of knowledge, and Dante's idea that the real problems are problems of the will. We may not know where we are, and we may understand that we are not happy with the situation in which we find ourselves, but we cannot quite solve these problems with knowledge alone because the problems here are problems of willing.

Let me present a simple explanation of the philosophical stances to which Dante is responding here. First, there is a Socratic scheme whereby all issues are issues of an intellectual sort. I know, and therefore I am virtuous. I know what justice is and the implication is that I'm just. That's a false implication because if I ask all of my students to give me a definition of justice, they'll all tell me something different: that justice is within the self, that justice is a way I relate to my family, or justice is a way I relate to the city, or justice is a way I take care of societal problems of the world in which I find myself. Dante will say that this is not knowledge of what justice is, that the definition of justice cannot make you just.

The other scheme that Dante opposes to this Socratic idea is one of the will. In the Letter to the Romans, St. Paul writes, "The good that I will do, that I do not do. The evil that I would not do, that I do" (7:19). He draws attention to the essential existential problem, the problem of the self. My will is divided against itself. I may know what to do, but I do not really know, and even if I do know, I am not sure that I will it. That's the fatality of life. We all think we know what's good. How many of us go around choosing and doing what we know is not good for us, what is not the best possible thing to do in terms of our judgment of our situation? So it's the perspective of the will that becomes Dante's perspective in coming to terms with the limitations of philosophy and intellectual knowledge.

We shall see that Dante talks about the will in a number of ways. In the last chapter, on the *Vita nuova,* I began to explain that for Dante the will is even better than an unwilling action, and yet the best experiences of life seem to be those that one does not want to happen, such as a dream, for instance. He certainly did not want the death of Beatrice, and yet he understands that as soon as he focuses on Beatrice as a figure, the real contingent historical figure of his love, then he has to give a direction to his own desires, he has to define his will. Already we have an anticipation of some of the problems of the will.

Now he will start exploring other such problems, both as they relate to the self, to the psychology of the character, and as they relate to politics, for instance to a vision of the world as an act of and the projection of our own wills. The world is the way we want it to be, and the people are, too. For the time being, though, Dante takes the will as his own perspective.

He finds out that he cannot go up the hill that he has seen. Three beasts, a leopard, a she-wolf, and a lion will block his journey, and so he's going right back where he started. He's back into the deepest despair possible because now there really seems to be no exit.

But then he sees something: "When I was ruining down to the depth there appeared before me one who seemed faint through long silence. When I saw him in that vast desert, I cried to him," and these are the first words that Dante the pilgrim will speak in the text, "'Have pity on me whatever you are, shade or living man!'"[5] The words "Have pity on me" are taken from King David in Psalms, so he's prostrating himself, and I stress this because the Davidic voice will constitute an important strain in this narrative. How does Dante talk? That's one of the ways, and we shall see how it appears again further along in the poem.

To return to the text, Dante has seen the three beasts, but we don't know what they are. Are they sins? Are they dispositions to sins? They are animals, and therefore they stand for animal projections of our desires, of his desires, and that's all we can tell about them. Then he meets a figure, and it's unclear if it's a shade or a man. He's dramatizing what medieval thought and literature called the land of dissimilitude, the land of an un-likeness. He finds himself in a world where things are not what they seem, where there seems to be a disparity between signs and their meanings, and part of his effort is thus to literally stitch back together this break between symbols and what they represent.

At any rate, his first meeting is with this figure by the name of Virgil, who will become his guide. He's the author of *The Aeneid,* but how he presents himself is crucial: " 'No, not a living man, though once I was,' he answered me, 'and my parents were Lombards, both Mantuans by birth. I was born *sub Iulio,*'" meaning "under Caesar," which is true, "although late." He is giving us an autobiography, a presentation of his life, his historical circumstances, and his works. He gives us a sense of how he came into this world and what his life amounted to. This is what it all comes down to, this is really the sense of my birth, and he speaks about his own birth. But then he will turn away from himself, turning his attention instead to Dante, his interlocutor: "I lived at Rome under the good Augustus, in the time of the false and lying gods. I was a poet, and I sang of that just son of Anchises who came from Troy after proud Iliam was burned. But you, why do you return to such woe? Why do you not climb the delectable mountain, the source and cause of every happiness?"—meaning the mountain of Purgatory that will take him to Eden, where all things started, according to the biblical version of cosmology.[6]

Dante will respond, " 'Are you, then, that Virgil, that fount which pours forth so broad a stream of speech?' I answered him, my brow covered with shame. 'O glory and light of other poets, may the long study and the great love that have made me search your volume avail me! You are my master and my author. You alone are he from whom I took the fair style that has done me honor."[7] As a teacher, I can say that every teacher would love, years after the students have been studying with the teacher, to receive this kind of great acknowledgment: how I remember your teaching. We can call this move on Dante's part the rhetoric of capturing the benevolence of the interlocutor. It's clear that the exchange involves the recognition of Virgil as a poet, but Dante is doing more than meets the eye with this praise of Virgil.

Virgil, as the poet of *The Aeneid,* clearly crafted the story of a grand epic journey. But that's not how he was known in twelfth-century Europe, in the culture immediately preceding Dante's time. Virgil, more than as a poet, was known as a philosopher. He was a Neoplatonic philosopher, one who had written a poem wherein the substance was not the fiction about the burning of Troy and the subsequent journey of Aeneas as an exile looking for a new land with his father on his back and his son Ascanius by his side. Rather, it had serious philosophical depth. *The Aeneid* was a way of acknowledging that poetry is capable of providing philosophical illumination. What was the philosophical message? I call it Neoplatonic because it was very much like what the Neoplatonists thought of *The Odyssey* at that time: the Neoplatonists, the allegorists, viewed it as a metaphor for the journey and the experience of the soul. It was the story of the soul that goes away from the point of origin, one's home, the place where one can find oneself somehow, where one is familiar and comfortable. Ulysses leaves Ithaca, goes to Troy, goes through life, and then he has to purify himself in order to go back. In so doing he traces a Neoplatonic circle back to the point of origin. And the Neoplatonists do the same thing with *The Aeneid.* Fulgentius in the sixth century, and Bernard Sylvester and John of Salisbury in the twelfth, write about *The Aeneid* as the story of a hero who is born in Troy and then goes through the stages of life. Each book represents a stage of life: childhood, youth, maturity, with all the temptations of the flesh that happened with Dido, and then Aeneas arrives in Italy, plans to build a new home there, and that's the sixth book. They would never really bother reading the other books.

So, *The Aeneid* was viewed as a philosophical text illustrating the pattern and the movement of life. It was telling us that we all, like Aeneas, are born here, but with care and prudence we can reach the Promised Land. Dante changes this interpretation by insisting that Virgil is a poet. He replaces the philosophical promises with the idea of poetry, in the belief that poetry is better than philosophy, for philosophy stumbles against its own limits: it cannot quite reach the depths, the heights, and the enlightenment it seeks and that make it so that happiness or the safe harbor is within reach of everybody. And Dante believes that it says nothing at all about the reality and the individuality of his life. Poetic language is, for him, the language that addresses these issues, and therefore poetry here is seen as a version of history. You are the writer, he says to Virgil, who wrote the poem dealing with Roman history. Poetry and history deal with the world of contingency and not the world of universal, and therefore potentially empty, promises. That's the great new interpretation of Virgil that Dante is advancing.

For these reasons Dante calls Virgil his master and a great sage and all that. And Virgil tells him, "This is very simple. You must take another road. You are going the wrong way." This is what I referred to as the idea that Canto 1 is a rehearsal of the whole poem. It tells the story of a journey that fails because that's not the way Dante is supposed to go. You find yourself lost, and what do you do? You try to go quickly up to your destination. You climb up the hill, and you think you can make it. No, no, no. Virgil asserts that Dante has to go a different way. He may reach the same point, the same destination, the world of justice, the vision of God, the idea of love, the good as he calls it, but he must go down to get there. Dante has to go through the whole spiral, through the horrors and the suffering of Hell, through Purgatory, in order to be able to reach the beatific vision. The way up is down, and this reversal marks the difference between philosophical presumption and the notion of a spiritual Christian humility that he has to pursue and wants to pursue. So now, at last, the journey may begin, and "then he set out and [Dante] followed after him."[8]

That's the end of Canto 1, and so we come to Canto 2. When are we, though? If this has to be a historical, reducible, and essentially biographical experience, Dante has to be very careful. He will give us the time, the precise time and place of this experience. The poem starts on the evening of Good Friday in the year 1300. Dante's experience is thus an imitation of the experience of Christ, because Dante will also emerge to the light of Purgatory on Easter Sunday.

But Dante is not yet ready to attempt this extraordinary journey. He questions why he should be the one to venture forth. "Poet," he says, "you who guide me, consider if my strength is sufficient, before you trust me to the deep way. You tell how the father of Sylvius went, while still mortal, to the immortal world"—meaning Aeneas, and then Virgil also speaks of Paul. "But I," Dante asks, "why do I come there? And who allows it? I am not Aeneas, I am not Paul."[9] First of all, these are the imaginative coordinates for Dante's own journey: Aeneas, the hero who brings about the foundation of Rome, and Paul, the apostle to the gentiles, who also goes to Rome and who was the spiritual domain of the Church. But who is *he?* That's the first question Dante must answer. I'm not Aeneas, I'm not Paul, so who am I? This whole part of this story is to find out who he is, and part of this journey is to find out if he can bring some degree of redemption and clarity to the world with his poem. He really believes in this "salvific" role of his own voice, though not without irony, not without discouragement, not without a sense that this may indeed be a proud arrogant kind sort of posture.

Yet, this whole idea about self-understanding is immediately countered by a reflection on his divided will. I want to cite this thematically: "And like one who unwills what he has willed and with new thoughts changes his resolve, so that he quite gives up the thing he had begun, such did I become on that dark slope, for by thinking on it I rendered null the undertaking that had been so suddenly embarked upon."[10] It would take me too long to give you a sense of an appropriate gloss to these lines. They are lines about the limitations of willing. Dante begins by claiming the importance of the will in the act of knowledge and we do see that he is so aware of it. Some might say that Dante's a voluntarist, but Dante doesn't believe in philosophy and intellect, not quite. He believes that the two faculties of the soul, intellect and will, are like the feet of one's body. If you really want to walk fast and safely, you have to use both. Similarly you have to use both the intellect and the will. So, as soon as he claims the importance of the will, which the Socratic experience had somehow neglected, he begins to reflect about the limitations of the will. What are the limitations? One is that the will can be divided against itself. The second is that the will needs something to regulate it because I can will anything, so how do I order what I will? The third limitation of the will is that I can never really go faster than my own will. I'm its prisoner. If the will is weak and slow and divided, that's what I am. I can't go past some of the difficulties it creates. Thus, when he asks in Canto 2 the great question of who he is, he sheds light on the first internal issue that he must cure, namely the divided will.

And then we come to Canto 3, in which Dante crosses the gate of Hell, with its famous warning that scares him quite a lot. On the other side Dante meets the first sinners of the text, the so-called neutral angels: "And I, my head circled with error, said, 'Master, what is this I hear? And what people are these who seem so overcome by pain?' And he to me, 'Such is the miserable condition of the sorry souls of those who lived without infamy and without praise. They are mingled with that base band of angels who were neither rebellious nor faithful to God, but stood apart.'" These are the angels who, during the great cosmic battle between God and the satanic forces with which the world begins, just became spectators. In other words, Dante begins his vision of Hell by dramatizing that which to him is the most serious of sins: being disengaged, not taking sides in the belief that you can wait and see what the outcome is and then you can take a side. He responds to them by saying that "these have no hope of death," that "mercy and justice disdain them. Let us not speak of them, but look, and pass on."[11] He won't even name them because to name them would be to bring them into reality, and the neutrality is a sign of the way in which they de-realize the world. They reduce the world to a pure show of their own, for their own spectatorship.

He goes on from here, and the second action in Hell is that he boards the ferry and sees Charon, who will transport all the souls. Dante gives an extraordinary description of this figure and the souls on his boat: "As the leaves fall away in autumn, one after another, till the bough sees all its spoils upon the ground, so there the evil seed of Adam: one by one they cast themselves from that shore at signals, like a bird at its call. Thus they go over the dark water, and before they have landed on the other shore, on this side a new throng gathers. 'My son,' said the courteous master, 'those who die in the wrath of God all come together here from every land; and they are eager to cross the stream.'"[12] I really want to focus on this image of the dead souls as autumn leaves. It's an image that Dante takes straight from *The Aeneid*, though Virgil himself had taken this image from Homer. In book 6, Virgil describes the descent of Aeneas into Hades, and there he waits and sees the souls waiting for metempsychosis, a term that refers to the reincarnation of souls. The souls are waiting to be reincarnated, and then they will come back, in an endless cycle.

Dante changes the thrust of Virgil's image, because Virgil has a Pythagorean understanding of existence, that is to say, the idea that life is a continuous circle, Plato's wheel of becoming. There is nothing really unique about us because we die, and then we can wait for the reincarnation of our soul. Death in Virgil is an elegiac experience: it's never really tragic and cannot be tragic, because it lacks that edge that comes from the perception that something particular and special has been happening to the world because I am here, and will disappear. Dante changes this idea of circularity that we have in Virgil, where you die and yet you can come back because, just as leaves fall in the autumn, you can wait for the spring when leaves very much like those that have just fallen will return. Dante instead focuses on the uniqueness of every leaf. For Dante, our souls are like leaves, but a leaf can be described as a soul only if you insist on its own uniqueness and the fact that it will never return. In formal terms, this means that Dante is replacing the notion of epic circularity that you find in the classics with a linear novel. The life of human beings is best described formally by a novel, in the sense that we are caught in a journey. It's unique, and it will reach its destination, whatever that may be.

Of course, as soon as Dante reveals a linearity to his text, he immediately enters into a circle, the garden where he begins Canto 4. Dante comes to Limbo, a word that comes from the Latin *limbus,* which means "the edge." So, he comes to an area of Hell that is really outside of Hell. In fact, it's very much like the Virgilian afterlife of the virtuous. It's described as a garden, one of three or four gardens that we find in the text, and it acts as a sort of prefiguration of the earthly paradise and gardens in Purgatory, as well as of the world of Paradise, where the city Jerusalem is also described as a garden. Such a place is often called a *locus amoenus,* an idyllic place, a term that belongs very much to the world of epic, in which there is always the story of a hero who reaches this idyllic, bucolic place in order to be able to relax. It's the place of the breakdown of the errancy of the hero, of the adventurous spirit, and it always reveals (or maybe it's just the irony inherent in these literary structures) that whenever heroes seem to look for a break from the quest by reaching the garden and relaxing, that's where they find out that they are in the most dangerous situation. Whenever you think that you are safe, and there's the running cool water of the river, there's the shade, there's the fragrance of the landscape, that's exactly when the snake will appear. That's exactly when the enemy will be capable of reaching you and overwhelming you. These are all places of temptation, and that's what happens here.

Dante arrives in this particular *locus amoenus,* and he sees the great poets, all virtuous heathens. He enumerates the characters, scientists, and philosophers from the Greek and Roman world, but he puts them a little at the edge of the scene. They really don't seem to have much impact on the situation here. But then the drama heightens when he notices the classical poets from Homer to Horace to Ovid: "'O you who honor science and art, who are these that have such honor that it sets them apart from the condition of the rest?' And he to me"—Virgil is speaking here—"'Their honored fame, which resounds in your life above, wins grace in Heaven, which thus advances them.' Meanwhile I heard a voice which said, 'Honor the great Poet! His shade, which had departed, now returns.' After the voice had ceased and was still, I saw four great shades coming to us, in semblance neither sad nor joyful."[13] As befits Limbo, it's clearly like life here. That's what the afterlife is in Dante's conception, an extension of what we choose to do on this earth. If you really think that the beauty of life is having endless seminars on aesthetics or poetry, as these poets do, that's what your afterlife is. You sit down on the grass and go on talking about beautiful things.

Virgil then describes these shades to Dante: "Note him there with sword in hand who comes before the other three as their lord. He is Homer, sovereign poet; next is Horace, satirist; Ovid comes third, and Lucan last'"—a famous epic poet whom Dante will again celebrate in Purgatory. "'Since each shares with me the name the single voice has uttered, they do me honor, and in that they do well.' Thus I saw assembled the fair school of that lord of highest song"—Homer—"who, like an eagle, soars above the rest."[14] The irony, of course, is that he's blind and the eagle has such sharp vision, but Homer's is an inner vision. He's blind because he's looking inward in order to know what the song he is to sing will be about.

Dante continues, "After they had talked awhile together, they turned to me with sign of salutation, at which my master smiled; and far more honor still they showed me, for they made me one of their company, so that I was sixth amid so much wisdom. Thus we went onward to the light, talking of things it is well to pass in silence, even as it was well to speak of them there."[15] Here is Dante. He inscribes himself in the history of Western poets, and he counts himself as sixth among them. We could say a number of things about what they are talking about. He says that he can't say. We can easily infer, however, that they talk about poetry, about their craft. This is the way Dante's imagination works, so that the reader has to pull together things that don't seem to be described.

Still, we know they are in the garden, and there's a kind of self-absorption about this setting. There is a kind of self-enclosure about this kind of poetry. It's a little scene that reflects on what the spiritual condition may have been like, but what is the most surprising and what constitutes the temptation of the scene for the pilgrim's own spiritual pilgrimage is that he claims to be "sixth amid so much wisdom." Do you see how this is jarring? Dante is going downward for redemption. He is descending in humility, and yet now he talks with a poetic voice that elevates itself. There seems to be a kind of discrepancy between the two, and that's the great temptation of Dante, to believe that poetry is better than philosophy, that poetry is like history. It's a form of hubris, and we'll explore it in more depth in the next chapter, since Canto 5 proves to be an extended reflection on the dangers of such a claim and the responsibility of writing poetry.

Ultimately, then, Canto 4 reveals a generic ambiguity to the *Comedy.* I have been defining the poem as novelistic vis-à-vis the circular structure of the "eternal return" and reincarnation of the souls encapsulated in the great Virgilian notion of what an epic is, and Dante will continue mixing his genres. As soon as you formulate something, Dante has a way of under-cutting that formulation.

Canto 4 ends with a miniature representation of the epic quality of this text. It enumerates all the souls that Dante can see, in a manner similar to the scene in *The Iliad* where Helen numbers all the Greek ships for Priam: "There before me, on the enameled green, the great spirits were shown to me, so that I glory within me for having seen them. I saw Electra with many companions, among whom I knew Hector, and Aeneas, and falcon-eyed Caesar armed. I saw Camilla and Penthesilea; and on the other side I saw King Latinus, who sat with his daughter Lavinia. I saw that Brutus who drove out the Tarquin, I saw Lucretia, Julia, Marcia, and Cornelia; and by himself apart I saw Saladin. When I raised my eyes a little higher, I saw the Master of those who know, seated in a philosophic family . . . Socrates . . . Plato . . . Democritus . . . Diogenes"—all the Greek philosophers and then Orpheus, Cicero, Linus, Seneca, Euclid, Ptolemy.[16]

Here we have a version of the classical encyclopedia—all of the knowl-edge is gathered here—and yet Dante has a way of saying that traditional encyclopedias have something wanting about them. They never tell you how you can really educate yourself. They never describe the process of education. Epic enumerations like this one always imply the wish of a nar-rative to encompass the whole of reality, as encyclopedias aim to do. The intellectual reality of it, though, is that enumerations, simply by being enu-merations, imply that no totalization is possible. There is always something that escapes the formal ordering that the encyclopedias want to reach. There is always something left unsaid.

CHAPTER 4

Inferno 5–7

The drama that unfolds in Canto 5, ostensibly a drama of desire, stems directly from the crisis in the pilgrim's mind in Canto 4 of *Inferno*. In what way? It is as if the experience of hubris, the celebration of one's own power and prowess as a poet, now has to confront the consequences of that claim. Dante will come literally face to face with a reader of his poetry, one who understands his poetry in a way that was not necessarily the one intended by its author, one of the most famous women in literature: Francesca. But before we explore this drama, we need to set the scene.

Where are we located in Canto 5? We are in the second circle. We're in the larger area of incontinence, and I should emphasize something about the moral topography of Hell before we consider what that means. What is the distribution of sins and sinfulness in Hell? For that matter, what is sin? For Dante, the will is the locus of sin. You cannot really sin intellectually; you cannot commit sins with your mind. Your mind can become an accomplice of the will, but it's primarily in the will, in voluntary action, that you find sinfulness. So, the first thing we should note is that Hell's geography depends on this conception of sin.

The shape of the soul for Dante is classical, ancient, Aristotelian. It's figured as a triangle that has the will on the left side and reason on the right. Where the two faculties of the soul, which are like the two feet of the body, meet is referred to in the Middle Ages as *synderesis,* using a classical term. This is the area where free will is produced; in other words, in free will you have a conjunction of both will and reason, and that's the beginning of the moral life. Only when your will is free can you start making decisions and getting engaged in the world around you.

Now the soul can also be further subdivided in a tripartite structure. At the bottom, we find the concupiscent appetites, which are what Francesca and the other sinners in "upper Hell" experience: lust, gluttony, avarice, prodigality. In the middle area, you have the sensitive appetite, which is the middle ground of Dante's Hell—violence and the kind of bestiality that takes over the human mind. And then the third area consists of the rational appetites. The order—the geometry and geography—of Hell is patterned on this systematization of the soul, but in an inverted form.

Thus we find ourselves beginning in the area of concupiscence, the area of lust. It's the area of the sinners who have inverted the hierarchical order of the reason and the will. They have invested pleasure with supreme lordship over the order of rationality. So, reason, though somehow dimmed, is always going to be used as a rationale to explain the passion of Francesca. I should mention a few details about the particular landscape that Dante evokes in this area. First of all, it's a landscape of souls that go swirling around in a circular structure. You have to be careful as you read the poem, even about the directions of the pilgrim. For instance, which way is Dante descending into this spiraled Hell? When you move in a spiral, it's very difficult to see if you're going left or right, of course, but Dante goes out of his way to say that he's always going leftward. And as soon as we get to Purgatory, he goes out of his way to tell us that he's now going rightward, which is to say, that Hell is the inverted cosmos of *Purgatorio*.

The other important detail about the landscape involves the ancient symbolism of the circle. There are a number of ways of understanding direction in the Middle Ages. For instance, the linear direction implies that of human beings, who are caught in time and who are going toward some kind of purpose or precise destination. The angels, instead, are those who circle around the throne of God, so that the circle implies the plentitude and perfection of movement. Clearly, Francesca and the other souls here are caught in a whirl of love, and they enact a caricature of the circular, perfect movement of the mind and of the angels around the divinity. The spiral, here the movement of the pilgrim, combines line and circle and implies that Dante is proceeding in a circular fashion around the divinity, but he also has a purpose, an aim to reach. Francesca and Paolo, to the contrary, are swirling in endless circles, and they will never rest.

The fundamental principle behind this representation of desire is displacement, something that Dante valorizes greatly, revealing the ambiguity of Dante's thinking. Desire is displacement because in this case Paolo and Francesca get nowhere, and yet it's exactly this displacement that makes us aware that we are never where we should be, that our hearts are always out of place. It's what Augustine says in *The Confessions,* which he begins by admitting his awareness that his heart is unquiet, and this disquiet renders the heart out of place. So, Dante is moving within the larger pattern of Augustine's thinking about desire.

To return to the text, however, Dante begins this canto with a number of avian metaphors, and around line 30, he writes of a "hellish hurricane." It's the externalizing of the storm inside, which, "never resting, sweeps along the spirits with its rapine; whirling and smiting, it torments them." It continues, "As their wings bear the starlings along in the cold season, in wide, dense flocks, so does that blast the sinful spirits; hither, thither, downward, upward, it drives them. No hope of less pain, not to say of rest, ever comforts them." And then there are cranes. Finally, Dante asks Virgil, "Master, who are these people that are so lashed by the black air?"[1]

Following these aerial images we have an enumeration, another epic device. The epic is always driven by the desire for totality, to include all things within the compass of its representation. It always has the enumerative style, and now here we have a number of figures that Virgil points out, beginning with several queens who are founders of cities. Keep this status in mind, because one of the issues that Dante is raising in this canto is the relationship between eros and politics, pleasure and the city. What is the place of pleasure in the economy of the city?

But who are the queens in this list? One is the "empress of many tongues," who "was so given to lechery that she made lust licit in her law, to take away the blame she had incurred." The emphasis of the line is this lust becoming lawful, lust becoming public and accepted. We learn that this empress is Semiramis, of Assyria, "of whom we read that she succeeded Ninus."[2] The next one is Dido, who in many ways is Virgil's invention in *The Aeneid.* Dante cannot but think about how Rome's conquest would appear to be the result of the libido of power, and he's playing with the idea that Rome, *Roma* here, is a *boustrophedon.* Boustrophedon is a Greek term meaning a reversal. *Roma,* as in a mirror, becomes *Amor,* and Venus is the mother of Aeneas. There is this idea again of an inner link between love and politics and the city. Virgil writes *The Aeneid* as a love poem, with an ideology of Rome based on desire.

Augustine will counter this conception of love by saying that it is not really love in these instances, but rather lust for power. The antagonism between lust and love becomes clear in Augustine. An African native but a Roman thinker, Augustine was really writing about and reflecting on the great myths of Rome. This is true in *The Confessions,* but it is especially true in *The City of God,* where he juxtaposes and opposes the earthly city, Rome, to the heavenly city, Jerusalem. He reflects on Rome as a city based on lust for power, and from that point of view, he considers it to be no different from any other empire. The Persian Empire, the Greek claims for empire, and so on, they're all Rome, and they're all part of a long sequel of violence and imperial fantasies. Dante is thinking along these lines, as well, and we shall soon see where that will take him.

Next on the list of queens is Cleopatra of Egypt, then Helen and the story of the fall of Troy. Then, finally, we find the story of Tristan and Isolde, which is a medieval invention. The presence of Tristan reveals that all the heroes and heroines of antiquity are viewed through the lenses of medieval romances. They may belong to the grand epics of the classical world, but Dante will see them through that optic of romance, the literature of desire. "And more than a thousand shades whom love had parted from our life he showed me, pointing them out and naming them."[3] Thus concludes the epic catalog.

Dante continues by describing his reaction to the catalog: "When I heard my teacher name the ladies and the knights of old, pity overcame me and I was as one bewildered."[4] Now this is really the first time that Dante introduces the notion of pity in the poem. And by the end of the canto, he is going to be overwhelmed by pity; he is going to faint after he hears the story of Francesca. He will be so overwhelmed that he will fall "like a dead body" falls. It's sympathy, maybe it's a little bit of self-recognition, maybe it's a way of coming to grips with his own responsibilities. The point here is that Dante is reflecting, and will go on reflecting, on the relationship between pity and justice. Does justice require pity, or is there a kind of justice that can be pitiless, that has no place for compassion? Are the two necessarily antagonistic, or is there some meeting point between them? This is but the first time that he considers this idea of pity, the recognition that it could be him in that position.

And with pity in his heart he says to Virgil, "Poet . . . willingly would I speak with those two that go together and seem to be so light upon the wind." He doesn't talk to any of the major classical figures. He chooses two ordinary people from his own time, from the area near where he eventually went to live, Ravenna. Virgil responds, " 'You shall see when they are nearer to us; and do you entreat them then by that love which leads them, and they will come.' As soon as the wind bent them to us, I raised my voice, 'O wearied souls! come and speak with us, if Another forbid it not.' As doves called by desire, with wings raised and steady, come through the air, borne by their will to the sweet nest, so did these issue from the troop where Dido is." Again we find the presence of Dido and with it the other possibility of Rome: Virgil is writing about the great battle between Carthage and Rome as two ways of choosing a civilization, two ways of experimenting with cities. And finally Paolo and Francesca arrive, "coming to us through the malignant air, such force had my compassionate cry."[5]

Now Francesca speaks, "O living creature, gracious and benign, that goes through the black air visiting us who stained the world with blood." She died, by the way, at the hands of her husband, who caught Francesca and his brother Paolo in a tryst, so that's why that allusion to the blood is there. "If the King of the universe were friendly to us," she continues, "we would pray Him for your peace, since you have pity on our perverse ill. Of that which it pleases you to hear and to speak, we will hear and speak with you, while the wind, as now, is silent."[6] Then she begins a description of her life and where she was born. Most of the narratives in *Inferno* begin with this idea of birth. We saw that in the case of Virgil and we see it once more in the case of Francesca. They begin with birth for a number of reasons, but primarily because birth is for Dante the event that could potentially impart a different direction to the world, or that could end in nothing, as in the case of Francesca.

She then starts to talk about her city in terms that clearly contrast with the movement of the souls caught in the storm. She implies that what she really wants is rest: "The city where I was born lies on that shore where the Po descends to be at peace with its followers."[7] Here we have an image of stability in a city she has lost.

Next we have three tercets in Italian that all begin with the word *amor*, love, love made into a kind of transcendent divinity. This love is the great subject of Francesca's experience: "Love, which is quickly kindled in a gentle heart, seized this one for the fair form that was taken from me—and the way of it afflicts me still. Love, which absolves no loved one from loving, seized me so strongly with delight in him that, as you see, it does not leave me even now. Love brought us to one death."[8] What is she saying here? First of all, she's actually quoting some important works of literature. The first line, "Love, which is quickly kindled in a gentle heart," is a quotation from one of Dante's sonnets in the *Vita nuova*, mentioned in chapter 2. Dante writes, "Love and the gracious heart are a single thing," using the poetics of the sweet new style. He tells us that "one can no more be without the other / than can the reasoning mind without its reason."[9] Francesca clearly intends to flatter the sensible authorship of the poet himself. It's part of a seductive strategy that she uses.

The second image—the ideas that love does not allow anyone who loves to return to his or her previous state and that love is reciprocal—comes from the so-called rules of love that Marie de Champagne dictates in book 3 of Andreas Capellanus's *The Art of Courtly Love*. The first rule: "Marriage is no real excuse for not loving," which is a way of saying that adultery is the law of courtly love. Rule two: "He who is not jealous cannot love." Seven: "When one lover dies, a widowhood of two years is required of the survivor." Eight: "No one should be deprived of love by the very best of reasons." And nine: "No one can love unless one is impelled by somebody else's love," which is the line that Francesca mentions. Francesca imagines herself as a courtly love heroine. She lives in the world of kings; she's in the court of the king of love, and thus these rules of love in *The Art of Courtly Love* apply to her.

But what is she saying by quoting these rules? What Andreas, first of all, does by having these rules of love and thereby reducing love to an art is acknowledge that love is the most transgressive and disruptive of all experiences. As a result, it needs to be formalized. Love needs to be contained. It may be made part of a game, as is perhaps the thrust of Andreas Cappellanus's thinking, or part of an acceptable ceremony, which is a possible reading of what is happening here. Francesca falls completely, squarely within this tradition of believing that she lives in a world of love where there is no possible resistance to love. In effect, these tercets about love, love, and love are meant to cast love as a transcendent force that no one can really withstand—or that Francesca, at least, cannot withstand. She is abdicating the power of her will to the irresistible, omnipotent, presence of this love. It's part of a strategy of not acknowledging any responsibility for her actions, of finding an alibi instead. She's telling Dante that his works and the works of Andreas Cappellanus were filters of love, that they were to blame for what happened between her and her brother-in-law. It's a way for Dante to show Francesca's blindness to the reality of her situation, as well as an unwillingness on her part to give up that which is really the defining trait of sin: habit. Sin is sin in the measure in which it has become a habit, a way of clinging to an action and refusing to acknowledge that there may be an alternative to it.

When she finishes, Dante entertains her arguments and asks for more information:

When I answered I began: "Alas! How many sweet thoughts, what great desire, brought them to the woeful pass!" Then I turned again to them, and I began: "Francesca, your torments make me weep for grief and pity; but tell me, in the time of the sweet sighs, by what and how did Love grant you to know the dubious desires?" And she to me, "There is no greater sorrow than to recall, in wretchedness, the happy time; and this your teacher knows. But if you have such great desire to know the first root of our love, I will tell as one who weeps and tells. One day, for pastime, we read of Lancelot, how love constrained him; we were alone, suspecting nothing. Several times that reading urged our eyes to meet and took the color from our faces, but one moment alone it was that overcame us. When we read how the longed-for smile was kissed by so great a lover, this one, who never shall be parted from me, kissed my mouth all trembling. A Gallehault was the book and he who wrote it; that day we read no farther in it." While the one spirit said this, the other [Paolo] wept, so that for pity I swooned, as if in death, and fell as a dead body falls.[10]

And that's the end of the canto. It's an amazing story she tells, and the first thing to notice here is that this is a story of reading. She reads, they read, one day they were reading for delight, and that's probably one of the concerns that Dante has. How should we read if we read for delight? Is there some other way of reading?

More specifically, she's reading the story of Lancelot and Guinevere, a story of adultery at court. Lancelot is the secret lover of the queen, clearly out of the desire to supplant the king, Arthur. There's a triangle here, a triangle of desire, and Francesca will imitate this triangle. The story of Lancelot, like all the stories Chrétien de Troyes, begins on one of the great feasts of Christianity, which are the Ascension, Easter, the Pentecost. And the heroes are sitting around boasting about themselves. Not one of them is doing anything heroic, but they all talk about how great they were. It's a little bit like a parodic version of the argument between Ulysses and Ajax in one of the last books of *The Aeneid,* where they talk about who is the hero worthy of inheriting the arms of the great Achilles, based not on their present prowess but on what they once were. Thus, in the story of Chrétien, the idea is that the heroic age is over and done with. The whole romance explores the reasons why the heroic age may have come to an end.

Why did it come to an end? The secret love affair between Lancelot and Guinevere. When the story starts, they're all sitting around drinking ale and talking, and a mysterious figure comes from the outside and kidnaps the queen. The knights don't move, and everybody's expecting Lancelot to get up and go to rescue the queen, but he won't out of fear that the secret affair that he has with the queen will be discovered.

That hesitation, that moral hesitation of Lancelot's, is the emblem of the fall from aristocratic virtues. There is now the intrusion of a temporal wedge between the thought and the action, and furthermore Lancelot would have to go on that famous cart of shame, exposed to the ridicule of the whole town, before he could really even attempt to rescue the queen. If you think about it, then, Chrétien is already reflecting on the crisis of the city in terms of private passion. Something is really gnawing at the heart of the city, and it's the inability to distinguish between the public and the private, an inability aptly demonstrated in Canto 5 by Francesca.

Dante is exploring reading here, so Francesca is reading the text of Lancelot and lapses into an imitative strategy of reading. She wants to be like the heroine about whom she is reading. She refuses to take an interpretative distance from this specular image; she wants to feel like a queen. She also thinks Paolo can be like Lancelot, and this pattern of mirroring is what we call the mimetic quality of the text, to use the term of René Girard, who has written about this question of the imitative structure of desire. Between us and the object of desire there is always a mediator, and in this case the mediator is Lancelot for Paolo, and Guinevere for Francesca.

But there's more to this story. For instance, you cannot read the story without thinking about how Dante frames the experience of Francesca with the language of time. If you glance at the text, you will see just how many references there are to time. "There is no greater sorrow than to recall, in wretchedness, *the happy time*" (emphasis mine). Then she starts talking about her adventure: "*One day*, for pastime, we read of Lancelot," and then "*that day* we read no farther" (emphasis mine). It's all about time, about the question of time as an experience, but why is Francesca represented in this way? Why is her story presented in terms of time?

In effect, I think Francesca has one great passion, and that passion is to do away with time. She's expressing the desire that her prior happiness, a fleeting moment, may last an eternity. Or she may be expressing the insight that one moment of happiness is well worth an eternity of pain. Or maybe she's just saying that it's not too bad that the love story that I had only lasted the briefest possible time. At any rate, what this shows is primarily that

Francesca not only abdicated choice and not only thought that her own will was powerless vis-à-vis the irresistible force of this transcendent idea of love, but above all, she has betrayed the order of necessity and time. Her passion violates the order of time. From this point of view, Dante is forced to reflect upon his responsibilities as an author when he's confronted with the reader. What have I done? What have I written? What I wrote has been understood in a way that is not necessarily the one that I intended, according to the meaning that I meant to assign to the *Vita nuova.* Dante has to reconsider the impact he has on his readers.

These concerns continue to figure into Canto 6, which is not unlike what we have been describing here. Whatever Dante has found out about passion, about desire, about the world of appetites, and whatever he has decided about himself and the meaning that this may have for him as a poet, he will use these discoveries as the premise for other concerns raised in Canto 6, a more political canto. He now aims to find out how authentic his earlier findings may be. He moves into a public realm, from the world of the court, the private world of Francesca, to the world of the city, of Florence, where we are still talking about incontinence but in a different form. Here we find the question of gluttony and politics.

His entrance into the circle of the gluttonous begins, "At the return of my mind which had closed itself before the piteousness of the two kinsfolk that had quite overwhelmed me with sadness, I see about me new torments and new tormented souls, whichever way I move and turn about to gaze."[11] First of all, I find the presence of the word *mind* in line 1 very suggestive. Canto 6 is all about bodies, about gluttonous souls who were once bodies and who cared only about their bodies. Dante uses as a counterpoint to these souls the question of the mind, as if the sin of these gluttonous individuals was the sin of not thinking of their minds, for the mind is seen as a necessary complement to the presence of bodies. The word *mind,* in Italian *mente,* comes from the Latin *mens,* or "measure." The mind is that which measures, which gives a sense of the measure of our own desires. We are asked to measure what is missing in the prevailingly biological reflection of Canto 6, a reflection about the biology of politics. Normally we have the pride of minds when we think about all the megalomaniacs in politics, but here it's really a question of politics in terms of the inexhaustible appetites of bodies.

The mythological figure that presides over the political bodies of this canto is the three-headed dog, a monstrous animal whose voraciousness and many mouths hint at the canto's themes. The landscape is stinking under an endless rain, a tellingly repulsive form of waste and food. Dante sets the scene: "As the dog that barking craves, and then grows quiet when he snaps up his food, straining and struggling only to devour it, such became the foul faces of the demon Cerberus, who so thunders on the souls that they would fain be deaf. We were passing over the shades whom the heavy rain subdues, and we were setting our feet upon their emptiness, which seems real bodies."[12] This is a great description and figuration of gluttony, bodies that are always empty now. They are punished to be empty, to exist as empty forms, and they only *seem* to possess real bodies.

One of these empty entities sits up and says, "O you that are led through this Hell . . . recognize me if you can: you were made before I was unmade." This is Ciacco, a name that means "pig," his nickname in the streets of Florence. Dante answers him, "The anguish you endure perhaps takes you from my memory, so that I do not seem ever to have seen you; but tell me who you are, who are set in a place so grievous and who suffer such punishment, that, if any is greater, none is so loathsome." And Ciacco says to Dante, "Your city"—he is talking about Florence, and his use of "*your* city" rather than "our city" suggests that Ciacco views himself as not really occupying a place within Florentine society—"which is so full of envy that already the sack runs over, held me in it, in the bright life. You citizens"—once again the distance of Ciacco from the city of Florence—"called me Ciacco: for the ruinous fault of gluttony, as you see, I am broken by the rain; and I, in my misery, am not alone, for all these endure the same penalty for the same fault."[13] So, in this passage we are given the sinner's stance on the city, but we do not yet know Dante's position.

The basic conceit in this canto is that of the city and the body. In the classical world the typical conceit involved the correlation between the *soul* and the city, but for Dante this is a soulless city. The only way to talk about it is to tell the story of the city as a body, as a corporate structure. Some of you may recall that in Shakespeare's *Coriolanus,* the title character makes a similar speech about the city and the body. But this image really goes back to a Roman historian whom Dante absolutely loves: Livy, who wrote a famous book about the foundation of Rome.

One of the stories that Livy tells is that of the famous civil war in Rome between the patricians and the plebeians. The plebeians, the workers, are tired of what is happening in the city. They are doing all the work, but they have few of the pleasures coming from living in the city, so they decide to secede. They retreat to the Aventine Hill, one of the seven hills of Rome, and the city is paralyzed, as you can imagine, so the patricians send an emissary, a man by the name of Menenius, to convince the plebeians to return to the city. Menenius manages to do this by telling the plebeians a famous fable. He explains that when you have a body, the hands work, the mouth enjoys and savors the great pleasures of foods, and the stomach can be full, but in truth whatever they produce and take in and ingest, they redistribute to the rest of the body, to the hands, the feet, and so on. In this sense the city is like a body, organized around a corporate structure. The plebeians are convinced by the comparison, and they go back to recompose the order of the city. This is the fundamental structure here.

Does Dante believe in the corporate structure of the city? Can it really hold together? I submit to you that he no longer believes in this conception of the city. When you read the canto you notice that all the body parts are literally littering the city. The nails, the hands, the heart, the beard, the hair, the mouth—they're all mentioned, and they're spread all over, as if to imply the impossibility of constituting these body parts into an organic unified totality.

Another issue that is being raised here is the question of civil war, a topic always at the center of Dante's political thought. Dante responds to Ciacco, "Your misery so weighs upon me that it bids me weep. But tell me, if you can, what the citizens of the divided city"—this is still Florence—"will come to; and if any one in it is just; and tell me why such discord has assailed it." An amazing image, discord, because it's a musical metaphor, but the word comes from the "heart"; discord makes the heart the receptacle where all these jealousies destroying the city are located. Ciacco replies, "After long contention they will come to blood, and the rustic party will drive out the other with much offense. Then, through the power of one who presently is temporizing"—meaning the pope—"that party is destined to fall within three years, and the other to prevail, long holding its head high and keeping the other under heavy burdens, however it may lament and feel the shame. Two men are just, and are not heeded there. Pride, envy and avarice are the three sparks that have inflamed their hearts."[14]

Dante follows this description of civil strife with a street scene in Florence, in which he asks about some other characters in the city: "I would have you instruct me further, and make me a gift of further speech: Farinata"—who will appear in Canto 10 of *Inferno*—"and Tegghiaio, who were so worthy, Jacopo Rusticucci, Arrigo, and Mosca, and the others who set their minds on doing good, tell me where they are and give me to know them, for great desire urges me to learn whether Heaven soothes or Hell envenoms them."[15] One should note, first and foremost, the language of gluttony throughout this passage: sweetness, bitterness, pleasant, unpleas-antness. This language runs through the canto and links together gluttony and politics. The men of such worth, though, where are they? They were so set on doing well in the city, but now they may be in Hell.

What Dante is dramatizing is the distance between human perspec-tive, the judgments that we make as human beings, and the divine judgment on the dealings and doings of these famous people; there is a discrepancy between the way they are judged here on earth and the reality of the worth and value of these people. They're farther down in the fire, and different faults weigh them down to the depths. What an extraordinary metaphor, the weight, the burden of sin, but it's really an image that goes back to the question of gravity. When you want to talk about the weight that we carry within us, the gravity we have within us, that gravity is love. There's a pas-sage in *The Confessions* of Augustine where Augustine says that he wants to exemplify why some people go up and other people go down, and he says it's like the gravity of objects around us. You drop a stone, and the stone goes downward on account of its own gravity, its own specific weight. A fire, he says, goes upward on account of its own specific weight. For humans, love is our gravity, and whether we go up or down depends on the direction of our desires.

So, this conversation with Ciacco provides a sense of all the reso-nances of this canto, but at the heart of it all, there is primarily the question of civil war, between the Guelphs and the Ghibellines, between patricians and plebeians. Dante sees the whole of history—Roman history, whether he is going to read Virgil, Lucan, Statius, Greek history, the story of Oedipus and Eteocles and Polynices—from the point of view of civil war. In his *Mo-narchia,* for instance, a treatise about the desirable form of a universal con-federation of states under one emperor, Dante considers the needed unity of all states, very much patterned on the Roman Empire. In fact, the Roman Empire becomes the model for this kind of unification that forms the basis of Dante's political vision. In effect, Dante sees history as a satanic form of civil war. So harsh is he about the realities of cities that you begin to wonder how and if he can elaborate a constructive theory of politics.

On this matter Dante does not agree with Virgil, nor does he agree with Virgil's greatest critic, Augustine, in *The City of God.* For Virgil, Rome is the providential empire, an empire that can unify the whole world. Au-gustine writes against Virgil and says even Rome is part of the history of violence. Dante comes along and pulls together within the *Divine Comedy* the idea of Rome and the necessary empire and the idea of civil war. What is it that connects them? Dante's argument is the following: Virgil is right to believe in the unity of all mankind, in a stoic idea that we all live in a "cosmopolis," a city of the world where we all find a place. And Augustine is right to claim that the empire is built on libido and lust. They are both right, and yet they are both wrong, precisely because they contradict each other. What Dante says in response to Augustine is that if there is no empire, then we are living in a world of disorder and lawlessness. The empire becomes the necessary remedy to the evils of the civil war. The civil war is the condition where my own brother, my own neighbor, can become my enemy. Augustine does not acknowledge this reality. It's the famous Christian response to the historical evil of empires: let me retreat into myself and find within myself some kind of comfort and some kind of shelter. And Dante will say that's not enough, because you may have retreated into yourself but the civil war will still reach into you.

And thus the movement from Canto 5 to Canto 6 of *Inferno* is a movement away from the internal world of desires that seem to be so private and personal to the outside world. As I said, Dante has to go outside of himself to test the authenticity of his discoveries in Canto 5. Canto 6, the political canto, will reveal that there is no comfort zone of one soul in the world, that the inner world is necessarily part of the outside world, and that the outside world will encroach upon and enter into the inner world. The terms for this kind of movement between the inner and the outer come from Virgil and Augustine, Virgil with the idea of the defense of the empire, Augustine with his undermining of the notion of the necessity of the empire. Dante will continuously attempt to harmonize the two visions, and he will ultimately endorse the idea of the empire, aware that that's the best (and only) response to the tragedy of civil wars.

Now we move from the warring masses to Canto 7, the only canto without individualized sinners. Here Dante meets the avaricious and the prodigals, and there's no individual figuration for them. It is as if these sins became an anonymous, and therefore a more collective, kind of problem, which he represents in terms of the countermovement of Scylla and Charybdis, and here we have the great figuration of Fortune as a woman turning the Wheel of Fortune while blindfolded. Dante uses the image to illustrate how the avaricious and the prodigals can turn against each other. And he asks how this can be possible. He asks why we are so attached to the things of the world.

Dante explains that God "for worldly splendors . . . ordained a general minister and guide who should in due time transfer the vain goods from race to race, and from one to another blood, beyond the prevention of human wit, so that one race rules and another languishes, pursuant to her judgment. . . . She foresees, judges, and pursues her reign, as theirs the other gods. Her changes know no truce. Necessity compels her to be swift, so fast do men come to their turns. This is she who is much reviled even by those who ought to praise her, but do wrongfully blame her and defame her. But she is blest and does not hear it. Happy with the other primal creatures she turns her sphere and rejoices in her bliss."[16] It's Fortune at the wheel, but this is a figuration that in many ways needs some explaining.

How can Dante believe in God as Fortuna? How can he refer to this pagan deity, Lady Luck? How can he live in a world of providentiality, where fortune is an intelligence of God? Fortune is blindfolded, yes, but there is still an intelligence, there is still a will and a meditation behind her turning of the wheel. Furthermore, there is a reason why Canto 7 begins with an allusion to the great war in heaven, to the primal struggle between the angels that disrupted the order of the cosmos. In other words, Fortune is for Dante the divinity that rules over this sublunary world of corruption. She is a minister only within the world of the fall.

But what can we do about Fortune? What is up will inevitably come down, in an endless rotation of her wheel. We are always precariously poised on the curve. We are never quite stable in our own achievements. Dante implies that the only way to conquer fortune is to give up one's attachment to the things of this world. Thus, Canto 7 offers multiple means of avoiding a contradiction in terms with regard to fortune and divine providence, while grappling with several of the weighty issues raised in the preceding two cantos.

CHAPTER 5

Inferno 9–11

Now Dante and Virgil are moving, and we with them, away from the area of incontinence and toward the gates of the city of Dis, where the pilgrim experiences a serious impediment, an impasse. He cannot go any farther. The guidance of Virgil fails him, and we are going to examine why it fails him along with the problem that the pilgrim will have to solve.

Once he is within the city of Dis in Canto 9, the first sinners he meets are the heretics, heresiarchs, chief among whom is Epicurus, the Epicureans, and already it is possible to establish a link between the city and Epicurean philosophers. To clarify this connection, one should be aware that Dante acknowledges, in a philosophical text that he wrote called the *Convivio,* three schools of philosophy: the academics or Aristotelians, the Stoics, and the Epicureans. In *Inferno* he examines who these Epicureans are, and for him they appear as those who are guilty of a form of intellectual pride, since heresy is a question of intellect and not of will. They deny the immortality of the soul, but in a certain sense it's still a problem to figure out why Dante should think of them as sinners at all. In antiquity the Epicureans were viewed as simply one more school of philosophical opinion, so why should they be punished? Dante's answer is that they should be punished for their intellect, although the logic of Dante's own idea of sinfulness is that the will has to be involved. The will is at the center of the habit to sin.

Let us return, though, to the crisis of Canto 9 as Dante is progressing in this journey. He reaches the gate of Dis, and three Furies, the three Erinyes of Greek mythology—Alecto, Tisiphone, and Megaera—appear and stop him. They tell him that he cannot go into the city, which is described as very similar to a medieval city. (In fact, it's built near a kind of swamp for reasons that have nothing to do with ecology but with the medieval idea that the land was always more malleable near swamps and had an easy supply of water.) At any rate, the three Furies call on Medusa, who doesn't come, but they threaten the pilgrim with the sight of Medusa all the same. They make a threat of petrifaction, of course, because according to the myth, if you gaze at the face of Medusa, you turn to stone. Medusa was a great virginal beauty, a vestal in the temple of Neptune, but then Neptune violated her, and Minerva took revenge on her by metamorphosing her into this ugly, repulsive figure with her hair turned into snakes. And yet she has a magic power to turn all onlookers into stone. The drama here involves the pilgrim directly; this threat is aimed at him. Virgil intervenes: "Turn your back and keep your eyes shut; for should the Gorgon"—Medusa—"show herself and you see her, there would be no returning above."[1] The guide offers his guidance, but then a fundamental shift occurs.

Dante continues: "Thus said the master, and he himself turned me round and, not trusting to my hands, covered my face with his own hands as well." Then the poet interrupts the narrative and talks to us as a poet. This is the first address to the reader. That is to say, this is no longer part of the action, no longer the story of the pilgrim, but the poet who is sitting in his study. He says, "O you who have sound understanding, mark the doctrine that is hidden under the veil of the strange verses!"[2] The poet, assuming authority, turns to us readers, and in a sense, he needs readers so that his authority can be constituted, and he warns us. He admonishes us to engage in what clearly appears as an allegorical operation. We have to know how to read underneath the veil of language, there's something hidden underneath this. So, what is the allegory about?

To better lift the veil, we return to the myth of Medusa. In another part of that tale, Medusa is conquered. She is defeated by the poet Perseus, who rides upon Pegasus, the winged horse of poetry. Perseus uses the mirrored shield Minerva has given him, and by not looking at Medusa directly but at a reflected image in this shield, he manages to see her and slay her. Within the Ovidian narrative, this is clearly a means to evoke for us the need for a mediated vision. Only through the mediation of the shield can Perseus be victorious and take flight on the back of Pegasus. For us, the shield of Minerva is the text, because at this point there is a direct divergence between what the pilgrim is enjoined to do and what we as readers are asked to do. Virgil tells him to shut his eyes, and not trusting the pilgrim, who must have been awed by this situation, Virgil covers the pilgrim's eyes for him. In turn, the poet addresses us and tells us to open our eyes. We can do this because we have the shield of Minerva, this textual mediation that will allow us to escape the direct threat of Medusa. After this command is issued, Mercury, who is the messenger, the figure of the interpreter, comes and manages to make a breach in the wall of the city so that the pilgrim and the guide can continue their descent. But we are still left wondering what this allegory really is.

Let me say a few things about the technique of allegory. Whenever you read the *Divine Comedy,* many scholars will tell you that the text is a vision, which it is, and that it's allegorical, which at times it is, and this allegory is supposed to explain everything that the pilgrim finds while lost in the woods. They're not just woods, though; they are also said to be a state of sin, and there he meets three beasts that stand for pride, and wrath, and whatnot. But the significance of that initial landscape, as you may recall, is not all that clear, and that's part of the problem. That's what I call the land of unlikeness, as John Freccero called it, within which the pilgrim will find himself. There is a marked inability to join together signs and their significations, an awareness that there are no signs so self-transparent as to be understood or decoded in a particular way. What is this idea of allegory? Dante is clearly telling us that it is an allegory at work: "You readers, who have good understanding and healthy minds, open your eyes and look beneath the veil of the strange verse." Why is it strange? What's going on here?

What is allegory, first of all? *Allegory* means "to speak otherwise." It's a figure related to, but not quite the same as, the enigmas found in rhetorical primers from medieval and classical times: enigmas, irony, when you say one thing and you mean another. But to define allegory in this way is to say very little because Dante has been very thoughtful. He has probed this issue very deeply in a couple of his works: in the letter to Cangrande that he sends as an introduction to the first ten cantos of *Paradiso,* Cangrande being the lord of Verona where Dante had lived for a while, and also in the *Convivio,* where he explores the idea of how one can arrive at meaning. He has been saying to himself: "I have a statement. How can I go on drawing a particular significance, or more than one significance, out of a statement?"

Dante ultimately distinguishes two types of allegory in answer to this question. One is the allegory of poets, the other the allegory of theologians. How does he distinguish them? The allegory of poets is an allegory that, in the literal sense, is a fable, a fiction. For example, Dante refers to Orpheus, who moved stones with the power of his language. This story really means that the power of the voice of the poet manages to edify cities. Orpheus also tamed lions with the power of his words. What that means is that whatever ferociousness we have inside us can partly be tamed by music, song, poetry, and so forth. That's an allegory of poets.

An allegory of theologians is completely different. The example that Dante gives sends us to the biblical story of Exodus. This is the story where the Jews escape the bondage of Egypt, go through the desert, and reach the Promised Land. According to Dante, this happened historically, it's true. This is not a fiction. The Red Sea did open up, and the Jews could pass through the Red Sea that way. In the allegory of theologians, the literal level must be historical. It must be an event. This is the distinction.

Within the allegory of theologians, they distinguish four levels of exegesis, a term that means interpretation. Four levels: the literal we have covered. Then there is the allegorical or figurative. An allegory tells you what to do, it teaches you. It has an ethics involved. The third level is the tropological, telling you what the story means in terms of your whole life, not just an action in a particular case. Finally, there is the anagogical or eschatological level, wherein the last spiritual realities are historically figured through the story of the Jews crossing the wilderness and reaching Jerusalem, which means having a kind of spiritual conversion. It means that this is really the way that life ought to go. You go from sin to glory or the peace of the city, and then anagogically, this is the story of the soul. It prefigures what the soul ought to be. In the case of the allegory of poets, you instead only have two levels, the literal and the moral.

There are a lot of difficulties with this way of distinguishing between the two types of allegory because even if the allegory of theologians refers to events, it's still words that we are reading. As a result, there is a way in which Dante seems to dodge the whole issue of how one can distinguish between the two modes. He will say that the true difference is in how you take the literal sense. You may, as an act of faith, take the literal sense of the Bible as the word of God, and then you are reading it theologically. But if you decide instead to say that the Bible is actually a collection of extraordinary poetic stories, then you are reading it according to the allegory of poets.

How does Dante circumvent this issue? By saying that his story may well be taken as an allegory of poets, but it's also an allegory of theologians because the literal sense is encapsulated in the "I" of the text. The historical sense is in Dante himself. "I" am the historical cipher moving through these experiences, and therefore, it is my life to which they will give a particular sense. I am the history that will give a particular truth-value to the poetic fables I relate.

Still, at this point we have only taken care of one little problem here, very external to the story, the allegory of poets or the allegory of theologians. It is time to decide what is really going on here, how we are to understand this threat of petrification. The fact is that Dante had written in his youth a number of poems for a so-called stone lady, *donna petra* in the Italian. They describe a love that was unrequited, but the passion for this woman was such that Dante felt that his intellect would be petrified by it. It's a statement of despair, a sense that death is going to take over and he is going to be paralyzed in his will, petrified. This is what I think is happening here as well. Dante is engaged in retrospection to an experience of his past, and that experience of his past is now ahead of him threatening him once again. What can he do? He has to cleanse himself, and he has to move beyond it.

To better explain this concept and to prepare us all to move beyond the wall and into Canto 10, I will turn to a little scene from *The Confessions* of Augustine, a book that Dante knew very well. Dante quotes it at very strategic places, so there's no issue of bringing it in gratuitously to explain this passage. Forgive the reversal, but it could even be viewed as a gloss on what Dante will write next.

The Confessions is an intellectual autobiography, the story of a young man who is fascinated by various schools of philosophy. He's a Manichean, and then he turns into a Neoplatonist, very flattered by the skeptical, rhetorical mode. He's a professor of rhetoric, and he has a rhetorical way of dealing with values and the world around him. Augustine also reflects a great deal about his love of shows, his love of theater, and his critique of the theater. He asks how to explain the fact that there may be some well-meaning young man who sees the maid in distress on stage and jumps into the scene to free her. He asks what it means to be a spectator. These are some of his primary concerns.

But let us turn to a specific little scene in the text involving a friend of his, Alypius, who is a Greek intellectual in the best sense of the word, a man who believes in intellectual self-mastery, a young man who witnesses Augustine's own experiences. In narratives you always have a Sancho to accompany Don Quixote; there's always the Other, more or less skeptical, who gives authenticity and makes claims for the truth-value of what the narrator or the protagonist experiences. In this case, the Sancho figure is

Alypius, who grew up with Augustine and who is about to meet back up with his friend.

Augustine goes to Rome, where Alypius will rejoin him, and from there they will go to Milan. When in Rome, the first thing that Alypius wants to do is to go and watch the games played at the amphitheater at the Colosseum, but the games are horrifying to Augustine. He asks, "How can an intellectual such as you want to go to games where actual human beings are being thrown, for the delight of the crowds, to beasts?" Alypius, of course, tries to justify himself: "I will go but because I'm an intellectual, I promise that at the crucial moment when the sign is given for the animal to devour the human being lying there I will not watch. I'm going to turn my eyes away and I will shut my eyes." But what actually happens?

A scholar of romance philology by the name of Eric Auerbach wrote a book called *Mimesis,* in which he reflects on this scene in Augustine, though he doesn't connect it with Dante. Auerbach says that this story marks the end of Hellenic rationalism. With that in mind, let's consider the story itself before seeing how it applies to Dante:

> [Alypius] had gone before me to Rome to study law, and there he was carried away incredibly with an incredible eagerness after the shows of gladiators. For being utterly adverse to and detesting such spectacles, he was one day by chance met by diverse of his acquaintances and fellow students coming from dinner, and they with a familiar violence, haled him, vehemently refusing and resisting, into the Amphitheatre, during these cruel and deadly shows, he thus protesting, "Though you hale my body to that place, and there set me, can you force me also to turn my mind or my eyes to those shows? I shall then be absent while present, and so shall overcome both you and them." They, hearing this, led him on nevertheless, desirous perchance to try that very thing, whether he could do as he said. When they were come thither, and had taken their places as they could, the whole place kindled with that savage pastime. But he, closing the passages of his eyes, forbade his mind to range abroad after such evils; and would he had stopped his ears also! For in the fight, when one fell, a mighty cry of the whole people striking him strongly, overcome by curiosity, and as if prepared to despise and be superior to it whatsoever it were, even when seen, he opened his

eyes, and was stricken with a deeper wound in his soul than the other, whom he desired to behold, was in his body; and he fell more miserably than he upon whose fall that mighty noise was raised, which entered through his ears, and unlocked his eyes, to make way for the striking and beating down of a soul, bold rather than resolute, and the weaker in that it had presumed on itself, which ought to have relied on Thee. For so soon as he saw that blood, he therewith drunk down savageness; nor turned away, but fixed his eye, drinking in frenzy, unawares, and was delighted with that guilty fight and intoxicated with the bloody pastime. Nor was he now the man he came, but one of the throng he came unto, yea, a true associate of theirs that brought him thither. Why say more? He beheld, shouted, kindled, carried thence with him, the madness which should goad him to return not only with them who first drew him thither, but also before them, yea and to draw in others. Yet, thence didst Thou with a most strong and most merciful hand pluck him, and taught him to have confidence not in himself but in Thee.[3]

So, that's the story, but what does it mean? In *The Confessions,* Augustine is very clear about its meaning: the failure of the mind to master its own will. It's about that crisis. It's about the weakness of the will to begin with, but it's also about pride: the belief that one can rise above the contingency of temptations and be in control of oneself. Yet, it's also a story of a temptation that Alypius cannot quite resist. And I think that this is exactly what's happening in Canto 9. Dante is dramatizing not only the failure of the intellect, which he's already discussed in the early part of the canto with the failure of Virgil to guide him, but also the failure of his will, at least as an event of the past but probably also as something that can happen to him again.

The passage to the city can take place after this scene, and now he enters into the City of Dis and finds the Epicureans, those who do not believe in the mortality of the soul. Let me gloss the Epicureans a little bit more than I did before. There are two types of Epicureans. Whenever we think about the Epicureans, we tend to think about those vulgar Epicureans who worship their stomachs and the pleasures of food. I think that Dante has already dramatized that kind of Epicurean in Canto 6 when he meets, as you may remember, Ciacco, whose name means "pig." But then there is the noble version of the Epicureans here in Canto 10, those who are interested in intellectual pleasures, the pleasures of conversations, friendship, and meditation. They are those who remove themselves to the garden in the belief that they should cultivate their soul and their own pursuits. These are the noble, philosophical Epicureans, not the vulgar sort that believe in the supremacy of bodily pleasures.

Nonetheless, personal pleasure is always the aim of an Epicurean ethics. Virgil continues, "In this part Epicurus with all his followers, who make the soul die with the body, have their burial-place."[4] How fitting is the punishment for this crime, this sin. It's perfect because these people never really believed in the immortality of the soul, and they are condemned to be dead forever. They dwell in sarcophagi, entombed. Sometimes we may wonder about the appropriateness of a punishment for a particular sin, but here we have no reason at all to be surprised by this destiny reserved for the Epicureans.

"Therefore, to the question which you ask me," Virgil explains, "you shall soon have satisfaction here within, and also to the wish which you hold from me."[5] Then they're interrupted. All of a sudden, Dante is once again involved in what's happening in Hell. And we are no longer truly discussing the immortality of souls, but rather the political implications of believing in the immortality of the soul. How is this refracted onto the political scene? Again, therefore, this is almost a Platonic conceit, the relationship now no longer between bodies and cities, as we saw in *Inferno* 6, but here between souls and cities. The resultant considerations abound. Is this a soulless city? How do we experience it? Is it livable? What is the relationship between the various people who inhabit it? Dante will soon seek answers to his myriad questions.

He singles out two people to question, one a Guelph and one a Ghibelline. We are in the middle of the civil war of Florence once again. It's going to be Farinata, a Ghibelline, and the elder Cavalcanti, a Guelph. The two souls are also related to each other because Cavalcanti's son, Dante's best friend—you may remember that he dedicates his *Vita nuova* to Guido and calls him "my first friend Guido Cavalcanti"—had married Farinata's daughter. In Hell they lie in their tombs, ignoring each other, ignoring the other's pangs, worries, and perplexities. It's a symbolic picture of what could be "any city." But this is the city in the beyond, where everybody's squabbling. Nobody's paying attention to anybody else, and everybody believes that one's own passion is paramount. It's a canto that, interestingly enough, is marked by interruptions: one soul is speaking, and the other says to quit it because it's his turn now. And so the scene enacts a little vignette of Florence in the year 1300 (possibly later, but 1300 is a good estimate).

Virgil and Dante are the first to be interrupted here, by Farinata, who appears from the navel up in his tomb and says, "O Tuscan, who go alive through the city of fire speaking thus modestly, may it please you to stop in this place. Your speech clearly shows you a native of that noble fatherland to which I perhaps did too much harm."[6] A little historical detail will help to explain Farinata's physical position here. When Dante went on an embassy to Rome, he could have seen the Church of the Holy Cross in Jerusalem, which, according to the legend, was built with stones from Jerusalem that had been brought to Rome by Constantine's mother, Helena. In the basement of that church, which would be opened only once a year around the Easter season, there was a mosaic showing the rising Christ from the navel up, and the representation of Farinata from the navel up is clearly meant as a caricature of the belief in the Resurrection. This is the story of a man who doesn't believe in the Resurrection, but iconographically Dante will go on focusing on the counterpoint. The description of Farinata is clearly meant to evoke these contradictions.

So, there is a great exchange between Dante and Farinata: who defeated whom, the continuous battles between Guelphs and Ghibellines, and Dante's claim that his own family managed to take good revenge when the time came, with a clear implication that more revenge will be necessary. But then they're also interrupted, this time by the old man Cavalcanti. This is what happens, an extraordinary scene: "Then there arose to sight alongside of him a shade, visible to the chin: I think he had raised himself on his knees. He looked round about me as though he wished to see whether someone was with me, but when his expectation was quite spent, he said, weeping, 'If you go through this blind prison by reason of high genius, where is my son, and why is he not with you?'"[7]

The reference is to Dante's best friend, Guido, whose name implies that he should be the one guiding Dante. The old father was hoping that his son, according to his name, could really be leading the younger poet, as he had led him in his early poetic experiments in Florence. Ultimately, then, Farinata worries about his ancestors, and Cavalcanti worries about his son. These are Epicureans with a sense of dynastic continuity, all within the immanence of personal concerns and family. They move beyond the fragmentations of the self from the Other. They seem to have an extended idea of themselves, in spite of themselves, in spite of their beliefs.

Dante answers Cavalcanti, "I come not of myself. He who waits yonder, whom perhaps your Guido had in disdain, is leading me through here." "His words and the manner of his punishment had read his name to me," Dante continues, "hence was my answer so full. Suddenly straightening up, he cried, 'How? Did you say 'he had'?" Dante uses the past preterite, "he had," and the old man infers from the verb tense that his son is already dead, which is a mistake, an equivocation: "'He had'? Does he not still live? Does the sweet light not strike his eyes?' And when he perceived that I made some delay in answering, he fell supine again and showed himself no more."[8] While Cavalcanti is no longer present, his conversation with Dante lingers beyond his disappearance.

Farinata, meanwhile, is utterly unconcerned with the whole discussion. He persists in arguing that the two sides of the Florentine civil war were engaged in a continuous back-and-forth. He keeps the subject strictly political, speaking only of Guelphs and Ghibellines, so that Dante has to ask him before leaving to reassure the old man Cavalcanti that his son is still alive, because in the year of Dante the pilgrim's journey, Guido was still alive, though he would die very soon afterward.

What is the meaning of this story of political disarray in Florence? And what are we to make of the story of the memory of Dante's friend, whose friendship with Dante had just come to an end? One of the early and toughest decisions Dante had to make was to banish Guido Cavalcanti from Florence because he thought that Guido was the cause of some unrest in the city. Guido went into exile and never made it back. He died three months later in the swamps of Liguria, a little bit north of Tuscany. Dante lives in many ways with a sense of personal guilt about what happened. He won't talk openly about it, but the guilt exists, and his relationship with Guido will become a key to understanding the canto.

Who is Guido really? Guido is what we call an Averroist. Averroes, actually mentioned by Dante in Limbo, was an Arab philosopher and a famous commentator of Aristotle. And in the Middle Ages they would read the great classics of philosophy, especially very difficult texts like Aristotle's *On the Soul,* by following the commentators. In his interpretation of the text, Averroes argues that Aristotle does not believe in the immortality of the soul. He's going to be challenged by Aquinas and by many others, but Guido Cavalcanti follows Averroes' understanding of the soul. Thus, the one who is here among the heretics is not just the old man, but also Guido Cavalcanti himself.

What does heresy even mean? I did indicate that in antiquity it was never really thought of as a sin because it's a question of the mind. The word comes from the Greek *haeresis,* meaning "to choose." One who is a heretic is someone who makes a particular intellectual choice. To be viewed as a sinner, you also have to indicate an element of pride behind a particular belief, and so Guido is held responsible for disseminating this idea of Averroism.

What is Averroism? One of the ideas in his commentary on *On the Soul* is that we human beings are not even intrinsically capable of thinking. We are concupiscent entities and sensitive entities. We're also rational entities, but rationality occurs to us intermittently. Averroism emphasizes the fact that we don't think all the time, that occasionally thought comes to us. And when we think, we are existing in a discontinuity from the world of feeling. So, there's a fairly tragic understanding here, making human beings the object, rather than subjects, of thought. We live like animals more often than not: we eat, we drink, we sleep, and so on. Then occasionally we manage to disengage ourselves from all of this and become capable of contemplative thoughts. At that point we no longer really live, we are abstracted from ourselves.

Not only did Guido believe in these ideas, they also shape one of his poems, one of the most beautiful poems written in that epoch, a poem called "A Lady Asks Me." It's a poem where there's a fiction: the poet Guido Cavalcanti imagines that a woman asks him to define love. She says that poets are always talking about love, and she doesn't understand what they mean by love, nor what the effects of love are. Cavalcanti responds with a long song talking about the nature of love, the function of love, and the effects of love. He proceeds almost scholastically, taking one case after the other. He begins by saying, in the exposition, that love is a passion that comes from Mars, not from Venus. That is to say, the nature of love is always to be one of conflict, of war and chaos, not one of order. He continues in this vein, saying that love induces death and is characterized by deliriums of the mind. It's a very grim idea of love that Cavalcanti offers this curious woman.

What Dante is ultimately doing in Canto 10 is connecting these Cavalcantian ideas of love with the politics of civil war. He finds that there is a strict, necessary correlation between them. And he opposes Guido Cavalcanti's thoughts on love. As you know from the *Vita nuova,* he believes that Beatrice can lead him to God and to the knowledge of God, in the persuasion that it is not by truth that you come to the knowledge of God. If you cannot come to the knowledge of God by truth, then how do you come to the knowledge of God? By love, by thinking about love: that's the way of the ascent. Furthermore, Dante will have this idea that civil disorder, the civil war, is nothing else but the phenomenon of a theory put forth by the Averroist, by Guido Cavalcanti. This is the double focus of this canto: love and politics and the connection between them, a connection that, by the way, the Averroists whom Dante links with the Epicureans, deny. Dante makes this connection imaginatively, for it is a connection refuted by the philosophers themselves.

With Canto 11 Dante juxtaposes to the disorder of the city a rational reflection on the order that sustains Hell. It is as if there's a logic even to the disorder of evil. And the idea is that there is a tripartite division to the plan of Hell. All of the sins are divided into three parts: the area of the sins of incontinence, the middle area, which is called the area of violence, and then the third area, which contains the sins of fraud. Dante calls fraud the sin peculiar to human beings because it's not just a sin of the will, but there is also the premeditation of the mind, the complicity of the mind. Dante sees the conjunction of will and, at the same time, the order of reason in the performance of that evil.

The canto ends with a question. Dante says that this is all from the *Ethics* of Aristotle and then Dante turns to Virgil for more information: "O sun that heal every troubled vision, you do content me so, when you solve, that questioning, no less than knowing, pleases me." Then Dante asks him to say something about usury. Virgil's response: "Philosophy, for one who understands it . . . points out, not in one place alone, how Nature takes her course from divine Intellect and from Its art; and if you note well your *Physics*"—another Aristotelian text—"you will find, after not many pages, that your art, as far as it can, follows her, as the pupil does his master; so that your art is as it were grandchild to God. By these two, if you remember *Genesis* at the beginning, it behooves man to gain his bread and to prosper. But because the usurer takes another way, he contemns Nature in herself and in her follower, for he puts his hope elsewhere."[9] So, to explain the sin of usury, Dante puts forth a theory of art, as if usury were a violation of art.

But how does he understand art? What is art for Dante? He sees art as work, that's the best way to explain it. At the beginning of Genesis when Adam was thrown out of the Garden of Eden and was told that in order to recover the garden, he had to go back to work, that work becomes an ascetic exercise, not a punishment. Here, similarly, Dante doesn't see work as a punishment, but rather as an ascetic exercise whereby one can transform the wilderness into paradise. That's really the general thrust of the canto, but I believe more can be made of this connection.

What is art in the Middle Ages? Art is understood by the Scholastics as a virtue of the practical intellect, in the order of making. What is the practical intellect? How many intellects do we have? Well, there's a speculative intellect. When Dante talks about the immortality of the soul and those who do not believe in the immortality of the soul, that's a question of the speculative intellect. Suppose that I had this intellectual trait of indulging in thinking about justice, for instance, an abstract idea of justice, not particular cases of justice, then I'm involved in an exercise of the speculative intellect. Dante instead ends the canto with an emphasis on the practical intellect, which is the mind that worries about doing or making, and these, too, are not the same thing. To say that it's a virtue of practical intellect in the order of doing would be to worry about prudence: a virtue of doing, because it's not the artisan's work. To say that it's a virtue of practical intellect in the order of making means that the work of art is a thing that one elaborates. From this point of view, the issue is never really one of whether art tells the truth. It has its own "thingness"; it's a thing, the work of art is something made, and therefore as made, it has its own reality, its own laws, its own rigor.

We can use the metaphors in Virgil's explanation of usury to see more clearly how Dante understands art. On the face of it, he's saying that art must be an imitation of nature. Does Dante then have a mimetic idea of art? Not at all, because if you look more closely, you note that he's using *two* metaphors. "Your art, as far as it can, follows her, as the pupil does his master; so that your art is as it were grandchild to God" because art follows nature, which is the child of God, so art is a grandchild. The whole image is one of fecundity and fertility. You can finally see why Dante opposes art to usury. Usury is viewed as a sterile activity, an activity that produces only symbols, money out of money. It's a symbolic operation, and Dante opposes to it the virtue of art as work, one of production, one of generation: the "grandchild" of God.

Then there is this other metaphor, as the pupil follows the master, which is not gratuitous because, after all, within the context, Dante has Virgil teaching him, so there is almost a kind of flattery here. He implies the educational aspect of art. Art educates, in the sense that it leads us out of a particular state of barbarity, ignorance, and darkness, so it has an educational and a nonmimetic role because art imitates the productive rhythms of the natural world. Dante believes in an art that is open to beginnings, to life. This idea comes from Genesis, an art that always leads us back to the thought of origins because only then can we understand the endings, only then can we arrive at our goals.

In the course of moving from Canto 9 to Canto 11, then, we have moved from concerns about the pride of the mind—which we could even call the wound of the intellect and the weakness of the will—to an idea of art. And I think that this idea of art is also, in Dante's eyes, a remedy for the evils to which we are prone. Dante thinks that should we apply to ourselves the same kind of care and rigor with which an artist produces the work of art, and then the cultivation of our souls may indeed begin to take place. Thus, Dante's attention to art is part of an ascetic exercise that he advocates as an escape from an infernal fate.

CHAPTER 6

Inferno 12–16

From Canto 12 to Canto 16 we are still in the middle region of Hell. We are in the area of violence, or as Dante also calls it, of bestiality, between the area of incontinence, the subject of the last few chapters, and that of malice. What I want to draw your attention to first is the fact that Dante's presiding symbols in this area are all hybrid figures: the Minotaur and the Centaurs in Canto 12; the Harpies, the filthy, foul monsters with the faces of women devouring the foliage and the trees, in Canto 13; and there are other emblems of doubleness as well in this part of the *Inferno*.

What is the importance of these figures? They are Neoplatonic images understood to signify the doubleness of human beings, our capacity to join within ourselves both the human and the bestial. In Neoplatonic thinking, the whole idea is that human beings are copular or neutral entities who have the potential of this doubleness within them. We can become fully rational or we can descend into bestiality. Our position in the ladder of being is one of utter indeterminacy. In the twelfth century, this is not the view most commonly held, however. Rather, it is still believed that there are creatures forever fixed who contain within themselves these dual impulses and natures simultaneously. Dante, though, seems to be aware that these symbols do not completely characterize what human beings truly are, that we can redeem ourselves, we can free ourselves from a certain state, or we can plunge into the opposite state. For Dante there's a difference between the symbols and actual human beings.

In Canto 12, we see where Dante places tyrants. It's really (and the irony is overt) a canto without outstanding and overwhelming characters. There are no great personalities here. Dante does name many of the tyrants

66

past and present: Dionysius of Syracuse, Alexander, the Ezzolino of his own time in Padua, and so on. These are clear figures of tyranny, but he places them next to educators like Chiron. This is a slightly ironic move because it comes straight after Dante's exemplary representation of Virgil's own teaching in Canto 11. Here now a reversal occurs: over and against the exemplariness of Virgil's teaching, as he usually does in the economy of the poem, Dante takes on the other perspective, that which he views now as the tyranny of teaching, that is to say, a sort of teaching that does not allow freedom, the freedom that the presiding figures of this canto also seem to deny: these creatures who are forever man and beast. Dante claims that teaching has to allow the freedom to move, either in the direction of rationality or in the opposite direction. This is the substance of Canto 12.

And now we come to Canto 13, which is one of the most remarkable cantos of *Inferno*. It's the canto of the suicides, and Dante encounters here a very well-known poet of the middle part of the thirteenth century named Pier delle Vigne. Throughout the canto, Dante puns on both parts of that name. The soul thinks of himself as a figure of Peter, one who holds the two keys of the kingdom, the keys of power, but there is also the last name, delle Vigne, meaning "of the vineyards." We are going to witness the metamorphosis of a human being into a vegetable, a plant. He is one of the souls who have been punished for their sins of violence against the self in the story of the suicides that unfolds in this canto.

The canto begins in "a wood which was not marked by any path." Here, there seem to be no directions at all, almost as if Dante were revisiting Canto 1 of *Inferno*. We find the same idea of a sense of loss of self, adumbrating what suicide may also be at some level: a loss of some idea of one's own being, of what one is or should be. Then Dante shifts to a description of the natural landscape, the world of nature; he highlights a peculiar stylistic move and I want to emphasize this style, this figuration of style. First of all, he uses a series of antitheses, but also negative anaphoras: "No green leaves, but of dusky hue; no smooth boughs, but gnarled and warped," antithetical but at the same time, with the repetition of this "no," anaphoric. "No fruits were there, but thorns with poison. These wild beasts that hate tilled lands between Cecina and Corneto do not have thickets so rough or dense."[1] There is a technical term for the rhetoric Dante deploys in his description of this place; it's called *privatio*, which simply means a privation. It's a means of emphasizing that there's nothing positive in the scene, but it's also a way of representing, not in terms of positive substances, but in terms of what is missing in the landscape, what should be there rather than what is there. It involves repeatedly taking away from any substantial description of the landscape, making us think about how the world *might* be, rather than how it *is*.

Who inhabits this barren land? "Here [are] the foul Harpies"—hybrid figures "who drove the Trojans from the Strophades with dismal announcement of future ill; they have broad wings, and human necks and faces, feet with claws, and their great bellies are feathered; they make lament on the strange trees."[2] We are in a world of negation and privation, a world of monstrosities. What is happening to human beings here? The whole scene recasts an important episode in book 3 of *The Aeneid* and dramatizes a major confrontation between Dante and Virgil about some of these issues. What is a metamorphosis? What is nature? What is the place of human beings within nature? Dante and Virgil think in sharply different ways about these concerns.

The scene that Dante is recalling is the scene in book 3 of *The Aeneid* where Polydorus, a cousin of Aeneas, has been killed. Aeneas arrives in Thracia, which is Asia Minor, and he thinks that this must be the place that the gods have assigned to him, and he does that which he knows has to be done, wherever and whenever one wants to build a city. He has to consecrate the ground by building an altar and by purifying the ground through fire. As he tries to do this, he's plucking a bough and he hears a mysterious voice. He shudders, he's scared, and the voice comes again. It's Polydorus, his cousin, in the form of a talking tree, who tells the story that he has been killed because of sacrileges that have been committed. The consecration, Virgil wants us to believe, cannot be carried out because a sacrilege has occurred: the killing of Polydorus on account of the gold that he carried. Polydorus simply asks that a proper burial be given to him so that he can descend peacefully into Hades. Aeneas complies and leaves that place in the knowledge that it is not the place assigned to him after all. He cannot found a city on the place of such an atrocious crime.

The good master, Virgil, the creator of that scene, encourages Dante to study his surroundings: "Before you enter farther, know that you are in the second ring, and shall be, until you come to the horrible sand. Look well, therefore, and you shall see things that would make my words incredible."[3] In a sense, this is the reason why Virgil is the authority and why he is guiding Dante through this infernal landscape. He has seen, imaginatively at least, some of the things that Dante is experiencing, and what Dante will see, the reality of it all, will exceed Virgil's own abilities to tell of it. Virgil is adopting a stance of humility on the part of the teacher. Therefore, we get a mild correction of the claims about teaching in Canto 12.

Dante begins to describe his experience in this part of Hell, saying, "I heard wailings uttered on every side, and saw no one who made them; wherefore, all bewildered, I stopped." And then we get another conceit, to which we shall return: "I believe that he believed that I believed." We call it amplification, a way of playing with one verb but also inferring what the belief of the other would be. It's a descent into the boundaries of one's own mind, a way in which Dante dramatizes the fact that there's no real conversation going on between him and Virgil at this moment. We find ourselves within the loneliness of Dante's own thoughts. "I believe that he believed that I believed," he writes, "that all those voices from amid the trunks came from people who were hidden from us. Therefore the master said, 'If you break off a little branch from one of these plants, the thoughts you have will all be cut short.' Then I stretched my hand a little forward and plucked a twig from a great thornbush, and its stub cried." This is nearly identical to the way that book 3 of *The Aeneid* begins, so Virgil is forced to intervene in a scene much like the one he created: "If he, O wounded spirit, had been able to believe before . . . what he had never seen save in my verses"—*The Aeneid*—"he would not have stretched forth his hand against you, but the incredible thing made me prompt him to a deed that grieves me. But tell him who you were, so that by way of some amends he may refresh your fame in the world above, whither it is allowed him to return."[4] Virgil is ironic here, suggesting a revival of fame in a place where there is no possibility of revival, where the natural world is not capable of behaving naturally, where there is no real growth, no real change. A shadow of unnaturalness is cast over the scene.

In a sense, we already get the confrontation between Virgil and Dante in these lines: "if he had been able to believe before what he had never seen save in my verses." It is as if Dante wants to test the truth value of what he had read in his guide's text. He had read the scene in *The Aeneid,* and he finds out that what he witnesses is entirely different from Virgil's account. In a way he is really drawing our attention to the act of reading. How do we read? What do we believe when we read the story? When we read a story we yield, in many ways, to the story. We want the story that we read to read us as much as we want to read it. We want the story to explain us to ourselves, to hold a mirror up to us to see who we are, but Dante is implying the need to violate the letter of *The Aeneid*. Whatever Virgil described exceeded credibility, and Dante must test the reality of that scene.

The trunk responds to Virgil with a *captatio benevolentiae*: "You so allure me with your sweet words."[5] It's a great rhetorical trick. Whenever people speak to you in public, or even privately, they can engage in this way of capturing your benevolence by telling a story, by implying something about their modesty. With "allure," the tree suggests that Virgil's rhetorical powers are extremely effective. We are dealing with rhetoric, first of all, with style, and with the language of the exchange. It is as if the suicide has a lot to do with this characteristic of language.

Then this soul begins to tell its tale: "You so allure me with your sweet words that I cannot keep silent; and may it not burden you that I am enticed to talk a little. I am he who held both the keys of Frederick's heart, and turned them, locking and unlocking, so softly that from his secrets I kept almost every one."[6] Here is the aforementioned pun on Peter; it's as if he were a St. Peter who holds the two keys to the kingdom of Frederick's heart. All the language of belief, of faith, that has been going around in the previous lines of the canto seems to be gravitating around the figure of Frederick, the emperor who is a kind of god of the city, because that's what his name means. In Italian, you say *Fede*rico, which contains the idea of faith within it, as if all faith, all beliefs, have to converge and go toward this emperor of Sicily.

Pier delle Vigne, instead, was the chancellor of the empire, and he conceived the first state university in Europe, the University of Naples, because Frederick wanted a university that would prepare lawyers, diplomats, people who could go on state missions and write papers for the state. And it would not be one of the schools in the vein of the universities that were under the aegis of the canon lawyers or the theologians. This, then, was the first lay secular school in Europe. Pier delle Vigne was a poet, and he also compiled the so-called institutes of justice for the kingdom, all of which are inspired by the language of moderation, the idealistic language of order, and the natural law that could be used to organize the state. The reality clearly is that, by his suicide, an act that violates the fundamental premise of natural law, Pier delle Vigne shows that he doesn't believe in what he claims to be the principle underlying the legal organization of the state, namely, natural law. Finally, he is the secretary of the emperor, a role that becomes crucial throughout the Renaissance. He's a counselor, but *secretary* comes from the Latin for "to secrete." He's the figure who distills—secretes—that which the emperor keeps hidden in his heart. Through this distillation, he also knows what has to be shared and what has to be kept concealed from all others. Quite a figure of prestige, he views himself as, and he was, a strict collaborator of the emperor.

So, that's who the man was, but what does Pier delle Vigne say about his time in Federico's employ? He says, "So faithful was I to the glorious office that for it I lost both sleep and life." Now the question of fidelity in how we read the text, how we believe what we read, is brought into a sort of refracted loyalty as faithfulness to the emperor. The cause of Pier delle Vigne's tragic downfall and suicide is going to be compared to a harlot, the personification of envy, the sin that Aquinas, for one, views as the worst possible sin because it is really very close to hatred in the sense that it has nothing positive about it. Almost all sins have some positivity to them. If you are a glutton, it's because that piece of cake, there's something about it that lures you to it. If you are proud, it's because you really have some sense of your own excellence. It's not so much that you look at yourself as stretching the hand toward the divinity, the pride of Lucifer. The real sin is that you kick around those individuals whom you perceive as below you. So, all sins have some kind of positivity except for one, envy, because envy only likes nothing. It's not jealousy. When somebody can't stand the idea that the other guy is happy, that's envy. Jealousy is the fear of losing. Now the court, this microcosm of political order and idealism, has been poisoned by what Pier delle Vigne's class envies, "the harlot that never turned her whorish eyes."[7]

Pier delle Vigne is aware of the tragic nature of his downfall, of his fate as tragic: "My mind, in scornful temper, thinking by dying to escape from scorn, made me unjust against my just self."[8] Once again through the style of repetitions—anaphora—Pier delle Vigne constitutes himself into a closed circuit, and the doubling of language reflects the self-babbling. When you read the sentence: "My mind . . . made me unjust against my just self," the obvious question that I think we should ask is: how many selves are there in him? How many figures are there in this one Pier delle Vigne?

The text that best glosses this scene appears in book 1 of St. Augustine's *City of God,* where Augustine is telling the story of Rome, the end of the period of the monarchy, and the rape of Lucretia. Augustine is fierce about the fact that she commits suicide as a result of the guilt and shame that she experiences after Brutus violates her. And Augustine asks how she dares to take her own life, because here is the chaste Lucretia who is embarrassed about the unchaste Lucretia, and this is a sin of false transcendence. She believes that she does not coincide fully with who she is, so that she has to double herself. She has to see herself as different from what she is. She can do justice against herself. The doubling of Pier delle Vigne is a similar sin of false transcendence, inasmuch as suicide is playing God to oneself and punishing oneself for wrongs that the suicide perceives in himself or herself. This parallels the doubleness that Dante renders through his style in this scene.

The story of Pier delle Vigne exemplifies or dramatizes the story of the tragic experience of suicide: "By the new roots of this tree I swear to you that I never broke faith with my lord, who was so worthy of honor. And if one of you returns to the world, let him comfort my memory which still lies prostrate from the blow that envy gave it."[9] Dante here provides a precise theological account of suicide, considered from an Augustinian point of view. Of course, Lucretia herself can be found in Limbo, and Cato, another famous suicide, will make his appearance in Canto 1 of *Purgatory,* so Dante is making some crucial decisions and distinctions in his depiction of suicide. Dante knows well that the phenomenology of various acts is vast and cannot ever be reduced to one common element.

In another memorable canto, Canto 15, we encounter another man associated with the world of education, Dante's teacher, Brunetto Latini, a translator into the vernacular who adapted and commented upon Cicero's rhetorical works, and a teacher of the Florentines. He stands for the great values of the rhetorical humanistic, or Ciceronian, tradition. At one point he was sent on an embassy to France, and while he was gone, his political party and he were banned from Florence. He eventually returned to his city, but he's a figure that Dante takes as a model. Effectively, it's the teaching of Brunetto that guides him in the initial phase of his political concerns, though other intellectual experiences will later intervene and radically change Dante's thinking. Some extraordinary encounters that he had with theologians and philosophers in Florence gave him a completely different view from the one that Brunetto Latini instilled in him.

But what happens between the two of them in the text? We are once again in the area of violence, this time violence against nature, and Brunetto Latini is condemned to this area for the sin of sodomy. There is no evidence at all from any other sources that he committed such an act. And Dante also has a different understanding of sodomy (which appears as a form of violence against nature), and is more clearly understood when he comes to Purgatory. At any rate, though, that's not quite the stated reason for Brunetto's appearance in this particular region of the infernal topography.

The focus of the canto is once again the natural world: "Now one of the hard margins bears us on, and the vapor from the stream overshades, so that it shelters the water and the banks from fire." This natural world is one of sheer chaos and violence. Dante continues this description with a comparison to the Netherlands, so called because the surface of the land there is lower than that of the water, leading to the need for dikes in order to protect the land from the violence of the water: "As the Flemings between Wissant and Bruges, fearing the tide that rushes in on them, make the bulwark to drive back the sea; and as the Paduans do along the Brenta, to protect their towns and castles before Carentana feels the heat; in like fashion were these banks made, except that the builder, whoever he was, made them neither so high nor so thick."[10] So, the natural world can hardly be contained. The natural world is always going to overwhelm all efforts to impede its violence.

Then Dante gives us the background of this encounter: "We were already so far removed from the wood that I should not have seen where it was had I turned to look back, when we met a troop of souls that were coming alongside the bank, and each looked at us as men look at one another under a new moon at dusk." Dante seems to create a strange world of the night. "And they knit their brows at us as the old tailor does at the eye of his needle." What an extraordinary image. Dante will use something like this, not quite the same image, but an image of a tailor when he has to describe his vision of Paradise. It is as if the humblest experience in the city, with all its artists, is the only thing he can think about as he's approaching the most sublime of experiences, in Canto 33 of *Paradiso*. The tailor is an artisan who, in order to fit you properly, has to have your measurements, an idea of who you are. Notice the immediate familiarity in Dante's encounter with Brunetto: "Eyed thus by that company, I was recognized by one who took me by the hem, and cried, 'What a marvel!' And I, when he reached out his arm to me, fixed my eyes on his scorched face, so that the baked features did not prevent my knowing him, and reaching down my hand toward his face, I answered, 'Are you here, ser Brunetto?'"[11] This is a scene of recognition. In *Inferno* there are more scenes of recognition than first encounters. It is as if recognizing means knowing people that you thought you knew and giving them a kind of understanding—recognizing in that broader sense as well.

Brunetto responds, "O my son, let it not displease you if Brunetto Latini turns back a little with you, and lets the train go on." Twice Brunetto will refer to Dante as "my son." It's acknowledged in this affiliation that they share a kind of familiarity that goes beyond any form of discipleship. Dante will resist that affectionate solicitation, that familiarity, but he will nearly always refer to him as the image of a father. Dante answers in kind, "I beg it of you with all my heart . . . and if you wish me to sit with you, I will, if it please him there with whom I go."[12] Dante means Virgil but leaves him unmentioned, as if concealing from Brunetto Latini, *pro forma* to be sure, the shifted loyalty from one teacher to another. But in any case, the two decide to converse.

The spatial configuration of the scene is particularly significant. The disciple is above, the teacher below, so that the disciple has to bow in order to be able to speak to the teacher, which could be a sign of his reverence for the authority of the master, but at the same time, it indicates that the hierarchy between them goes in both directions. The hierarchy has been completely altered from the days when they were in the streets of Florence.

Brunetto's first question is quite telling: "What chance or destiny," he asks, "brings you down here before your last day, and who is this that shows the way?" Chance? Destiny? Brunetto has no understanding of the trajectory of Dante's life and adventure. This is the beginning of a series of misunderstandings between the teacher and the disciple. Two different value systems are being deployed, and they are going to collide with each other. Brunetto speaks like a true humanist, a man who espouses Ciceronian ethics, for whom the world is indeed one of chance encounters, of an overarching and even providential destiny that takes us one way or the other, with nothing providential in the Christian sense of the concept about any of it. Dante responds with a pithy summary of his experience in the past few hours, "There above, in the bright life . . . I went astray in a valley, before my age was at the full. Only yesterday morning I turned my back on it. He appeared to me, as I was returning into it, and by this path he leads me home."[13] These are extraordinary words because what home means for the politically minded, Florence-centered, sense of existence of Brunetto, is not the idea of what home means for Dante. For Dante, home is the place of the soul, and the place where the soul is at its most distended. For Brunetto, home can only be the city of Florence. One has a political frame of reference, the other one has a theological frame of reference, and the two are coming up against each other.

Next Brunetto offers some astrological advice that continues his emphasis on chance and destiny: "If you follow your star you cannot fail of a glorious port."[14] Again Dante is dramatizing the radical ambiguity of words that seem to be so bland, like "glorious": what "glorious" means to a humanist is not what it means to a theologically minded thinker. In theology, one thinks of nature, grace, and glory. Dante begins Canto 1 of *Paradiso* with the glory of Him who moves all things, while glory for Brunetto means happy endings and fame. From Brunetto's point of view, the source of Dante's whole spiritual crisis, the loss of self he experiences, can only be political. Brunetto makes the incredible mistake of believing that Dante's experience is a precise replica of his own. He lost the city, and now this is exactly what he thinks is happening to the pilgrim as well.

He prophesies Dante's exile: "Old report in the world calls them blind; it is a people avaricious, envious and proud. Your fortune holds for you such honor that the one party and the other shall be ravenous against you." In other words, the two parties, the Guelphs and the Ghibellines, will both turn against him. And Dante answers, "If my prayer were all fulfilled, . . . you would not yet be banished from human nature, for in my memory is fixed, and now saddens my heart, the dear, kind, paternal image of you, when in the world hour by hour you taught me how man makes himself eternal; and how much I hold it in gratitude it behooves me, while I live, to declare it in my speech. That which you tell me of my course I write, and keep with a text to be glossed by a lady who will know how, if I reach her."[15]

Clearly, he is making an allusion to Beatrice, but it will not be Beatrice who will make another prophecy of Dante's exile; rather, it will be Dante's grandfather Cacciaguida who does so, in the symmetrically connected cantos 15 and 16 of *Paradiso*. Thus the distinction between this fictional figure of a self-claimed spiritual father, Brunetto, and the heroic grandfather, Cacciaguida, offers a marked antithesis. In the acknowledgment that Dante gives of Brunetto's teaching there is also a little bit of a critique, a little distance that Dante establishes between himself and Brunetto. For the true poetry of Dante's experience is that man does not make himself immortal. Of course, when a bold stroke works, maybe there are many other forms of achieving some degree of immortality: for example, one can make children, build a fortune, erect a monument to oneself to become immortal (at least in a provisional sense), but from Dante's point of view, immortality is not manmade. It can only come about through the salvation of the soul.

Therefore, the scene offers us a sense of a difference between these two men, and misunderstandings will, in fact, be the defining trait of this encounter. But there is still the matter of Brunetto's sodomy that we ought to try to understand. First, it's linked to violence, for we're in the world of violence, and so Dante wants to know who the other sinners are. Brunetto says that they're all clerks and great and famous scholars. And he mentions them all, "in the world defiled by one same sin," Priscian, a famous grammarian, Francesco d'Accorso, "such scurf." But then he comes to an abrupt conclusion: "I would say more, but my going and my speech must not be longer, for I see yonder a new smoke rising from the sand: people are coming with whom I must not be. Let my *Treasure,* in which I yet live, be commended to you, and I ask no more." He's not quite done, for like a true teacher, he gives a bibliography at the end of his discourse. He says that Dante should go and read his book, not just anybody's book, but specifically his *Trésor,* or *Treasure,* "in which I yet live." Finally, though, he departs: "He turned back, and seemed like one of those who run for the green cloth in the field at Verona"—a ludic image, an image of a race which is run in Verona—"and of them seemed he who wins, not he who loses."[16] He leaves with the illusion that he is a precursor, as it were. He is in a race, and he seems to be ahead of them, but really he's behind them by one lap. That's the telling image with which Dante ends this encounter.

So, Brunetto recommends this *Treasure,* which is a French text that he wrote. It's one of the most important encyclopedias in the vernacular, and yet it is lacking in comparison to the poetic encyclopedia that we are reading. Dante is in the middle of a learning process, so his text is an encyclopedia with a path toward learning, unlike the abstract one that Brunetto had written. Furthermore, Brunetto wrote in French. In one of his philosophical reflections, Dante explains that we are all bound by natural affection for our own language, and because of that claim, there are those who have put forth the interpretation that Brunetto is in this part of Hell for violating the natural bonds of affection that human beings have with regard to their own natural language, to their "mother tongue," as it were. Regardless, Brunetto's bibliography undeniably dramatizes an incredible self-delusion on his part. Here he is, dead. Here he is, circling around under the reign of fire, and he still thinks he lives in his own text. He mistakes for reality the symbolic life that he has within a text. The language of images, the language of seeming that pervades this canto, has to be understood in terms of this confusion on the part of Brunetto. The bigger mistake that Brunetto makes here, though, is to believe that Dante's own life is a replica of his own: read my text because whatever it is that you have to know, it's already available to you in my own book. He never faces the difference between Dante and himself. He refuses to see that Dante's life can have its own development and its own destiny, a destiny which he cannot understand at all. Canto 15 ends with this idea, therefore, that the sin of sodomy can also be seen as a confusion between the real and the imaginary, a way of drawing the real world into one of fictions and imaginations.

As we approach Canto 16, we are reaching the end of the intermediate area, the realm of violence. I presume that some of you may be surprised that these sins fall in the middle of Hell's schema. Our culture seems to view violence in all of its forms and expressions as the worst possible crime. For Dante, instead, the worst crimes are the crimes of fraud, and he is about to encounter a strange figure, a monster who will grant him access to the even lower depths, the area of fraud.

This is the figure of Geryon, first seen at the end of Canto 16. Dante will climb onto Geryon, Virgil will sit behind him, and they will descend. It's an experience of wonder in Hell, an infernal sublime. Dante writes, "To that truth which has the face of a lie a man should always close his lips so far as he can"—that's fraud, a mixture of truth and deception, which can also be seen as what literature does. He continues, "For through no fault of his it brings reproach; but here I cannot be silent; and, reader, I swear to you by the strains of this Comedy . . . that I saw, through that thick and murky air, come swimming upwards a figure amazing to every steadfast heart, even as he returns who sometimes goes to down to loose the anchor that is caught on a reef or something else hidden in the sea, who stretches upward his arms and draws in his feet."[17] Here, then, we find the second address to the reader; you may remember that we saw one in Canto 9, and I explained it as part of Dante's strategy of authority. He wants us to trust his account of the approach of Geryon.

What I want to point out here are several metaphors. First, this is an aerial journey; Geryon is flapping his wings and going through the murky air, but Dante describes it as if it were a journey by sea. The metaphor he uses is swimming: "I saw, through that thick and murky air, come swimming upwards a figure," and he does this because for Dante it doesn't matter how you are traveling. All journeys are journeys to the same destination. All journeys are really journeys to the absolute. Here, Geryon seems only to play a ministerial function, serving Dante and his guide, but at the same time Dante acknowledges that there is still a plan, something of the absolute that he has to see. The second metaphor derives from the rotatory movement of Geryon through the air, for as I have previously noted, the circle and the spiral constitute all motion in *Inferno*. Finally, we have this idea of swearing by Dante's own text, which is thus given the value of a sacred object. Ultimately, then, we began this section of Hell with a violation of *The Aeneid,* and now Dante is fully opposing *The Aeneid.* He replaces it with a new text: the *Comedy* that we are currently reading.

CHAPTER 7

Inferno 17–26

Just as Dante jumps onto the back of Geryon in Canto 16, so too must we make some leaps as we proceed farther into the depths of Dante's Hell. I'll make brief mention of Canto 17, which is an extraordinary canto. It's the only time that Virgil leaves Dante alone, and Dante has to meet the usurers without any guidance. It is as if he had to discover by himself and by his own powers what those temptations are and what the implications of usury would be for him. Let me offer a biographical resonance, in the sense that not only is the poet edging toward the condition of the usurer by engaging in illusory re-creations, but his own father was also engaged in that sort of activity.

Because of time constraints we go to Canto 19. Here we have an experience of the shifts in Dante's voice. In Canto 19 Dante assumes what I do not hesitate to call a prophetic voice. He sees himself as playing a public role. The departure from the political rhetorical tone used in the encounter with Brunetto could not be sharper or more radical. What does it mean to be a prophet for Dante? How can one take on this sort of voice? How does a prophet talk? One thing that you may want to keep in mind as I go on, to understand this canto, is that the pattern for all of this is the voice of the biblical prophets. But do not make the mistake of thinking for a moment that prophets are those who foretell the future, as that's not really their role. In fact, Dante later goes out of his way in Canto 20 to highlight the differences between prophets and diviners. The diviners are those who predict the future, while the prophets are literally readers of the present. For Dante, the biblical prophets are those who read the present history in its unfolding from the perspective of what they perceive to have been God's promise to Israel and to them. The prophets are, in a way, commentators. To be a commentator requires an exercise of memory, a way of bringing ancient memories to bear on the present. That's the way Dante understands the prophetic voice.

Another background detail that will prove useful as we proceed is that Dante was a writer of many epistles; he was a letter writer. We do not know the letters he wrote on behalf of his patrons, but we do know the letters that he wrote in his own name. One of his most noteworthy letters was written to the Italian cardinals who were in conclave, meaning that they were shut under lock and key and kept in a place where they could make decisions about electing, from within themselves or from the outside, a pope. In this case they could not agree about whom to choose. Dante begins the letter by addressing them, saying that perhaps they will wonder who this man is, who gives him the authority to speak to them and to spur us on to action. Doesn't he remember the possible objection to the intervention of a layman's voice in sacred things? Doesn't he remember the lesson of the biblical prophet who, on seeing the Ark of the Covenant tottering as it was being carried into the city of Jerusalem, stretches out his hand to try to protect it? God intervened with lightning and killed him. The point of these statements is to make clear that Dante is aware of the danger of taking on the prophetic voice.

He's aware of the possible profanation in which he is engaged, in addressing the so-called simonists in Canto 19. Who are the simonists? The simonists are the followers of Simon, who was called a *magus*, a sorcerer, or a magician. We call this phenomenon, when you have a name that creates a trend or a way of thinking, an eponym. So, Dante begins this story with reference to a founding event in the constitution of the Church. It goes back to the Acts of the Apostles, where there is a story of a sorcerer, a man engaged in witchcraft and illusions, Simon, who wants to buy the gift of prophecy and the power of making miracles from Peter. And therefore he challenges him to see who can fly, and they go up on a tower and try to fly. Simon, of course, will plummet and die. What Dante is doing here is lambasting the popes of his own time: Nicholas III, Boniface VIII, and Clement V. These three popes during Dante's life are all engaged in simony, a sacrilege, the act, exactly like that of Simon in the Acts of the Apostles, who wanted to buy the gift of prophecy. It is the sin of making commerce of sacred things and thereby engaging in blasphemy.

The question, then, is what does Dante think the sacred is? It's a constant theme in his reflections. What is the sacred? How do we determine it?
What does it mean to violate the sacred? Simon violates the sacred. The
popes now, who are of his own time, are engaged in the same kind of blasphemy and profanation. To further complicate matters, let me give you a
little detail that might help you to appreciate this ambiguity. The other
name of Peter is Simon, so in fact he's known as Simon Peter. It is as if by
having both a magician called Simon and the first pope called Simon Peter,
we arrive at metonymic proximity, the nearness between the prophetic
mode and the profanation of that same prophetic mode. How precarious is
the boundary line that divides the two? Regardless, Dante will straddle this
precarious border as he explores the sacred.

Now, let's see how he dramatizes all of these concerns. The first question is: how do prophets talk? "O Simon Magus" right at the start, is an
apostrophe, and the technique is one of several apostrophes in this canto. It
is followed in the opening line by another address: "O you his wretched followers that, rapacious, prostitute for gold and silver the things of God
which ought to be the brides of righteousness."[1] That's the definition of simony, which is viewed as adultery, a corruption of the chastity of the marriage between God and the soul. We will see other invocations here, and
I'm not so sure that we can quite differentiate between an invocation, which
is obviously a prayer, and an apostrophe, a calling on, an address. Apostrophes are also forms of lament. "O Simon"—as you can hear, it expresses a
kind of mourning. It's the language of grief, primarily, but there is also,
from a linguistic point of view, a crucial indeterminacy to this rhetorical
device. It's not really language. It says nothing on its own. It's a shout, a
need to break the silence. In other words, you use apostrophe because you
cannot be quiet, and that's exactly what makes this aspect of prophetic language so critical. It lies between silence, when one is overcome by the enor-
mity of what one sees, and the refusal to acquiesce. The whole canto is
punctuated by this rhetorical form that wants to break the silence and cannot quite find the words.

After the initial invocations, Dante begins to describe his surroundings: "Upon the sides and upon the bottom I saw the livid stone full of
holes, all of one size and each was round. They seemed to me not less wide
or larger than those that are made for the baptizings in my beautiful San
Giovanni," the Baptistery in Florence. He is referring to the wells where
baptisms take place, which are usually octagonal in shape. Dante reports,
"Not many years ago, I broke [a baptismal font] to save one who was drown-

ing in it—and let this be the seal to undeceive all men."[2] What Dante is doing here is acknowledging what could have been seen as an act of profanation. It is really figurative, though, because these fonts are huge, and you would need ten people to break them apart, so it's a figurative idea that he stretched his hand into holy things and violated them. He did it, and that's the excuse he's giving, that he did it in order to save someone's life. There is nothing gratuitous in Dante's own intervention, which is called an *interventio in sacris,* stretching profane hands into holy things. One could dismiss it as a gratuitous act, but it is not, so he must provide us with a description of it in order to establish its validity.

From here Dante begins to note the sinners in this part of Hell: "From the mouth of each projected the feet of a sinner and his legs as far as the calf, and the rest was within."[3] He's representing the popes, who were placed upside down, which is the way Simon fell, and also the position that, according to legend, St. Peter wanted for himself. Peter asked that he be buried upside down because he wanted to demonstrate the true direction needed for souls to arrive at the perfection of being. We live in an inverted world, and therefore when you have your head down, you are actually right side up. You're going toward your proper destination. Dante is playing with this iconographic motif of Peter, who asks to be crucified upside down, and the story of Simon who, very much like this soul, suffers a punishment with his head upside down.

How else are these particular souls punished? In an overt parody of the Pentecost, with flames. There is a rain of fire that comes down upon them, and they have flames running along their feet. This is a horrible inversion and perversion of prophecy and of the gift of languages, for we are all capable of speaking everybody else's language. I'm sure that there are polyglots among you, but we all speak the language of charity, and therefore we can all understand each other that way. These souls, instead, have no gift of language at all.

Dante asks Virgil to identify a specific sinner who "writhes himself, twitching more than all his fellows, . . . and who is sucked by a ruddier flame," and in the process of discovering the soul's identity, a series of inversions is introduced. "I," Dante says, "was standing there like the friar," but he is a layman, so we are witnessing a role reversal, and the pope is going to unveil his own identity in a moment; he is revealed to be like an assassin. They've traded places. This inverted pope is Nicholas III, and he soon admits a highly suggestive misunderstanding. He tells Dante that the reigning pope at the time of Dante's writing, Boniface VIII, of the Orsini family, one of the great Roman families, has already arrived. He asks Dante, "Are you already standing there, Bonifazio? By several years the writ has lied to me. Are you so quickly sated with those gains for which you did not fear to take by guile the beautiful Lady, and then to do her outrage?"[4] This is the kind of accusation that Dante can launch at powerful figures now, via his text, by acting as a prophet who takes on power and unveils its abusers.

Dante is unsure at first how to respond to his confused interlocutor, but Virgil urges him to correct Boniface's misconception about Dante's identity, which leads to the former pope's haughty reply, "Then what is it you ask of me? If to know who I am concerns you so much that you have for that come down the bank, know that I was vested with the great mantle." Dante will respond to this pompous self-importance with a general attack, which is really the prophetic moment: "I do not know if here I was over-bold, in answering him in just this strain, 'Pray now tell me how much treasure did our Lord require of Saint Peter before he put the keys into his keeping? Surely he asked nothing save: "Follow me." Nor did Peter or the others take gold or silver of Matthias when he was chosen for the office which the guilty soul had lost.'"[5] Dante feels that he ought to speak in this manner because he finds himself in the presence of an eclipse of authority. He thinks that it is incumbent upon him to take on that authority that is lacking in Boniface, in order to make up for what he thinks is missing.

This whole problem of the confusion of orders, the confusion between the secular and the sacred, can be traced to one great event, the so-called Donation of Constantine. The Donation of Constantine was a fourth-century document that stated that Emperor Constantine gave control of the land of the Roman Empire to the pope, Sylvester I. In other words, it made the pope the ruler of a secular domain. To Dante, this was a confusion of registers and of responsibilities, for the pope should be engaged only in spiritual pursuits and spiritual matters. So, the sin of simony is certainly a problem that has to do with the Donation of Constantine.

The problem is complicated by the fact that the document was a forgery. But this issue won't be clarified until the fifteenth century, when two people begin to uncover the truth. One was Nicholas of Cusa, who repeatedly emphasized the moral arguments against the Donation of Constantine, as much as Dante does here. But the one who really proved the falseness of the documents with which Constantine supposedly made the donation to the pope was Lorenzo Valla, a philologist who thoroughly examined the language of that text, and thereby found out that the document could not possibly have been written in the fourth century because it bore the traces of eleventh-century Latin. With extraordinary linguistic precision, Valla specified all the signs that the Donation had been a forgery and that the forgery had been committed in a convent in the south of France.

But these discoveries are all after Dante's time, so why is this Donation so important to Dante? Dante makes it such a central concern precisely because it represents the confusion of the spiritual and the secular that simony embodies, and simony crystallizes the crucial crisis of his own time. Dante also wrote a political text called *Monarchia,* which is really an argument in favor of the separation between these two orders, the church and the state. It had to be neatly divided, both to protect the state from the intrusions of the church and to protect the church from the likely intrusions of the state. So, it's really an argument that goes in two directions, and it's the most critical argument of Canto 19.

A different question of registers is on display in Canto 21, which merits a brief comment. Dante goes out of his way in Canto 21 to speak of the humble style of his *Comedy.* It is as if he wants to free himself from the shackles and the complications of using a lofty language or of taking on the extraordinary position of being the prophet of his own times. This use of comedy is also linked to a peculiar experience in this canto: the fear of falling. The devils are chasing him, and he calls them Ghibellines. These demons are like his enemies who are trying to throw him down, and the point is that comedy is always flanked with the idea of the fall. Laughter, as it were, begins at the moment when someone slips and falls.

But the chase concludes, and the fear of falling is dissipated in the latter part of this section of the *Inferno.* In Cantos 24 and 25 Dante passes through the realm of the thieves, and he is overwhelmed by the metamorphoses he witnesses: the form of punishment of these thieves, who are forced to change form over and over again. They are human beings bitten by snakes, then they become snakes, then they turn into ashes, and then they recompose themselves, in an endless cycle: "As the lizard under the great scourge of the dog days, darting from hedge to hedge, seems a lightning-flash, if it cross the way, so appeared, making for the bellies of the other two, a small fiery serpent, livid and black as a peppercorn; and it transfixed in one of them that part by which we first receive our nourishment, then fell down before him, stretched out. The transfixed one gazed at it, but said nothing, only standing there yawning as if sleep or fever had come upon him. He eyed the reptile, the reptile him; the one from his wound, the other from its mouth, smoked violently, and their smoke met."[6]

Following this description, though, Dante breaks the chronicle of what he has seen, the witnessing. Instead he speaks of other poets, saying, "Let Lucan now be silent, where he tells of the wretched Sabellus and of Nasidius, and let him wait to hear what now comes forth. Concerning Cadmus and Arethusa let Ovid be silent, for if he, poetizing, converts the one into a serpent and the other into a fountain, I envy him not; for two natures front to front he never so transmuted that both forms were prompt to exchange their substance."[7] On the face of it Dante is saying that the kind of metamorphosis he's describing is more horrifying than anything that Ovid or Lucan could create. Ovid, the author of *The Metamorphoses,* always guided his metamorphoses by a belief in the bond between human beings and the natural world. There is a kind of serene transformation happening in Ovid. Dante also says that he's different from Lucan, another author of scenes of metamorphosis in his story about the Roman civil war. What is really crucial here is that Dante's vision of metamorphosis is a *different* one from those of his predecessors.

Dante is repeating and reenacting exactly the kind of aesthetic temptation that we already witnessed in Canto 4 of *Inferno,* in Limbo. Dante met the poets, and he was taken with the great temptation of sitting with Homer, Virgil, Horace, Lucan, and Ovid, exactly the people that he mentions here. And yet, the scene of harmony that Canto 4 seemed to convey is now being utterly overthrown. Here what Dante is really saying is that he is their rival, he is even better, he is seeing things that they didn't even imagine. If you had the illusion of an idyllic relationship among these poets before, Dante disabuses you at this point. Once again Dante is descending, performing a descent of spiritual humility, and yet his voice seems to be going in an opposite direction, one of hubris. This is exactly the same kind of temptation that he had in Canto 4. The structure repeats itself.

In another parallel, in Canto 4 Dante claimed that he built fellowship with the great poets, and then he came into Canto 5 and had to confront the responsibilities of being a writer through his encounter with Francesca, a reader of his own sort of writing. Similarly, when Dante leaves Canto 25 and enters Canto 26, he meets none other than Ulysses, the master rhetorician, whose experience and whose journey will lead Ulysses and his companions to a tragic end. For Dante this is an extraordinary moment, for a number of reasons. Ulysses is a steady point of reference for his own adventure. He will keep thinking of him in Canto 19 of *Purgatorio* and in Canto 28 of *Paradise,* when Dante is about to move beyond the entire physical universe. He looks back to see the distance he has traveled, and the only thing that he sees is really that passageway where Ulysses violated all boundaries. Ulysses is a mode of being, a possibility of being, for Dante himself.

Every school child in antiquity and in Dante's own time knew that Ulysses was a famous Greek hero, polytropic as Homer calls him: a man of many turns, a man who had been seasoned in all experiences, a man who knew it all. They knew that he had gone to the war at Troy, that he was the one to suggest the building of the Trojan Horse and the stealing of the Palladium, which was a simulacrum of Minerva. And everybody knew that it took him ten years to return to Ithaca. This is the story of *The Odyssey*. Ulysses returns, completing the *nostos* as the Greeks call it, the journey of return. He becomes the hero of nostalgia.

In antiquity, in particular, they knew it very well because then the story of Ulysses had become a philosophical allegory of the fate of the soul. The idea of Ulysses, who goes from Ithaca to Troy and then, after a war of ten years, undergoes another ten years of vicissitudes, cleansing and testing himself in order to reach his hometown, was really the story of the soul. The soul incarnates itself, it travels past the various planets and gets tainted by their attributes (some of us are lunatics, others are mercurial, others are saturnine), but then, by cleansing ourselves, the soul can go back to its place of origin. That's the circle of the return, and that's the way the Alexandrian Neoplatonists understood the allegory of *The Odyssey*. An overarching theme in this canto will be Dante's divergent reading of this story and of the Greek world in general.

Dante almost immediately violates the standard version of Ulysses' tale. Dante begins, instead, with a Ulysses who has already returned to Ithaca and who is about to start his journeys of exploration all over again. The idea of the eternal return, the idea of closure at home, is not part of Dante's imaginative sensibility. He is a truly restless poet, always placing himself and his heroes on some kind of quest, on the road toward a place, or toward an idea, like those philosophers who are always thinking about some way of reaching wisdom and truth. That's what happens with the story of Ulysses in Dante's hands. In the *Comedy* Ulysses starts all over again. He's involved in a journey that is absolutely gratuitous, a quest for wisdom in the unpeopled world. And he dies as a result. That's it.

The first thing you will notice is that it's not Dante who conducts the interview with Ulysses. It is Virgil, the poet of Latin antiquity; they speak Greek. It is the poet of *The Aeneid* who thinks of himself as the fitting interlocutor of the great Greek hero. Dante's excluded; he just watches their exchange. But there's more to this idea of stylistic decorum. This reinterpretation of Ulysses' story is, in fact, as tragic as a text could ever get, arriving even at the tragic sublime, and Virgil was the author of a tragedy, rather than a comedy. The sublime style is also present in the words of Ulysses, who speaks in the loftiest way possible. In a certain sense, Ulysses tells the story of his life as if he were Aeneas. If you ask readers of Virgil and Homer, some of them will probably will tell you that while Virgil is a good poet, the first six books of *The Aeneid* are just *The Odyssey,* and the second set of books are just *The Iliad.* Not at all. The difference between the two heroes is clear: Ulysses has a place to which he can return. He goes from Ithaca to Troy and then back to Ithaca. Aeneas has no place to go. His is the open-ended road, the open-ended journey, and this is the way Ulysses will think of himself in the *Inferno.* This beguiling self-depiction is just one example of the extraordinary ambiguity with which Dante represents Ulysses. From the very beginning, Ulysses is a philosopher and a rhetorician. He is someone who can manipulate all knowledge for his own ends, and it is this alluring ambiguity that Dante emphasizes in his characterization of Ulysses in Canto 26.

The canto starts with a topical allusion. Dante is drawing our attention to a specific place, to the city of Florence. It is as if he wants to moor himself, to anchor himself to something as concrete as his own native place. And it's an apostrophe to Florence: "Rejoice, O Florence, since you are so great." The antithetical use of "great" or of "tall and small" at the same time is a common feature of this canto, a rhetorical move intended to make us wonder what the relationship is between that which claims to be so large and that which claims to be so small. Ulysses obviously thinks of himself in terms of loftiness, and Dante now rhetorically starts with Florence as "so great." The satire is obvious as he continues, "Over land and sea you beat your wings, and your name is spread through Hell!"[8] The whole point is that he has seen some Florentine thieves, even named them, so Florence's "greatness" is questionable, at best.

In one of the next few lines, Dante makes a telling shift of verb tenses: "I sorrowed then and sorrow now again." He sorrowed then, in the past tense, when he was a pilgrim, watching and witnessing the stories that he is going to tell, and he sorrows now, in the present tense, as a writer. There's a double focus that Dante's using: the focus of the pilgrim and the focus of the narrator. "I sorrowed then and I sorrow now again," he continues, "when I turn my mind to what I saw; and I curb my genius more than I am wont, lest it run where virtue does not guide it."[9] At least Dante attempts to curb his powers as he pays witness to a story of the immoderate hunger for knowledge that comes from a flight of the mind.

The flight of the mind is like the flight of Icarus. It seems to know no boundaries. Ulysses is he who transgresses all boundaries, but doesn't Dante also transgress boundaries? He won't say so here, for he wants it to seem that he is taking Ulysses as an exemplary figure who could lead him to curtail his abilities. Similarly, the language of running here is that of horses, specifically the horses of the soul, and virtue is the ability to rein in both the black horse and the white horse of the chariot, to hold them together. That's the allusion that Dante is making with his Neoplatonic language.

Then we get the first description of the landscape, a somber landscape indeed: "As many as the fireflies which the peasant, resting on the hill—in the season when he that lights the world least hides his face from us, and at the hour when the fly yields to the mosquito—sees down along the valley, there perhaps where he gathers the grapes and tills: with so many flames the eighth ditch was all agleam, as I perceived as soon as I came where the bottom could be seen. And as he who was avenged by the bears saw Elijah's chariot at its departure, when the horses rose erect to heaven—for he could not so follow it with his eyes so as to see aught save the flame alone, like a little cloud ascending: so each flame moves along the gullet of the ditch, for not one shows its theft, and each steals away a sinner."[10] Dante's not comparing himself to Elijah here; he's comparing himself to someone who watches Elijah. Elijah is also engaged in a flight of the soul, exactly like Ulysses, though Elijah is going to be represented as the antithesis to Ulysses. But Dante is claiming to be unlike either of them. Rather, he is like Eliseus, the one who inherits the mantle of prophecy from Elijah, and the one who witnesses, who watches. Dante is trying to avoid the extremes of both the prophet and the rhetorician.

Virgil goes on to tell Dante that within the flames are spirits. Inside a forked flame there are two souls: Ulysses and Diomedes. Except in the case of the suicides, Dante always sees pairs of sinners. Here's Diomedes, who doesn't talk, and here's Ulysses, as well, and I suppose that the reason is that Dante really wants us to know about the social quality of a moral violation. A moral violation always implies the presence of somebody else. Except for the suicide, which has a peculiar form because you have witness, homicide, and victim all in one, you always have a witness, somebody else who has been touched by the sin, or an accomplice of the sinner.

Dante describes the flame as "so divided at its top that it seems to rise from the pyre where Eteocles was laid with his brother," and in so doing already makes a connection to ancient Greece.[11] The story is *The Thebaid*, and the two brothers, Eteocles and Polynices, were enemies. In Greek mythology the story of Thebes, which Dante knows through Statius, reveals the idea of the tragic city. Thebes becomes the term for a tragic city because in effect it presents birth, specifically the birth of Eteocles and Polynices, the children of Oedipus and Jocasta, as a tragic event. In this sense, the Greek idea of cities and birth is radically distinguished from Virgil's idea of birth as something to be celebrated all the time. Already, then, these flames have an aura of tragedy about them.

Dante asks to speak with the fiery souls—"Master, I earnestly pray you, and pray again, that my prayer avail a thousand, that you deny me not to wait until the horned flame comes hither: you see how with desire I bend towards it"—and Virgil responds, "Your prayer deserves much praise and therefore I accept it; but do you restrain your tongue." Earlier Virgil wanted to curb Dante's powers, now he asks him to curb his speech: "Leave speech to me, for I have understood what you wish—and perhaps, since they were Greeks, they would be disdainful of your words."[12] We have a sense of the hierarchy of styles beginning to take shape: Virgil and Ulysses, and then in Canto 27 it will be Guido da Montefeltro and Dante.

Virgil requests to hear the tale of one of these sinners, and Ulysses speaks with a tongue of flame, whipping in the wind. He says, "I departed from Circe, who had detained me more than a year there near Gaeta, before Aeneas had so named it." Clearly, Ulysses tells his story through the myth of Aeneas, claiming priority over Aeneas. But Ulysses lacks Aeneas's human connections, for Aeneas is a founder of cities, and he names the city of Gaeta after his nurse, whereas for Ulysses, "neither fondness for my son, nor reverence for my aged father, nor the due love which would have made Penelope glad, could conquer in me the longing that I had to gain experience of the world, and of human vice and worth."[13] The heavily ethical language here suggests an ethical quest, and nothing can stand in the way of this virtuous action.

Ulysses sets sail aboard a single ship, and he begins to mention places he sees on his travels. He always mentions cities—in Spain, Morocco, Sardinia, Ceuta—on the other side of the Mediterranean. It is as if he is a man who lives in space; as if he never really knew his own place in the world. He's always looking for something and doesn't know where he belongs.

These aimless wanderings continue for a long time, and then, "my companions were old and slow when we came to that narrow outlet where Hercules set up his markers, that men should not pass beyond." And now we are treated to the speech that he makes to these companions. Look at the rhetorical wisdom with which he moves. He addresses them as brothers, which is the biggest possible *captatio benevolentiae:* we are all together, there is no hierarchy here, I'm not your leader, I'm not your king. His next rhetorical move is hyperbole. If you want to seduce people to come with you, you have to tell them that theirs are mighty actions and then magnify all the possible perils. He says, "O brothers . . . who through a hundred thousand dangers have reached the west"—not a definite place, the west, it is a vague place and yet lofty—"to this so brief vigil of our senses that remains to us, choose not to deny experience."[14] He enacts modesty, the oscillation between hyperbole and litotes, as it were, the recoiling into the sense of ordinariness and smallness. And then he uses this extraordinary word, "experience," which, etymologically speaking, refers to a journey, a going-through. Knowledge is tied to displacement and travel; potential wisdom is used as a lure. His rhetoric is a snare.

And then Ulysses appeals to his companions' sense of self-worth in order to seal the deal. He advises them to "consider [their] origin." If you want to know the end of things, you have to know the beginnings, the seeds. This is Ulysses' perception, and because he is of a noble seed, there is a natural determination in his own mind that he will reach, indeed, a noble end. And the same for his men: "You were not made to live as brutes, but to pursue virtue and knowledge."[15] That's a remarkable line. In what is perhaps an allusion to the metamorphosis of Circe, who had changed these same companions into the hogs of Epicurus wallowing in voluptuary experiences, Ulysses promises not only to restore in them the fullness of their human image but also to bring them to virtue and knowledge. It's almost an impossible promise; it may not even be a correct promise, because he's stating that virtue is knowledge. I say I will lead you to virtue and knowledge, but they may not be the same thing. I may have knowledge, but it doesn't mean that I have the virtue that I claim to have knowledge about. I can know what prudence is, but that doesn't really make me prudent. It is with these false promises, then, that Ulysses leads his men to their doom.

Ulysses' sin is to have counseled his companions to go beyond the boundaries of knowledge. Let me say that for Dante there's no figure more interesting, more important, for whom he has so many questions, than the figure of the counselor. One counselor was, of course, Pier delle Vigne. How does he take the pressure of the court? What does he offer as advice to Frederick the Great, his emperor? And then we're going to see other counselors. We're going to find, in *Inferno* 28, a Provençal poet who literally advises war between father and son. He breaches the unity of the body politic.

Here, though, Ulysses is the counselor who gives the wrong advice to his followers. He makes rhetorical promises that he knows he cannot quite keep. They are grand questions, but what do they amount to? Furthermore, Dante places Ulysses and his companions on the point of going beyond the Pillars of Hercules. It is as if Dante implies, if one were to read the full trajectory of the *Divine Comedy,* that there is no knowledge worthy of its name unless it is connected to some degree of transgression, that somehow transgression is part of an original and new knowing.

Ulysses has to go beyond the limits of the known world in order to discover something new that nobody else knew. That makes him, as they say, a Renaissance figure *avant la lettre.* Dante doesn't seem to be terribly bothered by the transgression, however, since he himself, in different circumstances, is engaged in exactly the same kind of transgression of the perimeter. Dante surpasses even the cosmic perimeter as he goes beyond the sun, goes farther than Daedalus and certainly farther than Icarus. But the promise Ulysses makes to his compatriots remains a faulty one. Dante will refer to it, with a famous metaphor, as a "mad flight."

Dante makes us aware of Ulysses' madness by underscoring the political consequences of the promises that he makes. The whole of Canto 26 is littered with fallen cities. It begins with Florence. Dante apostrophizes against the city, which he describes as spreading its wings as if cities were like heroes, engaged in great flights. That is a clear desire on Dante's part to have us connect the story of Ulysses' self-degradation and turpitude with the story of Florence. Ulysses' own fall is linked to that of Dante's native city. Then there is a reference to the city of Troy. There is a reference to Thebes through Eteocles and Polynices. There is also a reference to Rome. The canto is full of references to cities from this perspective. Canto 26 is a brief version of the epic because the impulse of the epic is always political. There is no epic that exists that doesn't attempt to represent falling cities and the edification of new cities or the placement of a city in a great metaphysical drama. It could be Heavenly Jerusalem, Rome, Carthage, or Thebes, but it's always about falling and rising cities, and so, too, is the strategy of Dante. In particular, he aims to show how the grand philosophical claims of Ulysses have effects that make them appear to be empty rhetoric.

Dante places Ulysses nowhere, somewhere in the ocean without a particular place. He goes from one city to another, and at the same time, because of this, he doesn't seem to be able to deliver on what he has promised. It's a reflection on one particular aspect of the tragic story of Ulysses. It's the tragedy of language, a language that contains all the most incredible mirages and yet falls short of reality. Ulysses is placed in the empty ocean away from all responsibilities and locations, and it is this gratuitousness of his quest that results in his being in Hell among the evil counselors. He has led his men to nothing after having promised them everything.

But Ulysses will appear again in the *Comedy*. He plays a pivotal role in Dante's imagination. He has a paradigmatic role. Dante can't quite get over the phantasm of Ulysses. Ulysses shows up in his dreams in Canto 19 of *Purgatorio,* and then he will also make an appearance when Dante has to measure the great imaginative distance that he traveled when he's at the border of the physical and the metaphysical worlds in *Paradiso.* He looks back, and he will see Ulysses, or he will see the place that has been the place of Ulysses' transgression. The figure of Ulysses haunts Dante, and as a result, he also haunts the *Divine Comedy.*

CHAPTER 8

Inferno 27–29

We turn now to Canto 27, which really ought to be read in conjunction with Canto 26, because here we have what I would call a countermyth to the story of Ulysses. There is a contraction of focus; there's even a revision of the claims of epic grandeur that we have in Canto 26. Dante meets and becomes the interlocutor of Guido da Montefeltro, an extraordinary figure, a military and political leader who experienced a conversion. He became a Franciscan friar, and Pope Boniface VIII, whose name you may recall, summoned him. The pope was not someone that Dante really held in the highest esteem, but Boniface VIII, in an inversion of the relations between high priest and cleric, asks Guido da Montefeltro for some advice. We are dealing again with evil counselors, and the pope's request is equally wicked: you are a great man of arms, so you have to teach me the strategies I should pursue in order to conquer and destroy Palestrina, a small town near Rome.

And so we enter into a Machiavellian world of counselors. It's actually the language of Machiavelli *avant la lettre;* Machiavelli takes for himself the language that Guido uses. At one point Guido says his works were not those of a lion but those of a fox, and these are the two attributes that the perfect prince ought to have in Machiavelli's most well-known work, *The Prince.* That is to say, the perfect prince is one who knows how to use strength, but also how to use slyness, when to be crafty and foxy and when to be violent and leonine. These two images clearly originate from Cicero—they are not Dante's own invention—and it's likely that Machiavelli got them from Cicero, as well as from this canto.

The connections between the two cantos extend well beyond their shared depiction of malevolent counselors, however. First of all, Canto 27 begins with a reference to the Sicilian bull, clearly a counter to the Trojan Horse of the previous canto: "As the Sicilian bull (which bellowed first with the cry of him—and that was right—who had shaped it with his file) was wont to bellow with the voice of the victim, so that, though it was of brass, yet it seemed transfixed with pain."[1] What is the story here? It's a demotic, vulgar version of what happened to Ulysses. Ulysses is condemned to be held prisoner of the flames and the two tongues of fire, because he was a rhetorician, a philosopher, a Neoplatonist trying to persuade others of his ideas, and very proud of his success at persuasion until he gets caught by his own tongue. It's the temptation of the artist himself; it's Daedalus who builds the labyrinth and gets caught by it. It's the story of the artist who becomes a captive of that which he himself constructed. Here Dante begins with a story of the Sicilian bull, the first victim of which was the artisan who made it. I think it's clearly a way of reflecting on the scene that precedes it.

Suddenly, following this description, Virgil and Dante are interrupted by a voice that asks to talk with the one speaking Lombard, namely Dante. What an extraordinary little misreading of the language and rhetoric deployed in the previous canto, where Virgil goes out of his way to say Dante should not talk to these people, for they are Greeks, so Virgil should be the one to talk to them. But now, from the perspective of Guido da Montefeltro, they are no longer speaking some kind of Homeric, Attic Greek, but an Italian dialect. This shift demonstrates that language is not a question of the style you are using, for language always reveals some sort of inner essence. It shows you where you are in the ladder of values and the distance that you have from the world of truth, or the proximity that you may have to some self-complacency, as in the case of Ulysses. At any rate, the soul pleads, "If you are but now fallen into this blind world from that sweet land of Italy whence I bring all my guilt, tell me if the Romagnoles have peace or war; for I was of the mountains there between Urbino and the chain from which the Tiber springs."[2] As opposed to the lofty rhetoric of Ulysses, who speaks through the grandest generalities about the destination and the fate of human beings, here the language involves a deliberate diminution, a contraction of focus, as if it becomes local, the language of peace and war between neighboring towns. And then, as a way of adjusting the stylistic register, Virgil will tell Dante to converse with Guido, as he is Italian.

Once again, on the surface, the degrees of style and the laws of rhetorical decorum are always observed, and now the pilgrim will inform Guido da Montefeltro about the situation in Italy. Guido responds, "If I thought that my answer were to one who might ever return to the world, this flame would shake no more; but since from this depth none ever returned alive, if what I hear is true, I answer you without fear of infamy." This is a passage that you may recognize, since T. S. Eliot uses it as an epigraph, an epitaph actually, for "The Love Song of J. Alfred Prufrock." What I want to emphasize here, though, at the level of style, is *how* Guido speaks: curses, hypothetical sentences, parenthetical remarks, not just a style that deliberately goes contrary to the smooth high style of Ulysses in the preceding canto. He says, "I was a man of arms, and then a corded friar, trusting, so girt, to make amends; and certainly my hope would have come full, but for the High Priest"—here is the curse against Boniface—"may ill befall him!—who set me back in my first sins: and how and wherefore I would have you hear from me."[3] We get another reference to birth, with which, as you know, characters start telling us their story. They tell of this birth, the first major event of their lives, and then of whatever happens next, whatever biographical account may be a descent from or a deviation from the promises that birth may have held.

Guido contends that his actions "were not those of the lion, but of the fox." This is the Machiavellian language we mentioned before. We are moving into the secret halls of power, where big deals are struck, where plans for the destruction of cities are made, where the pope will ask secret advice from his counselor, who "knew all wiles and covert ways, and plied the art of them."[4] I have to remark that Canto 26, which opens with the image of Florentine thieves, also makes use of a language of concealment and covertness. The image harks back to the canto of the thieves (*Inferno* 25). The resonance suggests a subtle bond between thievery and speech: Ulysses the master rhetorician is possessed by language; more generally, the language for thievery (26.39–41) conveys the insight into the furtiveness of language. Also, Dante in that canto spoke of the sun through a periphrasis, to say that it was hidden, that sinners are concealed from its sight in the tongues of fire. The language in these cantos is that of manipulation, of political stratagems and machinations, and in Canto 26 it becomes highlighted and made visible to us.

Guido's autobiography continues: "When I saw myself come to that part of my life when every man should lower the sails"—as if he were another mariner like Ulysses—"and coil up the ropes, that which before had pleased me grieved me then, and with repentance and confession I turned friar, and—woe is me!—it would have availed. The Prince of the new Pharisees, having war near the Lateran—and not with Saracens or with Jews, for his every enemy was Christian, and none had been to conquer Acre, nor been a merchant in the Soldan's land—regarded neither the supreme office and holy orders in himself, nor, in me, that cord which used to make its wearers leaner."[5] Now we are truly moving within the halls of what we would call the Vatican today, but at the time it was known as the Church of St. John the Lateran, which was the residence of the bishop of Rome. And it was famous then, as it is famous now, for the frescoes about Constantine's Donation to Pope Sylvester.

The whole issue of the temporal power of the papacy is glimpsed and underscored throughout this scene between Guido and Boniface. Boniface asks counsel of Guido, in an extraordinary caricature of the holy office, offering him an absolution before even the commission of the crime: "Let not your heart mistrust. I absolve you here and now, and do you teach me how I may cast Penestrino to the ground. I can lock and unlock"—the new Peter—"Heaven, as you know; for the keys are two, which my predecessor did not hold dear."[6] This is the famous story of Celestine V, who gave up the office of the papacy and who stands even in the historical recollections and scholarship of today as the embodiment of a figure who understood, maybe a little too dualistically, that drama always arises between power and holiness. The two forces, for Celestine, were really incommensurable, and it was impossible to create a dialectic between the two, so he gave up. Dante refers to him with a little bit of harshness for not being heroic enough to withstand the tide of corruption and deciding instead to retreat to a contemplative life.

Nor does Guido withstand the tides of corruption. He continues, "Thereon the weighty arguments pushed me to where silence seemed to me the worst, and I said"—and this is the advice he gives, spectacular in its simplicity—"'Father, since you do wash me of that sin into which I now must fall, long promise with short keeping will make you triumph on the High Seat.'"[7] Guido finds the request irresistible, especially because he has been guaranteed absolution, so he can do whatever he wants. So, there is not just a coercion of Guido, but also a kind of pleasure that he feels in committing the evil he will perpetrate. What does his advice mean? Make promises and plan not to keep them. Go and tell the people in Penestrino (Palestrina) that you are going to respect them, that you are going to make them rich, whatever you want to tell them. Then, of course, as soon as they open the gates of the city, don't keep any of these promises.

This is a restatement of a famous text about rhetoric that in the Middle Ages was thought to be Cicero's but is not really his. This rhetorical treatise, like many other treatises, is based on one premise, namely that rhetoric is the art of making the city and the citizens agree in order to keep the city going. In a properly governed city, promises are made and are always observed. It's a way of explaining rhetoric in moral terms. What Dante is saying here is that those dictates, those kinds of propositions, can easily be turned around, and they *are* being turned around in practice.

Finally, we find out what happened to Guido when his life came to an end. St. Francis arrived, and there was a little rivalry between Francis and the devil, fighting over the soul of Guido. Francis loses, and Guido is, of course, placed here in Hell. I mention these details because you will see that Dante picks up a genre of medieval disputation later in *Purgatorio.* There is a canto where Dante meets Guido's son, because in this poem fathers and sons do not necessarily belong in the same moral space, and sons do not necessarily follow in the footsteps of their fathers. You will see how Dante echoes this whole scene, which is a prefiguration of things to come.

Before we arrive in Purgatory, however, we must enter the most tragic section of the *Divine Comedy,* from Canto 28 to the end of *Inferno.* These cantos will tell us what Dante thinks of tragedy and how he envisions the tragic. After all, he calls the poem a comedy, so what is the role and the place of the tragic in a comedy? Is there room for the tragic vision here? The point, as we will repeatedly see in the following cantos, is that the tragic is never the final vision. The essence of tragedy for Dante is always linguistic; it has to do with issues of the inherent ambiguities of language, the impossibility of decoding and deciphering what is being said by one particular statement as opposed to another.

It is certainly language and tragedy that we find in Canto 28, where Dante encounters the figure of Bertran de Born, a Provençal poet whom Dante actually greatly admired. In Dante's treatise on language, the *De vulgari eloquentia* (On Eloquence in the Vernacular), Dante singles out Bertran de Born as a great poet because he knew how to write the most difficult genre. He knew how to rhyme and how to write war poems. This is really the most difficult type of poetry, aesthetically very difficult to sustain, and Bertran de Born was a genius at it. But in Canto 28 Dante places him among the so-called makers of discord in Hell.

This difficult canto begins with a reflection on war and a reference to ineffability: "Who could ever fully tell, even in unfettered words, though many times narrating, the blood and the wounds that I now saw? Surely every tongue would fail, because of our speech and our memory which have little capacity to comprehend so much. Were all the people assembled again who once in the fateful land of Apulia bewailed their blood shed by the Trojans, and those of the long war that made so vast a spoil of rings—as Livy writes, who does not err—together with those who felt the pain of blows in the struggle with Robert Guiscard, and those others whose bones are still heaped up at Ceperano, where every Apulian was false, and there by Tagliacozzo where old Alardo conquered without arms; and one should show his limb pierced through, and another his cut off, it would be nothing to equal the foul fashion of the ninth pouch."[8] What sort of metaphor is this? We could call it the adoption of the so-called ineffability topos. It's a poetic device, where the poet admits the difficulty, or even impossibility, of describing a particular reality. This ineffability involves the sublime; it usually has to do with, let's say, the vision of God. Whoever has seen God, whatever mystic may have had a vision, they always fall into the contingency of language that cannot quite grasp the sublime quality of what they have seen. Dante now deploys the same device for the world of evil. It is as if Hell now has its own sublime quality that is a parallel and counter to that which Dante will witness in the divine spectacles at the top of Paradise. Even in Hell, language cannot quite be adequate to the reality it wants to represent. Dante wants to describe the whole of Hell, but all the dismemberments of bodies from old wars cannot come close to what he has seen in this realm. The questions that arise in the face of this ineffability topos will only become further complicated and nuanced in the unfolding of the canto.

In the midst of all this language of the ineffable, however, there is also a little detail, a reference to Livy, a Roman historian. His voice and his authority are considered unquestionable. Livy cannot make mistakes. Livy and his fellow historians are unerring in their accounts of what they have seen, but somehow the poetic voice is not the same thing as the historian's voice. You can see this tension in the first few lines of the canto. But then it comes to a close with a different form of poetic reflection; Dante is describing something altogether different in the meeting of Bertran de Born. He says, "I stayed to view the troop, and saw a thing that I should be afraid even to relate without more proof."[9] We encounter the threat of the ineffable once again. The poet feels the difficulty of representing the extraordinary quality of what he has seen.

But he goes on: "Conscience, the good companion that emboldens a man under the hauberk of feeling itself pure, reassures me. Truly I saw, and seem to see it still, a trunk without the head going along as were the others of that dismal herd, and it was holding the severed head by the hair, swinging it in hand like a lantern, and it was gazing at us and saying: 'O me!' Of itself it was making a lamp for itself, and they were two in one and one in two."[10] He uses strangely mathematical language to describe the divided body of Bertran de Born, a maker of discord who is being punished by having his own body divided from itself. Two is one, and one is two, a mathematical language that implies the impossibility of equality here. This is exactly the language that he used for the metaphor earlier in the canto, with the description of all the battlefields and all the dead people, limbs accumulated one on top of the other. Dante's using once more an expression of quantity to make us question whether there is some rationale in the disparity of one being two. He claims not to have the answers. He claims that only God knows.

And then Bertran finally speaks: "See now my grievous penalty, you who, breathing, go to view the dead: see if any other is so great as this!" He is the first character in Hell who complains that the punishment inflicted on him is beyond all justice, that there's no proportionality between the punishment he receives and the crime he has committed. Bertran proceeds to explain: "And that you may carry news of me, know that I am Bertran de Born, he who to the young king gave the evil counsels. I made the father and the son rebel against each other. Ahithophel did not more with Absalom and David by his wicked instigations. Because I parted persons thus united, I carry my brain parted from its source, alas! which is in this trunk. Thus is the retribution observed in me."[11] Why should Bertran de Born bear a visible mark of division on his body? To his mind it is too "grievous."

The idea of a punishment in Hell is that a punishment is the prolongation of what one has chosen to do in this life. You did not believe in the mortality of the soul, so you are always going to be dead after death. You choose to create division, and you are divided. This is the justice that regulates this world of Hell. The word Dante uses for this retribution is *contrapasso,* which means "a counterpart" or "countersuffering." There is a fair correspondence between what you have done and what you are going to suffer. In a sense it's close to but not quite equivalent to the idea of an eye for an eye and a tooth for a tooth.

The whole point of this canto is that Bertran de Born divides father and son and thereby violates a fundamental principle of political theology. A great medieval historian, Ernst Kantorowicz, wrote a book called *The King's Two Bodies* that asks what a king really is. According to Kantorowicz, a king always has two bodies, the visible body that we all have and a mystical body of royalty. They used to say in the Middle Ages, and perhaps we still do, "The king is dead, long live the king." The king never dies precisely because he has two bodies. He may die as an incumbent, but the office of the king always remains. So, by dividing the father from the son, Dante has Bertran de Born breaching the unity of the mystical body of the king. The two, father and son, are really one.

The other metaphor that is behind all this, which we already traced in the canto of Ciacco, is the idea of the body politic, the idea that the city is constructed like a body, with an organic set of correspondences. There's no difference between patricians and plebeians; they're all part of one organic unified whole. That is true for the body politic, from a Roman point of view, but it's also the principle of the mystical body of the Church. Saint Paul, in the Letter to the Ephesians, refers to the church as the mystical body of Christ, and the state becomes a secular counter to and extension of this mystical body. We are all parts, some of us thumbs, others toes or hair, in this body of Christ. In Canto 28 you have a political focus on Rome, but also a reference to Muhammad. There are a lot of people who find it absolutely odious that Muhammad should be placed in this area of Hell, and the only argument that one can make on behalf of Dante is that Muhammad was actually a member of the Church who created a schism, which is different from heresy. The heretics are those who do not believe in certain tenets of the doctrine. The schismatics are those who want to divide it. So, whether of church or state, division is at the heart of all the images in Canto 28 of *Inferno.*

Where does Dante's idea of justice come from? How does it work? Dante is aware of the great commentary on Aristotle's *Ethics* by Thomas Aquinas. He keeps Aristotle and Aquinas and their discussion of justice in mind as he writes. Dante is clearly a poet of justice. He truly believes the whole point of his quest is to establish some degree of justice in his soul, to try to find justice in the city, and to probe the possibility of some universal justice, as opposed to Lucretian ideas of anarchy and chaos in the cosmos. In that way, there can be some continuity between the outer and the inner worlds. Thus, it makes sense that he would consider the thought of Aristotle and Aquinas on these matters.

What is their idea of justice? They usually discuss two types of justice: retributive justice, which is the one that we have in Hell, but also distributive justice. Is Dante aware of both? Yes, for it's impossible not to think of the representation of the Wheel of Fortune in *Inferno 7* as anything other than a case of distributive justice, which must follow an arithmetical model.

That is to say, if someone has five of something and you want to establish justice, you take some away from the one who has five and give them to another one who has zero and thereby create a kind of equality. Equality is always the aim of distributive justice. In retributive justice, things are a little bit different because—and Aquinas reflects on this, though it is not at all a concern of Aristotle—if I say "an eye for an eye, and a tooth for a tooth," am I really establishing justice, or am I just doubling the offense that has been perpetrated? If someone plucks out one of my eyes, and I do the same to whoever has damaged me, am I restored to my original state? No, that doesn't happen. So how can we even consider retributive justice? Aquinas, and here also Aristotle, admits that it's always very difficult to find exact counterparts between crime and punishment. If a clown were to slap the king, it's not enough for the king to slap the clown back, because there is also the violation of the office involved, which can never quite be restored simply by having the king slap the clown back. Both Aristotle and Aquinas say that's why money was invented, so that one can repay wrongs in other forms, with other punishments.

How does Dante reinterpret their stances on justice? First, it is crucial that Dante thinks about this fundamental problem of justice, which is the aim of the ethical structure of the poem (in *Inferno*, in particular), through the poet, through Bertran de Born. It's Dante himself who has just been announcing the impossibility of finding through language the right metaphor, the exact correspondence between a reality and its representation. What Dante is doing is telling us how arbitrary his own judgments in Hell are. He acknowledges that the way in which punishments and crimes are related is never quite reliable.

To make this clearer, I turn to the very beginning of Canto 29 because it works as a retrospective gloss on the problems that I've been trying to explain in Canto 28. Dante will enter the world of the falsifiers, those who are engaged in diabolical, unnatural mutations, personifications, and impersonations, but before he gets there, he has to get past the last canto. The narrative economy of each canto being what it is, Dante usually comes to the end of a canto and closes off with that particular sin or that particular sinner. This is an exception. Dante enters Canto 29, but the situation he has been describing in Canto 28 keeps reappearing. It worries him somehow.

Dante cannot stop looking back at what he has seen: "The many people and the strange wounds had made my eyes so drunken that they longed to stay and weep; but Virgil said to me, 'What are you still gazing at? Why does your sight still rest down there among the dismal maimed shades? You have not done so at the other pits. Consider, if you think to count them, that the valley circles two and twenty miles; and already the moon is beneath our feet. The time is now short that is allowed us, and there is more to see then you see here.'"[12] Once again we get numbers, arithmetical language. Why this particular measure? One great reader of *Inferno,* who actually began his career as a commentator of Dante, was Galileo, the scientist. He tried to find out what the actual size of the whole of *Inferno* was, just by using this little detail that Dante gives, the radius, and he comes up with the idea that Hell is as large as the city of Florence, which may be a mathematical proof or just his own joke. I'll leave it to you to decide.

The real reason for the constant backward glancing comes later. Dante says, "Within that hollow where I was but now holding my eyes so fixedly, I believe a spirit of my own blood laments the guilt that costs so dear down there." Dante knows that a relative of his is in this den of Hell. But Virgil tells him to move on, that he saw the soul "point at you and fiercely threaten with his finger, and I heard them call him Geri del Bello," but Dante was too distracted to see him. Dante responds, "The violent death which is not yet avenged for him by any who is partner in the shame made him indignant; wherefore, as I judge, he went on without speaking to me, and thereby has he made me pity him the more."[13]

It's fairly clear: Dante meets a kinsman of his who has been killed, and that death is unavenged and is going to stay unavenged. Dante is overwhelmed by pity and compassion, but he does not promise that he's going to go out and take revenge against the killers of his relative, Geri del Bello. He is redefining the notion that justice is a doubling of the crime. The idea of justice as revenge, as a way of establishing a precise similarity, is what Dante is giving up here completely. This is the beginning of Dante's worrying about the nature of God's justice, worrying about the arbitrariness of his own claim of authority in describing these very issues. He commences a tone of uncertainty, of doubt.

But that's not the only facet of Dante's text. As we know, he's also capable of taking on a prophetic voice, so that he appears as the one who has, by a singular grace of God, been chosen to explore the world in the beyond, which is captured and understood in the most physical and direct way. So, these two voices are simultaneously present, and I think that is really the poem's primary source of tension. Dante is both a prophet and a poet aware of the arbitrariness of his own construction. He's a poet-theologian and a poet-allegorist. In many ways, this duality makes the poem the actual experience of a pilgrimage. That is to say, the judgment you give of the realities that Dante is representing can reveal yourself to you: who you are and where you are. It's a way of shifting away from a journey guided by the voice of a master, who can tell you how things are, to an interpretative journey in which you decipher the text and constantly involve yourself in the story. This story, which is Dante's journey, can turn out to be your journey, too. Dante wants you to tell your own story. His conception of justice and his questioning of that same conception make you his equal. Justice, indeed.

CHAPTER 9

Inferno 30–34

As we conclude with *Inferno,* I'll be talking about Dante's tragic mode at the bottom of Hell. This tragic representation is a difficult enterprise, considering that this is a comedy. But that difficulty is somewhat mitigated because the tragic here is not an ending, not a final vision, but part of a larger discourse that Dante will develop, which is ultimately comical. He really has a comical vision, even of the divinity and certainly of the cosmos. There is a redemptive, happy, harmonious sense to the whole.

Another difficulty is that within the Christian vision that shapes Dante's poem, it's very difficult to locate the tragic: there is no such a thing as a Christian tragedy. And yet this issue may be just as nuanced, for within that Christian vision, we are always told that the only thing we know of God's presence in history is the Crucifixion. There's the story of the dying God, the story of the suffering of the divinity itself. It is not, once again, a final vision. So, there's a theological problem that Dante has to confront and there is also a larger aesthetic problem.

The ultimate resolution to the tragedy problem involves language and Dante's insight into what the tragic may be. To understand how this works, though, we have to look outside the text a little bit. Dante goes into exile in 1302. At that time, he had written only one book, the *Vita nuova.* It's a lyrical poem, self-enclosed: it's about the sense that the self is absolute, that love is an absolute itself and one cannot love "relatively." It does not allow for the intrusion of anything within its own orbit and perimeter, and Dante finishes it off with a vision, realizing that he has to do other things in order to continue writing.

He doesn't write much at that point, perhaps some songs. Instead he is involved in political life, in the footsteps of his teacher Brunetto Latini, and hoping that his life will really be very different from Latini's. Ironically, it's not better because it's actually even more tragic than Brunetto Latini's life; at least Brunetto Latini was politically involved in the history of Florence. He experienced exile, but he returned to Florence and could go on teaching Dante. He wrote encyclopedic texts, like the *Trésor* and autobiographical allegories about his life.

But when Dante goes into exile, the first thing that he writes is a treatise on language in Latin called *De vulgari eloquentia*. It's a text written from the perspective of exile, very much like the *Divine Comedy* because Dante will never go back to Florence. The reasons why he writes this kind of text are very unclear, in part because he never finished it. He wrote two books of it, but we don't even know how many he had conceived of writing. Let me give you a little bit of a summary of the text, and then you will see how it will reappear in the final cantos of *Inferno,* where in effect Dante rewrites it and gives a sense of the wholeness of this text and of why it could never have been finished. He starts very much in the manner of medieval treatises, from a metaphysical standpoint, from on high: What does human language do? Is language something human? And the answer that he gives is both yes and no. It is human because we are the only ones who can speak, though he makes room for certain animals that occasionally speak in a human voice and can be understood by human beings. He's not talking about parrots; he's talking about miraculous biblical scenes. He also notes that the angels do not speak, or at least they don't use the language we do. They communicate with the other angels or with God intuitively. So, there is a reality that escapes the language that we use. Thus, the language is only human, and yet it's not human at all because it's actually a gift from God. This is the metaphysical premise of Dante's treatise.

Who were the first people to speak? He says they were Adam and Eve in the Garden of Eden. That's biblical enough, it's clear. What was the first language that they spoke? Hebrew. Dante asserts that Hebrew was the primal language, and he will even go so far as to say that Hebrew was never extinguished by the fall of mankind, for instance, or by the building of the Tower of Babel. Furthermore, not only does this primal language survive the story of Nimrod, it has never really disappeared. Dante takes, and I'm only qualifying the statement, what we would call an ahistorical viewpoint.

It's almost as if Hebrew does not belong to the flow of history and the reality of the mutations to which all sublunary things are prone. I stress this fact because I'm going to return to it when I discuss *Paradiso* 26, where Dante meets Adam and blatantly changes his mind, as though something intervenes between the writing of the *De vulgari eloquentia* and the encounter with Adam, when Adam says that the Hebrew language he spoke completely vanished as soon as he ate the forbidden fruit. In other words, in *Paradiso,* Dante is ready to historicize the question of human language, unlike in the earlier treatise.

In book 2 of *De vulgari eloquentia,* Dante takes the treatise in an entirely different direction. He stops talking about the grammar of language, how language is ordered. Instead he talks about rhetoric and almost becomes a theorist of poetry and style. He explains, for instance, his three styles of writing poetry, which you may recall: the high style, the middle style, and the low style, or the style of tragedy, the style of elegy, and the style of comedy. He suggests that style should never be thought of as pure ornamentation. Dante implies that style is rather a mode of knowledge. He says there's a high style for high reality, a middle style for the middle reality of the mixed world, and so on; but what he really means is that if you want to understand those who are at the bottom of the social hierarchy—the fisherman, for instance, or clowns—you cannot treat them with the same decorum with which you treat the king. Kings speak differently, using the sublime kind of language. The style is tied to a specific exchange of ideas.

Dante also describes his theory of the canzone, which is the greatest poetic lyrical form and a way of bringing out the music of language. He is responding to a poetic revolution that had taken place in Sicily, at the court of Frederick II. Prior to that time, the Provençal poets would compose poetry and accompany their poems with the lute, the famous Provençal poets' instrument. The Sicilians, instead, divided those two modes. It was possible to write poetry in and of itself, without the accompaniment of music, in the persuasion that the art of poetry was the effort to bring out the inherent harmony of the language.

Dante discusses themes, too. What are the great themes of poetry? I alluded to that when I explained the background of Bertran de Born because Dante says Bertran de Born was the greatest writer of war poetry. Other important themes include the rectitude of the will, which is to say a sense of the ethical, and, of course, love. Then he ends with a great definition of poetry as the art that combines music and rhetoric. And that's all we have of the *De vulgari eloquentia.*

To return to the *Comedy,* then, since I'll be talking mainly about tragedy and language, I want to emphasize how much Dante retrieves of the *De vulgari eloquentia* here. There's a deliberate pattern of references, a retrospective view of his past, of some failure of his. He asks himself what was so impossible to accomplish about a particular task that he realized it was impossible to accomplish. These assorted connections between Dante's treatise on the vulgar tongue and the cantos of lower Hell will only become clearer as we proceed.

Where are we, by the way? These are the cantos of the lower Hell, in the general area of fraud. In Canto 11, where the ethical map of *Inferno* is provided, Dante distinguishes between the sins of fraud and the sins of treachery. Treachery is a subdivision of fraud because fraud can be found in rhetoricians, falsifiers in general, flatterers, and so on, but treachery is worse than that, and that's where we are now, in the realm of treachery. The treacherous sinners are those who engage in a deceptive violation of the trust others place in them, which is not necessarily true for all fraudulent people. Someone can perpetrate a fraud against you without knowing you or having anything to do with you. The question of treachery instead implies what Dante calls the erasure of the bonds of love because it involves one's friends, family, country, or hosts. Those who sin in this fashion annihilate all possible ties within a community, between the self and others.

As such, treachery is the language of nothing. It's a way of saying that nothing matters, that there's no such thing as a true attachment to another person. It's a severing of the self in the domain of pure arbitrariness. I may be above everything or perhaps below everything, but I certainly have no attachments to anything around me. And without attachments, without exchanges, there is no language at all.

So, Dante enters Canto 30, and he's talking about two experiences that define the tragic mode. First, he speaks of "the time when Juno was wroth for Semele," a mistress of Jupiter.[1] He's talking about the tragic text *The Thebaid*, in which the gods themselves within the classical world seem to have been wounded by exactly the same mad passions that drive human beings to destruction. This is Juno, who cannot die but who will suffer from the same passions as Semele or any other mortal. There's a language here of the tragic and the mythopoeic, with a classical theology being tied to it. Then we get the story of the Trojans again and, even farther along, the Ovidian story of Myrrha, a young woman who is inflamed by incestuous passion and impersonates somebody else in order to be able to sleep with her father. This is all part of the "tragic perimeter" of these cantos.

The defining tragic story here, however, is that of Sinon, who is an impersonator and a falsifier who convinced the Trojans to bring the infamous Horse within their walls. You don't really have to know a lot of Italian to know that Dante with this name is punning on *sì-non*, "yes-no." This man is the very representation of the falsification of personality. The tragic is thus tied to a sense of self-contradictory identity, people who do not know exactly who they are or whether they may take on another figuration or the reality of somebody else. This idea of ambiguity is already betrayed by Sinon's name, which truly serves to emphasize the connection between madness and tragedy.

Further echoes of the *De vulgari eloquentia* appear in Canto 31, where Dante meets the giants. The language Dante encounters here is nothing more than an amalgam of strange sounds. Every commentator will tell you that Dante's using gibberish here. Nobody knows what it means. These are the words: "'*Raphèl maì amecche zabì almi*,' the fierce mouth, to which sweeter psalms were not fitting, began to cry. And my leader towards him, 'Stupid soul, keep to your horn and with that vent yourself when rage or other passion takes you. Search at your neck and you will find the belt that holds it tied, O soul confused: see how it lies across your great chest.' Then he said to me, 'He is his own accuser: this is Nimrod, through whose ill thought one sole language is not used in the world. Let us leave him alone and not speak in vain, for every language is to him as his is to others, which is known to none.'"[2] And then Dante goes on to meet a number of other giants.

But why does Dante mention giants at all, either here or in the *De vulgari eloquentia*? There is a way in which the *De vulgari eloquentia* is written from the viewpoint of Nimrod because what Dante wants to do is something exactly like what Nimrod attempted. Nimrod wanted to combine all the possible languages, and the effort resulted in Babel and the confusion of tongues. He wanted to build a tower whereby human beings could reach heaven, the other side of the incarnational Word that joins heaven and earth. One is a descent, the other the pride of ascent. Nimrod wants to occupy a superior perspective; that's what his being a giant means. He aims at a perspective from which he can see the whole of the world around him and then transcend the world of contingency. The theological response is that you can't transcend by means of pride. You do it with humility. There is an undeniable connection between pride and perspective.

The *De vulgari eloquentia* is also a text of perspectivism. Perspectivism simply means the presence of various viewpoints, all of which one somehow manages to control or to know. In Dante, this is the way that the entire *Inferno* is written, for as we know, Dante uses all possible styles. He uses the courtly language and rhetoric of Francesca, the legal language of Pier della Vigna, the language of the schools, of Brunetto Latini, and the language of the prophets. He uses all perspectives. The whole of the *Divine Comedy* is such a perspectivist story.

Some might argue that I am using a language that doesn't belong to Dante's own culture. That would be a very legitimate objection because when we talk about perspective, we usually think about the revolutionary language of fifteenth-century art. Actually, there was a certain knowledge of perspective earlier than Dante, but even if they did not have a theory of perspective, they certainly had the *practice* of perspective. Perspective is usually tied to art, and we usually link it with a figure like Alberti, a fifteenth-century theorist of art who wrote a treatise called *De pictura* (On Painting) in 1436, in which he theorizes about what other painters were doing. What is perspective for Alberti? It simply means the discovery that the mode of representation practiced in the Middle Ages really lacked depth, and the belief that the world of appearance and the world of reality coincided in some way. Perspective means that the world that I see shifts and changes according to the position that I, the spectator, occupy in the field of vision. It also implies the possibility of manipulating the space that we witness as a particular space. We can change it according to distance, according to the laws of the eyes, the position of the eye, according to the hour of the day. These Renaissance men admitted that they were only going to be able to give a sense of the appearance of things, not of their reality. That's the revolutionary thought behind perspective.

Dante uses this perspectivism—which, I repeat, means a way of assembling various points of view—because he believes that he really has collected a variety of vantage points. He's in exile in 1302, he has been traveling all over Italy, and he thinks that he can forge the vernacular language of Italy. In the *De vulgari eloquentia,* for instance, he writes about the proximity of the Romance languages. He says that the way in which French, Provençal, Spanish, and Italian are connected involves a single particle: the way we use a single sound, like *sì,* to make an affirmative statement. This is how the families of languages have been knit together.

Dante is also continuing to respond to the story of Nimrod. The line that everybody thinks doesn't mean anything—"Raphèl maì amecche zabì almi"—actually does have meaning if you look at it carefully. It is an imperfect anagram of a Hebrew line from the Psalms, and a reference to "sweeter Psalms" in the following lines implies that Dante is giving up his source. The line in the psalm, Psalm 22, is "Eli, Eli, lama sabachthani." These are the words that Jesus utters on the cross, "Father, Father why have you forsaken me?"

So Dante is using Hebrew because, as he said in the *De vulgari eloquentia,* Hebrew is an inverted, twisted language as used by of the builder of the Tower of Babel, a language we are not supposed to understand, and yet, he indicates here, behind all the confusion there is still something intelligible. Specifically, it's the tragic moment of the Crucifixion, where the Son feels that he is completely abandoned and that the whole divine order is no longer responsive to him. It is a moment of theological despair. As a result, Dante is, I think, telling Nimrod obliquely that had he not been so stupid he would have known that by using this kind of language, he could have reached heaven.

Then there is a case of perspectival confusion. Dante is far away, and he mistakes the giants for towers, a reference to a famous town that still exists. If you go on the highway near Siena, you can still see Monteriggioni's towers, which is what Dante sees when he thinks that the giants are towers, because he lacks the correct perspective. In perspective, you see according to the distance between you and the object. This is the basic mathematics, the geometry that rules and sustains the theory of perspective.

But even after establishing his perspective, Dante has other problems to consider. At the outset of Canto 32, he writes, "If I had harsh and grating rhymes, as would befit the dismal hole on which all the other rocks converge and weigh, I would press out more fully the juice of my conception; but since I do not have them, it is not without fear that I bring myself to speak; for to describe the bottom of the whole universe is not an enterprise to be taken up in sport, nor for a tongue that cries mamma and daddy. But may those ladies aid my verse who aided Amphion to wall in Thebes, so that the telling may not be diverse from the fact. O you beyond all others misbegotten crowd who are in the place whereof it is hard to speak, better had you here been sheep or goats!"[3] Here Dante rehashes what I have called the ineffability topos. You may recall from the beginning of Canto 28 that Dante talked about a sort of parodic, inverted form of the sublime because the horror of what he was witnessing was such that he could not find the words and metaphors to describe it.

This is a variant of that conceit, but here Dante is looking for a style rather than specific words. There must be a unique style for this particular reality, and he starts by saying that he cannot go on using the language of familiarity. He cannot use words like *babbo* and *mamma,* the language of the child, because he is encountering the treacherous souls who have betrayed their families, so there is a tragic resonance surrounding that little motif of his. This scene cannot be told in the familiar language of the everyday because these sinners have betrayed all of that. It's possible that it cannot be told at all, because in this area of treachery and fraud, words and deeds do not necessarily belong together. So he appeals to Amphion and the building of Thebes. Once again, we find the tragic story of Thebes, and Dante is also indirectly alluding to something that he himself has written. Amphion was a poet who moved stones with the power of his language, a version of Orpheus who placated and tamed the savage beasts within our hearts, and Dante wants to emulate him. The fact is that Dante had written some "stony rhymes," *rime petrose,* and with the retrospective view established here, he realizes that the only style adequate to this infernal reality is the style of the poems he wrote during a time in his life when he was crazy for a certain *donna petra,* or "stone lady," who would change him into stone. Dante needs to return to and restore this stony style to depict justly the frozen iciness of Hell. There is no burning fire in lowest Hell, only cold, hard ice.

That ice is on full display at the end of the canto: "We had already left him when I saw two frozen in one hole so close that the head of the one was a hood for the other; and as bread is devoured for hunger, so the upper one set his teeth upon the other where the brain joins with the nape. Not otherwise did Tydeus gnaw the temples of Menalippus for rage than this one was doing to the skull and the other parts. 'O you who by so bestial a sign show hatred against him whom you devour, tell me the wherefore,' I said, 'on this condition, that if you with reason complain of him, I, knowing who you are and his offense, may yet requite you in the world above, if that with which I speak does not dry up."[4] To me, this is the most unbearable scene of *Inferno,* the cannibalization, one human being eating another. This is a truly tragic representation. And we are approaching a moment where silence envelops all possible representations. It's something that is not altogether capable of being stated. Dante places us at the boundary between speech and what cannot be said.

This liminal exchange follows at the outset of Canto 33: "From his savage repast the sinner raised his mouth, wiping it on the hair of the head he had spoiled behind, then began, 'You will have me renew desperate grief, which even to think of wrings my heart before I speak of it. But if my words are to be seed that may bear fruit of infamy to the traitor whom I gnaw, you shall see me speak and weep together.'" These lines are clearly an echo of *Inferno* 5 and Francesca's language there. But the language of love has become a language of hatred because Ugolino can't distinguish them, and that's part of his tragedy. Dante is echoing Francesca and her romance with Paolo in order to explain the hatred and blindness of Ugolino, who lacks any perspective on himself and on the world around him. He then continues, "I do not know who you are, nor by what means you have come down here; but truly you do seem to me Florentine when I hear you."[5] The focus is now on language, which is a part of the process of getting to know and understanding the Other. This soul may know the inflections of the Florentine dialect, but there's still no possible communication between the two of them.

If we were to name the rhetorical genre that Dante deploys here, it is what critics call a dramatic monologue. Ugolino speaks without pause as he tells us the story of his life the way he sees it, and therefore he does not expect, nor does he get, any response from his apparent interlocutor. In this way Ugolino can fictionalize himself, and furthermore, he believes that his perspective, the way he fictionalizes himself, will become reality. Dante entices Ugolino to do exactly that because he knows that such behavior is unavoidable in Hell, where the dead really believe that they can just tell their stories and others are going to believe them. They deceive themselves into thinking that the reality they construct will be everybody's accepted reality. This is one of the issues that we are going to confront repeatedly in this canto.

So, Ugolino's biographical moment begins. He says, "You have to know that I was Count Ugolino, and this is the Archbishop Ruggieri."[6] What an extraordinary line. It contains what we call attributes, or titles, and a crucial shift in verbal tense. Ugolino takes control of time by switching from the past tense to the present: "I *was* Count Ugolino, and this *is* the Archbishop." This rhetorical move implies that the object of his hatred is unalterable and timeless, while Ugolino himself has a history. And yet Ruggieri, that object of his hatred, is exactly what goes on defining him in the present. There is the secular and the sacred, if you wish: Guelphs and Ghibellines, with the idea that Ugolino had really betrayed his side. A Guelph became a Ghibelline, and a Ghibelline became a Guelph. In a certain sense, then, he represents a recapitulation of all the satanic sins we have seen so far in *Inferno*.

Ugolino continues his autobiographical tale, explaining that he was put as a prisoner in a tower, which we are meant to understand as a reference to other towers, like the Tower of Babel. Ugolino's particular tower was called the "tower of hunger," for reasons that will soon become evident.

There he has a dream, and the mistake he makes is to think that the dream is going to come true. And the dream is this: "This man appeared to me as master and lord, chasing the wolf and the whelps"—the word *Guelph* comes from "wolf," Guelph and Ghibellines—"upon the mountain for which the Pisans cannot see Lucca." He has this vision of destruction, the mutual destructions of the wolf and the hunter. And he awakens to his crying children, awaiting food that will never come, for the tower is being boarded up. He responds stoically to their doom: "I did not weep, so was I turned to stone within me. They wept."[7] However, shortly thereafter, we note a movement here between the horror of this tragedy and the tenderness, the pathos of it, primarily because Dante uses the diminutive Anselmuccio to refer to Ugolino's small child Anselmo.

But then the horror strikes again: "My poor little Anselm said, 'You look so, father, what ails you?' I shed no tear for that, nor did I answer all that day, nor the night after, until the next sun came forth on the world. As soon as a little ray made its way into the woeful prison, and I discerned by their four faces the aspect of my own, I bit both my hands for grief. And they, thinking I did it for hunger, suddenly rose up and said, 'Father, it will be far less painful to us if you eat of us; you did clothe us with this wretched flesh, and do you strip us of it!' Then I calmed myself in order not to make them sadder. That day and the next we stayed all silent: Ah, hard earth! why did you not open? When we had come to the fourth day Gaddo threw himself outstretched at my feet, saying: 'Father, why do you not help me?' "[8] I don't think it's farfetched to hear behind this child's question an echo of the prayer of Jesus on the cross that we discussed a few cantos back. There is a way in which the violence inflicted on Ugolino's children seems to repeat or reenact the great drama of the Christian sacrifice.

Inevitably, one by one, the children perish before Ugolino's eyes, and "I took me, already blind, to groping over each, and for two days called them after they were dead. Then fasting did more than grief had done."[9] Ugolino sees no more and thus lacks perspective. He no longer has any distance from anything, nor can he tell things apart. As a result, that final sentence—"fasting did more than grief had done"—is an extraordinarily ambiguous line, for we really cannot know with certainty what he is saying. According to Rodin, for instance, who will base a sculpture on this tale, the story is that Ugolino ate his own children. He yielded to his appetite, the urging of hunger, rather than to grief. But he may be saying something else. Maybe he's saying that fasting had more power than grief, that he died of hunger rather than from his grief. We don't know, and I think that part of the tragic mode that Dante is trying to convey to us is that we are left without a definitive answer. According to Borges's reading of this canto, Dante wants to leave us in suspension, to believe that it's possible that Ugolino may have eaten the children, but maybe he didn't. I think that Borges is right, that we are not supposed to be able to tell, that the ambiguity of that line is never going to be quite resolved. It's going to remain forever unknowable.

Dante expresses the tragic nature of these events in an apostrophe against Pisa. "Ah, Pisa," he writes, "shame of the peoples of the fair land where the *sì* is heard, since your neighbors are slow to punish you, let Capraia and Gorgona shift, and make a hedge for Arno at its mouth, so that it drown every soul in you!"[10] The *sì* offers another little echo of the *De vulgari eloquentia*. And yet, in the moment when Dante is dealing with treachery, the most nihilistic of all sins because it means that you declare null and void any bond that you may have with others, he uses an affirmative word. To me, the irony is glaring here, since he suggests a possible affirmation, when in fact there is no hope for one. What follows is really the kind of language that Ugolino had used before the tragedy, when he begged the earth for an earthquake, so that the earth might open up and swallow all of them. Dante appropriates this language out of horror, the terrifying realization that he is himself enmeshed in the same sort of tragic spectacle. He suddenly sees that the whole realm of Hell could actually be just an apocalyptic ending to the world he knows.

But the most tragic event of all is spelled out shortly thereafter: "For if Count Ugolino had the name of betraying you of your castles, you ought not to have put his children to such torture." In other words, this has been the crucifixion of innocence. "Their youthful years, you modern Thebes"— Pisa is the new Thebes, the scene of a new *Thebaid* that we have been witnessing just now—"made Uguccione and Brigata innocent, and the other two that my song names above."[11] The tragic nature of this occurrence is visible in the very presence of the Christological language in this canto, because the sacrifice of the cross means one thing and one thing only: now that all violence is finished and we have found a voluntary scapegoat, who says that we're all innocent and that he is the guilty one, we are redeemed, we are made innocent once again. The story here, reenacting and echoing the story of the cross, seems instead to announce the futility of that sacrifice. Retrospectively, Dante suggests that that sacrifice was just another one of the many senseless acts of violence that punctuate human history. Of course, this is not the end of the poem, but it's certainly the most desperate part of the poem, because Dante comes to believe that the law of history and the law of the world are truly tragic. And there is something absolute about them, something not quite escapable.

And so it is with true tragedy that Dante enters the final canto of the first part of his *Comedy*. Canto 34 is where Dante meets Satan. The encounter with Satan is, first of all, the source of the incredible coherence to the whole movement of *Inferno*, because, as you may recall, the story of *Inferno* began with the neutral angels, those who had been sitting, watching the spectacle of the disruption of the cosmos at the time of the Lucifer's rebellion against God. And now it ends with Lucifer, so it really has an angelic, cosmic proportionality to it.

The other thing that I have to say about Dante's depiction of Satan is that those of you who are readers of Milton and know what a brilliant rhetorician Lucifer is in *Paradise Lost* will be disappointed by Satan's silence here. In fact, T. S. Eliot, who wrote a commentary on this issue, recommends that first-time readers of the *Divine Comedy* skip Canto 34 because it's so strange that Lucifer doesn't speak. The problem, though, is that Eliot had probably never read the *De vulgari eloquentia*. Satan is not supposed to speak, according to Dante's treatise on language, because he's one of the angels (who do not use human language), and, more importantly, because he represents evil defeated.

From this point of view, Canto 34 stands in radical, sharp contrast to Canto 33. In Canto 33 we saw the sovereignty of evil. It was as if it were all-engulfing, hovering over all of reality. Here, we witness exactly the opposite, how Satan becomes a reified, dumb object and actually an instrument for the pilgrim's ascent. It's only by going along the body of Lucifer that the pilgrim can proceed. It's the only means by which he and Virgil can turn themselves upside down and finally reemerge into the light. It's the only way out of Hell.

The rest of the canto deals with a cosmological argument about the origin of Purgatory. Dante offers up an astonishing poetic myth. The myth that he invents is that when Lucifer fell at the time of the grand angelic disruption, the first rebellion against the Deity, the earth retreated out of fear at the approaching of this fallen angel and reemerged on the other side of the hemisphere, the southern hemisphere. That was the beginning of Purgatory.

Thus, an evil act is connected to a chance for redemption. In Dante's cosmos, there is no evil that cannot be utilized to the ends of the good. The real defeat of evil occurs when evil becomes a stepping stone over its own threshold, allowing one to reach the purgatorial island.

How does Dante's voyage through Hell conclude? The last line of *Inferno* is: "E quindi uscimmo a riveder le stelle," "and thence we issued forth to see again the stars."[12] There is a remarkable love of symmetry in Dante's poem, as each canticle will end with that same word "stelle"—stars, stars, and stars. So, each canticle ends with us looking up, reminding ourselves where we are, longing for the stars in the distance. And we, like Dante, can only shift our perspective and journey onward beneath that endless expanse.

CHAPTER 10

Purgatorio 1–2

Purgatorio, a word meaning "place of cleansing or purification," is the middle section of Dante's poem. It is a place of transition between the world of Hell and all the evil that we have witnessed and the realm of glory that Paradise is going to be. As an idea, the way Dante understands it, Purgatory is part of human geography. There are two hemispheres in medieval geography: the northern hemisphere, which is the one we inhabit, and the southern hemisphere, where we find the island of Purgatory. As discussed in the last chapter, Purgatory came into existence as Lucifer fell, causing the earth to tremble and retreat, thus creating the void that becomes Hades, the abyss, and the island of Purgatory, which emerges on the other side, in the southern hemisphere. At the top of the peak on that island, one finds the Garden of Eden, where God placed Adam and Eve. In sum, Purgatory is a place on the map.

From this point of view, Purgatory is part of human geography, but it has historically been inaccessible to human beings. One hero that we have already met, Ulysses, in *Inferno* 26, tries to approach an island, and retrospectively we can understand that that was the island of Purgatory, as if it were a place of immortality that Ulysses wanted to reach and could not. That journey of his ended tragically, in shipwreck. This island is not meant to be reached through merely human means.

Structurally, Dante's Purgatory is divided into three parts. The first part is the so-called ante-Purgatory, the zone for those souls who are waiting to go farther up. They're not really repenting yet, but simply waiting to be assigned a particular place along the ledges. Then there are the penitents before going through the process of cleansing. And finally, the third group, those who make their way through the various ledges, which begin with pride and end with lust just before the pilgrim gets into the Garden of Eden. The ordering of sins is an exact reversal of the ordering of sins we had in *Inferno*. Here you begin with a spiritual sin or intellectual sin, the question of pride, and end up with the most physical and material of them all, lust.

Another important characteristic of Purgatory is a moral trait. We are going to enter the realm of the reconstruction of the human, and it makes sense that Dante should place it immediately after Hell. Only by knowing, only by experiencing, as metaphorically as we can through the poetry of Dante, the nature of evil, the horror of it, can we begin to have an appreciation of the good toward which the pilgrim is going to climb. The perception of moral life and political life in *Inferno* was so satanic, so narrow, so terrible that Dante is going to have quite a challenge to explain the usefulness and the possibility of reconstructing a moral world, then a political world. He came very close to a total rejection of the historical and political world, and now he has to find out if reconstruction is even possible. The way he will do this is, literally, to go back to the natural world. Do not expect Dante to imagine a place where there is some kind of redemptive intervention from the outside that can tell us how we should act. The natural world must be capable of producing within itself at least some seeds of a need for the good. This self-sufficiency is going to be part of both Dante's strategy and his difficulties in implementing it.

A further trait of Purgatory that was really completely missing in *Inferno* is a sense of time. Time was the biological clock of the pilgrim, who was the only living creature, the only truly displaced figure, and he is the only displaced figure throughout the first part of Dante's poem. In *Purgatorio* he will find instead that all figures are displaced figures. So, it's a more human world, and the souls here have a sense of time. In fact, the first thing that we come to understand in Purgatory is what time is. In *Inferno* the present occupies no space, and there is only knowledge of the past and the future. In *Purgatorio*, we are given an existential sense of time, which is understood as future-oriented, as a projection into some kind of future, and, at the same time, a return to the past. After all, as the pilgrim moves ahead, he discovers that he's really going backward, to the Garden of Eden, exactly where God placed Adam and Eve in Genesis. This idea of time will truly become a leitmotif throughout *Purgatory*. The question of the relationship between the past and the future is constant: even the past was the future at some point, right? The future is the only thing that is going to matter, and the way it's related to the past will become the principal object of Dante's concerns as he moves through the various ledges of Purgatory.

But when is this happening for the pilgrim? What is the present moment? The story of the *Divine Comedy* begins on Holy Thursday, with Dante spending the first night in the dark woods, but the real journey begins on Good Friday, in a clear imitation of Christ's harrowing of Hell and emergence into the light on Easter Sunday. That's where we are now, Easter Sunday morning. The *Inferno* began at dusk, with the idea of the approaching night that represents the unknowability of whatever he was about to confront. Here, instead, we begin with dawn, and therefore Canto 1 of *Purgatorio* becomes that which in Provençal literature is called an *aubade,* from the word *aube, alba* in Italian, "dawn." This dawn song is, however, a song that in many ways reverses the grand tradition of the erotic lyrics of Provençal poetry where the dawn becomes the unhappy time for the parting of lovers. It's restored as a great time when, finally, the pilgrim can proceed and the poet can continue literally mapping the journey.

The second part of the *Comedy* begins with an image of water, and therefore it carries a motif of cleansing and purification. Dante writes, "To course over better waters the little bark of my genius now hoists her sails, leaving behind her a sea so cruel; and I will sing of that second realm where the human spirit is purged and becomes fit to ascend to Heaven. But here let dead poetry rise again, O holy Muses, since I am yours; and here let Calliope rise up somewhat, accompanying my song with that strain whose stroke the wretched Pies felt so that they despaired of pardon."[1] It's a brilliant proem to *Purgatorio,* for a number of reasons. First of all, Dante picks up the metaphor, the epic topos, of the journey with which the poem began, "in the middle of the journey of our life," as you may recall. But he also mentions sailing, recalling a specific journey, the doomed sea voyage of Ulysses. I also want to draw your attention to the use of a comparative adjective here, the "better waters." This is Dante's emphasis on the journey as a comparatively good one. It is not the best of waters; it is not the worst of waters; these are *better* waters. We are really on the way to better things. It's a world of degree that Dante introduces, for he truly believes in hierarchy, a hierarchy of values, of states, of powers, of beauty, of intellect. His is never a dualistic world divided between what's bad and what's good. There are many mediations and steps along the route to Paradise, and he has already introduced this notion with a single adjective.

Furthermore, this is not only a pilgrim's journey, it is also a journey of poetry. Dante specifically mentions "the little bark of my genius," which is a conventional way of describing the writing of poetry. He wants to highlight a motif that is going to be crucial throughout the rest of the poem, namely that there is no sharp, drastic discontinuity between the journey of the pilgrim and the journey of the poet. The journey of the poet is an extension of the other journey, but it, in itself, is also a journey of knowledge and discovery. Dante makes large claims for poetry, not just a commemoration of the past.

This opening is also the first time that Dante uses the future tense in the text: "I will sing." We're brought into a world open to futurity, and the only way of thinking about futurity is a belief in the new. If the future is exactly like today, then you really have no future, since everything would be released into the domain of sameness. Dante uses the future to imply that there is an alternative, a difference, a possibility of doing things in ways that have not been done before. This is going to be a new departure, a new departure for thought, a new departure for the imagination, and a new departure for poetry itself.

He couldn't say this in *Inferno*. He couldn't even say this in the *Vita nuova*. You remember that when we spoke of that great little autobiographical text at the beginning of the book, I indicated to you that the future tense is never used in it. It was entirely a book of memory, with all the difficulties and the dangers of memory, which can draw us into a world of phantasms. The only time that the future was used in the *Vita nuova* was in association with death and when Dante has a prophetic dream and hears a sort of oracle speaking to him, telling him that he too will die. Beatrice has just died and then the death of Beatrice brings to his mind the fear and threat of mortality. And the *Vita nuova* ends with a statement of hope, a hope to work and to write things whereby he can say things about Beatrice that had never been said about any woman. These are the two possibilities of the future that were available in the *Vita nuova*.

Then Dante offers up a prayer to the Muses, very much in the style of the epic tradition, especially since he invokes the muse of epic poetry, Calliope. The focus on Calliope retrospectively explains the earlier part of the abovementioned citation from the beginning of *Purgatorio*, "Let dead poetry rise again." The poem presents itself as Calliope, the mother of Orpheus, so by saying he will let dead poetry rise again from the dead, Dante presents himself as a sort of Orphic poet. An Orphic poet followed the tradition of Orpheus and wanted to conquer death. That's clearly not for Dante, the belief that poetry can do the trick, that through poetry we immortalize ourselves and conquer death. He is going to understand very soon that that's not the way he is going to approach poetry.

The second scene really gives you a different sense of the tonality of *Purgatorio,* because now not only do you have the morning and time, you also have light for the first time. These are not the spectacular shades of light, the blue, the reds, the greens, which he will dramatize in *Paradiso.* There we will see lights emanating from the various planets, the red of Mars, the white of Jupiter, the blue of Saturn; there will be a polychromic palette at work. Here it's a more human and natural world on display: "Sweet hue of oriental sapphire which was gathering in the serene face of the sky, pure even to the first circle, to my eyes restored delight, as soon as I issued forth from the dead air that had afflicted my eyes and breast. The fair planet that prompts to love"—Venus, the morning star—"was making the whole East smile, veiling the Fishes that were in her train. I turned to the right and gave heed to the other pole, and saw four stars never seen before but by the first people"—Adam and Eve. "The heavens seemed to rejoice in their flames. O northern widowed clime, that are deprived of beholding them!"[2] The northern hemisphere is where we are, while Dante is in the southern hemisphere. He is connecting with us, telling us what lights we are deprived of by having lost Paradise.

The other important detail here is one we've addressed before. Dante is now turning to the right, although it should be said that even while spiraling down in the world of Hell, he actually was going to the right. He said that he was going to the left, but he was going to the left because he was upside down. Now he is right side up, and the directions of the human world are restored. Dante literally orients himself: the metaphor he uses is of oriental light, and he's always orienting and reorienting himself according to it. How Dante knows where he is in *Purgatorio,* and also in *Paradiso,* is always by looking to the east. From this point of view Dante really retrieves an incredible metaphor that was available among the medieval mystics, thinkers like Boethius and Cassiodorus, who believe that we in the West can only truly think by looking toward the East. The only way in which we can orient ourselves is by trying to capture the source of that light. I mean this in the most metaphorical, and the widest, senses possible, but for now Dante is merely nodding at these implications.

In the midst of all this, it's incredible how the language has shifted between the first paragraph and the second. There is a contrast between his excitement for the light and his experience of Easter Sunday. Dante understands the Resurrection, and the tonality is elegiac, centered on the idea of what we have lost in the widowed region of the northern hemisphere. But it's also a provisional privilege for him to see any of this. As a result, Dante introduces the extraordinary poetic tension that abounds in *Purgatorio*. The pilgrim is caught in the middle, and we shall see the consequences of these currently merely tonal shifts as we progress through the *Divine Comedy*.

Eventually, Dante concludes his descriptions and meets his first purgatorial soul: "When I had withdrawn my gaze from them"—the stars—"turning a little to the other pole, there whence the Wain had already disappeared, I saw close to me an old man alone, worthy in his looks of so great reverence that no son owes more to his father. His beard was long and streaked with white, like his locks of which a double tress fell on his breast." This is Dante's encounter with Cato. Who is Cato? Dante describes him as an old man, and we also know that he's a Roman. He's a pagan and a man of laws. The first thing that he asks involves the possibility of rule-breaking on Dante's part: "Who are you that, against the blind stream, have fled the eternal prison? . . . Who has guided you, or what was a lamp to you issuing forth from the deep night that ever makes the infernal valley black? Are the laws of the abyss thus broken? Or is some new counsel changed in Heaven that though damned you come to my rocks?"[3] He is upholding a Roman tradition of the law. In a way this is a man who is a stranger to the world of Purgatory. He certainly doesn't seem to understand that heaven may have offered some grace, that Dante and his guide may be here because of some providential intervention that is not to be explained, either by the laws of nature or by manmade laws.

It is Virgil, Cato's fellow Roman, who responds, explaining, "I have shown him all the guilty people, and now I intend to show him those spirits that purge themselves under your charge. How I have brought him would be long to tell you: from on high descends power that aids me to conduct him to see you and to hear you. Now may it please you to approve his coming. He goes seeking freedom, which is so precious, as he knows who renounces life for it." The reference here is clearly to Cato himself, who historically committed suicide in the civil war because he refused to take sides between Pompey and Caesar, as is told in the great epic by Lucan, the Roman-Spanish poet, who wrote a text called *Pharsalia*, or *Civil War*, a text that is very polemical with regard to, among other things, Virgil. Dante's guide continues to clarify, "You know it, for death for its sake was not bitter to you in

Utica"—in North Africa—"where you did leave the raiment which on the great day will be so bright. The eternal edicts are not violated by us, for this one is alive and Minos does not bind me; but I am of the circle"—Limbo—"where are the chaste eyes of your Marcia"—his wife—"who in her look still prays you, O holy breast, that you hold her for your own. For love of her, then, incline yourself to us: let us go on through your seven realms. I will report to her your kindness, if you deign to be mentioned there below."[4] The first phase of their discussion ends here, however, for Cato maintains that his former wife can no longer move him.

This is an amazing beginning to this section of the poem because we are told that Cato is an old man, a pagan, and a suicide. These are the traits that Virgil singles out, obliquely referring to his adventures and clearly contradicting the world of *Purgatorio,* which is a Christian canticle. It is Easter Sunday, so why have this holy day inaugurated by the presence of a pagan who knew nothing of the Incarnation? It's the home of a renewed life, so why start it with a suicide? We saw what Dante thought of suicides in *Inferno,* with a number of suicidal souls inhabiting various regions of Hell, so why begin *Purgatorio* with an old man, a suicide, and a pagan? Usually, whenever you have representations of the beyond, you have a young man or woman who is welcoming new souls in order to indicate the renewed life, the novelty, the freshness of the scene. You certainly don't have an old man or a suicide. So why does Dante?

The question of the suicide is probably the easiest to determine because Cato's suicide is a suicide for freedom, and Purgatory is the domain of freedom. Dante is starting to explain a political and moral state. It's political because it's a refusal of the disarray and chaos brought in by the war between Pompey and Caesar, at the time of the civil war, but it is also a moral state because Cato decides to put an end to his life in a sacrificial move, as if to draw attention to the way in which the state had been destroyed by the rivalry between these two great figures. Freedom is the fundamental problem here, and Dante wants us to think of it in pagan intellectual terms from the very beginning of *Purgatorio.* The middle section of the *Comedy* ends with the pilgrim regaining his free will, so the whole poem really moves forward this idea of Cato's search for freedom.

Now there is an obvious relationship between freedom and the future. You cannot conceive of freedom unless you have an idea of beginnings and of the future. Nor can you conceive of novelty unless you have ideas of both the future and freedom. The notion of originality, even poetic originality, is impossible unless it's tied to a certain idea of freedom, the notion that things can be different. If I am slave to the past, if I am a slave to a political order, if I am slave to my own vices, as internalized as that quest can be, then I really have no freedom. Cato embodies one who refuses to live if that means living under the tyranny of civil war and violence, and thus in the impossibility of a moral life. We can also explain the notion of the old man here. Dante wants to draw our attention to the fact that the search for the future is not an alternative to the past but rather grows out of the past, so that the idea that there may be some sharp distinctions between the two is rejected. The seeds of the future are already contained in the past, in a figure like an old man, like Cato.

The third problem is the question of his being a pagan, and this brings me back to Dante's project in *Purgatorio*. He must make a careful distinction, which St. Augustine could not make in the *City of God*. Augustine distinguishes between the earthly city and the heavenly city, and the heavenly city may live on earth, but it's really a pilgrim Church approaching beatitude and the encounter with God. The earthly city is corrupt and in many ways not able to assimilate to the world of redemption. This, if you are an Augustinian and have a very supple view of Augustine, may strike you as crude, but I don't think that it violates the essence of that dual idea. Dante, instead, is talking in opposition to Augustinian dualism. There are in nature—that is within the pagan, secular, historical world—seeds that can become crucial for the making of a new moral life that will be consonant with the Christian redemption that Dante is seeking.

The best sign of this incredible tension—time, the meaning of freedom, the value of the pagan world, the insistence on the secular as capable of producing some kind of seed for the future—emerges in the second paragraph, when finally Virgil, to temper the harshness of Cato, asks him to let them through because he knows Cato's wife. It's very Italian of him: "I know your wife and I'm going to go back to where she is. I know who you are, so do me a favor because I'll be doing her a favor." What he is doing is appealing to Cato's affective memory, but it's a solicitation that Cato does not accept because he refuses to be determined by the past. Cato can only make sharp distinctions, and to his mind, Marcia can do nothing for him. Furthermore, in the history of Cato's life, Marcia had actually left him. She asked for a divorce because she wanted to marry somebody else, and at the death of the other husband Marcia asked Cato to take her back, and he did. Dante recounts this whole story in the *Convivio* and views it as a sign of the extraordinary generosity of this man. All of that lore plays into this reference to Cato, but from our point of view, it ultimately remains a question of the power of memory and the limits of memory.

After their brief exchange, Cato lists some rules that have to be followed in the process of cleansing: you must wash off the stains of Hell and gird your loins. Dante heeds his instructions, with the aid of Virgil: "When we came there where the dew strives with the sun, for being in a place where, in the breeze, it is little dispersed, my master gently laid both hands outspread on the grass. I therefore, aware of his purpose, reached toward him my tear-stained cheeks, and on them he wholly disclosed that color of mine which Hell had hidden. Then we came on to the desert shore, that never saw any man navigate its waters who afterwards had experience of return."[5] What is Dante referencing, yet again? He makes it very clear that Cato and Ulysses are both pagans, but he insinuates a distinction within the body of pagan culture: Ulysses, on the one hand, with his transgressive search for knowledge, and on the other hand, the experience of Cato.

Now Dante has another task to complete before he can proceed. He must gird his loins. Dante has to gird himself the way a journeyman, whether a biblical journeyman or a Roman one, would whenever he undertook a journey in antiquity, placing a girdle around himself. It's a moment of containment of self, and that's the ritual he has to undergo. But something surprising occurs when Virgil chooses a plant with which to cover Dante: "O marvel! that such as plucked the humble plant, even such did it instantly spring up again, there whence he had uprooted it."[6] Interestingly, the emphasis here falls on the power of the natural world to restore itself. There is an immediate emblem of the Resurrection here, but we're still in the natural world. There is no element of grace: the nature of the plant—in an inversion of what had happened in *Inferno* 13—is to rise again, to be born again. The power of nature remains an important element of this canto.

And now we come to Canto 2, in which the situation changes somewhat, but it starts with yet another search for orientation. Again Dante orients himself toward the east, the Orient, but now it becomes more clearly Jerusalem. Purgatory was considered to be at the antipodes of Jerusalem, against the feet of the heavenly city. Jerusalem was known as the navel, the center, of the earth and now we are at its outer limits. The holy city becomes an immediate point of reference as Dante ponders movement without acting on the possibility of moving: "The sun had now reached the horizon whose meridian circle covers Jerusalem with its highest point; and night, circling opposite to him, was issuing forth from Ganges with the Scales, which fall from her hand when she exceeds."[7] Aimed toward Jerusalem but unmoving, Dante is attempting to bridge the gap between his expectations and hopes and what is actually happening.

Suddenly, a rapid light appears, and he sees a fast boat carrying the souls of penitents who are reaching the banks of Purgatory. This image is the polar opposite of what we saw with Charon's boat in Hell, the boat of the sinful souls. And then an angel of God arrives, who "the brighter did he appear, so that close up my eyes could not endure him."[8] Dante looks downward as the ship comes to shore. He hears that the thousand spirits on board are singing a psalm, "In exitu Israel de Aegypto [When Israel came out of Egypt]," Psalm 113. It's the psalm in which the Jews are remembering their exodus from bondage in Egypt to freedom in Jerusalem. As a result, retrospectively, the reference to Jerusalem gives a kind of unity to the whole canto.

This psalm is the only text that Dante actually cites in the *Divine Comedy*. He makes references to the Bible all the time, but the only text of the Bible that Dante cites directly is the Psalms and the Song of Songs. Perhaps this move is meant to acknowledge that the Psalms are poetry and that he responds to that poetry. Furthermore, the Psalms are probably the text that offers the first representation of subjectivity in Western countries. It's the story of someone who is looking inward and finding out the diseases of the self, the appetites, the passions, and so on. And the pilgrim himself is engaged in that same sort of quest. Finally, the Psalms are basically lyrical recapitulations of the story of Exodus. Dante's saying that the *Divine Comedy* is the lyrical representation of the biblical story of Exodus, that his own human history is engaged in the same search for a path from slavery to liberty.

In Canto 1 of *Purgatorio* we saw a vision of Roman political, moral liberty, but now we have an idea that the whole of history is engaged in this exodus, this journey toward liberty. Thus there are two types of liberties—a Roman one and a Jewish one—to which Dante wants to connect. He understands that there are two traditions based on a quest for liberty that are worth exploring. There is a sense, in both of them, though in different ways, of a beginning that he must try to harmonize, that he must try to explore and probe in depth.

Also, the story of Exodus in many ways embodies and crystallizes the real intellectual issues of Purgatory. What is the story of Exodus about?

Leaving behind the house of bondage and taking along the gold of the Egyptians, which represents secular knowledge. That secular knowledge is also part of what we must carry with us in the journey toward freedom. But the Jews also stay in the desert for forty days. They feel that they're abandoned by Moses, who has come up to receive the tables of the law, and while they're feeling abandoned, they engage in idolatry. This is the story of Exodus, a story of a people caught between idolatry and revelation and prophetic promises. The idolatry shows itself as a statement or as an experience of nostalgia: that's what the making of the golden calf is. They are desperate and leaderless, so they engage in an act of desire, a longing for at least the safety, or what they perceive as the safety, of dwelling in Egypt, mindless of the fact that they were in bondage. It is as if the safety of living were preferable to them even if that safety exists in the shadow of tyranny. These are the concerns that Dante will have at heart as he comes into Purgatory.

The whole of *Purgatorio* becomes a means of looking back and forth between the future and the past, which are warring with each other for control of the mind of the pilgrim. The canto shifts away from grand historical concerns, these reflections on how the pagan world experiences beginnings and new departures, and they are possible only on the basis of an ideology of freedom. The narrative shifts, and it's all internalized.

The pilgrim moves within himself, and his first statement is that he does not know where he is, which is a way of alluding to his exilic predicament. He literally does not know where to go. His mind and body are split, an inner self-dislocation that persists. And the penitent souls are as lost as he is, so naturally they all ask him for directions. But they're in the desert. The desert is a place where you don't know which way to go. Typologically speaking, the desert is the unmapped space between Egypt and Jerusalem. It's an "in-between." You have no roots here; you have no paths. There are no carvings or markers left for you, so they ask Dante for directions. Virgil tells them the truth, that the souls are mistaken, for he and Dante are also strangers in Purgatory. That's what it means to be an exile, and that's what it means to write this poetry of exile. *Purgatorio* is a desert. There is even a spirituality of the desert in the text, and certainly a statement of the exilic condition. Dante tells us that we really don't belong anywhere. We are always displaced and going somewhere else. At the basis of Dante's own religious longing, there is a sense of displacement, of pilgrimage. There is a sense that our hearts are not where they ought to be.

Virgil continues to explain that they are equally lost, but Dante's living nature is soon made plain: "'We came but now, a little while before you, by another road which was so rough and hard that henceforth the climb will seem but play to us.' The souls, who had perceived from my breathing that I was yet alive, marveling grew pale; and as to a messenger who bears an olive-branch the people crowd to hear the news, and no one shows himself shy of trampling, so did all of these fortunate souls fix their eyes on my face, as though forgetting to go to make themselves fair."[9] As a result, Dante becomes an object of temptation for the penitent souls. They should be going somewhere, they should be going up the mountain, and yet, they stop where they are. They thus reveal another way of thinking about forgetfulness and the sense of having a place to reach.

One shade in particular steps forward and attempts to embrace Dante. Three times he tries and three times he fails. This little detail of the failed embraces is a way of acknowledging that the souls have no substantiality that can be grasped, a detail that will resurface a few more times in *Purgatorio*. The soul asks Dante to stand still, and there is a moment of recognition. It is Casella, a friend from Dante's youth, a musician who had probably even set Dante's poetry to music, and a man from Siena who clearly has died. This scene is clearly intended to relieve the hardship of the journey. It offers a moment of indulgence, a meeting with a friend, a little pastoral interlude if you wish, to break up the hardness of the desert and the implications of that metaphor. It is a pause that provides for reflection and crucial aesthetic relief.

Casella asks Dante why he is on his quest. The pilgrim responds, "My Casella, to return here once again where I am I make this journey . . . but how has so much time been taken from you?" Casella explains how he got to Purgatory. Questions answered, Dante makes an important request, which is clearly a reflection on the power and the limits of aesthetics: "If a new law does not take from you memory or practice of the songs of love which used to quiet in me all my longings, may it please you therewith to comfort my soul somewhat, which coming hither with its body is so wearied."[10] So, Casella starts singing a song that is actually a poem that Dante himself wrote, and he sets it to music as he may also have done during his life.

Dante constructs an aesthetic cloister with this song: "'*Love that discourses in my mind*,' he then began so sweetly that the sweetness still within me sounds."[11] Here sweetness is to be understood as an attribute of musical harmony, though, as will be indicated by the canto about the gluttons, it's also always the language of the palate, of savoring. Dante, Virgil, and all the souls savor the sweetness of the song, enraptured. And yet it remains a poem of Dante's own. The poet is listening to his own song, with a slight touch of narcissistic temptation. He believes that Casella is playing up to him, giving him a sense of himself, and reassuring him that someone else knows who he is. The danger in this sensation is apparent: they all forget about the ascent.

But then, of course, Cato comes, the ethical voice, the voice of the law, "the venerable old man, crying, 'What is this, you laggard spirits? What negligence, what stay is this? Haste to the mountain to strip off the slough that lets not God be manifest to you.'"[12] So we have a scene of conflict between aesthetics and ethics. How are they working against each other? Dante has forgotten the lesson that he just learned in his encounter with Cato. Therefore Cato intervenes, and his anger is the anger of the teacher, who says, "I *just* explained to you what the problems are with this behavior." Virgil had hoped that Cato could be swayed by the memory of the past, but Cato had rejected the power, the affection, and the pleasure of that memory.

In Canto 2 Dante is thus involved in an idolatrous moment. He witnesses something that he has been making, that he has built and composed, and he is so taken in by it that it essentially has the power to distract him from his own ascent. He has forgotten the reasons why he is here in Purgatory in the first place, and so *Purgatorio* begins with an explicit statement about the importance of new beginnings, new departures. Cato uses the word *negligence* to describe the particular failing of Dante and the penitent souls in this moment. "Negligence" means "not to choose," so Cato is reproaching the power of poetry to produce an atmosphere of nonchoice. Obliquely, then, that's what his ethics is. We are always engaged in an act of choice. He speaks from the perspective of a freedom that literature, the poetic text that Dante evokes, has the power to tame, and somehow, for a moment, to neutralize. A single word thus underscores the extraordinary degree of self-reflection and self-reflexiveness, from all points of view, that Dante puts on prominent display in the second part of his poem.

Purgatory is a place of moral purification, so Dante urges all the souls that had gathered around the song of Casella to move away. The language that he uses is that of dispersion: like doves or pigeons that disperse throughout the plain. In retrospect, what is apparent, I think, in all of these situations is Dante's insistence on the power and importance of a communal destiny. However, here this communal fate appears as defeated. In the case of Cato, Cato has been defeated by the civil war between Pompey and Caesar, to the point that he had to commit suicide. In the case of Casella's song, that poem had managed to gather around itself, not only Dante, but all the other souls who had become mindless of what they were supposed to be doing, continuing their climb up the mountain. Cato intervenes and shatters the illusory form of community. What I think that Dante's after is the following: there may have been defeats here, but these losses contain seeds that will be necessary for his rethinking how to renew and reconstruct his idea of a common historical destiny. There is value even in defeat.

CHAPTER 11

Purgatorio 5–10

I have been focusing on a Dante turned to the future, a Dante who thinks and reflects on hope. Nothing else really matters because everything else can only be understood as part of the future, even when it's past, with the logical underlying assumption that that which is past was once the future, the only reality of time. Dante understands in *Purgatorio* how time moves in one direction, which is future-oriented, though it turns out to be a return to the Garden of Eden as well.

In Canto 5, however, Dante meets souls who bring to the fore for him the power of retrospection. These are souls who manage to repent at the last minute. Again, it's a question of time, but a time that is pretty much inexhaustible. It's *always* possible to fall back, reflect, and turn one's life around. He meets a figure who identifies himself as Buonconte da Montefeltro, the son of Guido, whom we met in Canto 27 of *Inferno*. Buonconte represents a break between the past and the future, since a son or daughter is a statement about a project for the future. The elder da Montefeltro ends up in Hell, but the son ends up in this purgatorial ledge on the way to redemption, so there is no chain of natural necessity and causality between the past and the present and the future. There is a focus on freedom, because once you break that bond of necessity, you are really opening up and inaugurating the idea that we are free to make ourselves, regardless of what antecedents we may have behind us.

Buonconte says, "Ah, so may that desire be fulfilled which draws you up the lofty mountain"—we are in Dante's universe of desire, impelled by desire's lure—"do you with gracious pity help my own. I was of Montefeltro, I am Buonconte." Note the disjunction in tenses. I already pointed

those out for you in the canto of Ugolino, and here too Buonconte is assert-
ing his identity in the mode of the present and detaching himself, with the
use of the past tense, from his family history. Dante asks him, "What force
or what so carried you astray from Campaldino that your burial-place was
never known?"[1] Dante asks the soul to tell his tale.

What follows is an extraordinary scene, for one very autobiographical
reason: namely, Dante himself fought at this battle of Campaldino. It was a
moment of maturation for him, his great entering into the battlefield of life,
when he discovered that, because of the victory that the Florentines had
in Campaldino, he too could make claims about himself, his family, and
his political future. Here, though, he meets a victim. And there have been
those who have claimed, though with very little evidence, that maybe this
is someone that Dante killed in battle, that he brings him back in poetry
because he cannot do so in reality. Regardless, it is a paradoxically painful
autobiographical moment for Dante, a moment where he experienced war
as both perpetrated and suffered violence.

Rather than answering the question of the battle, Buonconte recounts
his death. This is generally a poem about births and the portentous quality
that being born implies, the kinds of alterations that we all bring on the
world around us by the very fact that we were born. But here he talks of
death: "At the foot of the Casentino a stream crosses, named the Archiano,
which rises in the Apennines above the Hermitage. To the place where its
name is lost I came, wounded in the throat, flying on foot and bloodying
the plain. There I lost my sight and speech. I ended on the name of Mary,
and there I fell, and my flesh remained alone. I will tell the truth, and do
you repeat it among the living. The Angel of God took me, and he from
Hell cried, 'O you from Heaven, why do you rob me?' "[2] This passage elucidates the notion of the power of time and the power of retrospection, looking back at that final moment in one's life, which is the decisive moment
that confers coherence and meaning on one's existence. We were born with
certain expectations of what we could do, but death becomes the revela-
tory event.

After this dialogue, the canto concludes with six extraordinary lines,
where we may even be seeing a subtle allusion to Dante's own wife. It's an
encounter with Pia de' Tolomei, a woman from Siena, and this little passage
is meant to remind us of Francesca in Canto 5 of *Inferno*, the canto that is
symmetrical to this one in *Purgatorio*. A new spirit approaches Dante with
a request, "Pray, when you have returned to the world and have rested from
your long journey, . . . remember me, who am la Pia."[3] These lines function

as an epitaph for la Pia, who was mistreated by her husband but remains incredibly forgiving. The passage tellingly ends with the word *gem,* which in Italian is *gemma,* Dante's wife's name. So, one may wonder if Pia doesn't also stand for or bring to mind the kind of wishful thinking on the part of Dante that his wife, whom he had been forced to leave behind because of his exile, may also forgive. Dante is, in any case, introducing the radical category of forgiveness, for if you want to begin again, then forgiveness is exactly what's demanded. Canto 5 becomes a canto of great pathos and intimacy, where Dante's really involved, really connected to the souls he encounters here.

Canto 6, instead, is a more public canto, a political canto like Canto 6 of *Inferno* and Canto 6 of *Paradiso.* You know by now that there's a principle of symmetry at work in the *Comedy.* Yet, while Canto 6 of *Inferno* is about the city of Florence, Canto 6 of *Purgatorio* is about Italy as a whole, and the disarray, the chaos, the disunity of the country. Dante writes, "When the game of hazard breaks up, the loser is left disconsolate, repeating the throws and sadly learns. With the other all the people go along: one goes in front, one plucks him from behind, and at his side one brings himself to mind. He does not stop, but listens to this one and that one; each to whom he reaches forth his hand presses on him no longer, and thus from the throng he defends himself. Such was I in that dense crowd, turning my face to them this way and that and, by promising, I got free from them."[4] It's a remarkable comparison. All the penitents are so surprised at seeing Dante alive in the beyond that they go after him, and there's a throng of people pressing on him. So, he is like the winner in a game of hazard. Dante's the winner, and they all go after him and neglect Virgil, who is the loser here.

It is as if Dante were speaking of his salvation, of the uniqueness of this journey that he is undertaking, in terms of a game of hazard. We have been thinking that this is a providential journey, and now he is casting it as if it were just a game of chance. It's an interesting metaphor from the point of view of the language of play. It's like a lottery. Someone loses, and someone wins, and Dante acknowledges that because he happened to be born after the Incarnation, he had the possibility of saving himself, while Virgil did not. This question of play in Dante's theological perception is an issue that I will talk about much more extensively when we reach *Paradiso.* But one thing is clear: Dante understands that the relationship between the soul and God is a one shaped by risk on both sides, and that this idea of risk that would seem to be a blind casting of the dice in effect constitutes the freedom of human beings. By using this language of hazard and chance, salvation is disengaged from the idea that God knows all and we are already determined in what we are doing.

To be more precise, many philosophers in antiquity, Boethius being the most important, would discuss the relationship between human freedom and God's foreknowledge. They would always present the case that God is outside of time. All times converge in God, so God sees all things in the present with a point of view that is transcendent and therefore synoptic for God, while we live in a diachronic world. We think that we live in a world where we do not know what tomorrow may bring us, but according to this logic, whatever decisions we make now have already been decided. The consequences, whether they're unpredictable or not, have been determined by things that escape our control, things that only God knows. This is the Boethian scheme of harmonizing God's foreknowledge and human freedom. It doesn't take too much to realize that this is really a little bit of a delusion, because either I'm free or I'm not. It may be that God knows all, but it doesn't mean that He wills that I do what I do. And yet, He knows and I don't know, so my own freedom is still somewhat rhetorical.

Dante approaches it differently, with a departure from Boethius. The relationship between God's foreknowledge and the soul's being in time is one that introduces the question of chance and hazard and that involves both God and the soul. He doesn't say it directly here, but as we work with the text, it will become very clear. The issue is that in a love relationship between God and the soul, we are always at risk. If you accept the principle of a love economy regulating the universe, which Dante certainly does, then you understand this notion of hazard not as a principle of chance in the sense of casual blind randomness, but in the sense of this risk element. Dante's universe is a universe of love, and that's how the creation of the universe and of human beings takes place. The involvement that every soul has with God is one of love. And just as in the relationship between, say, Beatrice and Dante, there is an element of risk in this loving. What is that risk? I can think of several. One loves, and one may not be reciprocated in that love, for instance. Certainly, it's a risk of God who creates and may not be loved, which is the story of what disobedience is. And this certainly is the existential experience of one person involved with another person. Dante likes figures such as St. Francis, who goes to pray on the cliffs at night because he wants to dramatize the idea that even a prayer puts you at risk of being hurt and disappointed, of discovering that the world does not go the way you want it to go. And that which is true of prayer is also true of love. Sometimes love hurts.

In the next part of Canto 6, this political canto, there is another encounter between two poets, Virgil and Sordello, who is a Mantuan poet. They share the same birthplace, Mantua, across the centuries. When they meet, the very idea of their birthplace becomes an immediate topic of discussion. Virgil starts to speak of Mantua but is cut off. Dante is clearly playing with a famous epitaph of Virgil's in Naples where he was buried, which says: "Mantua made me and the south, Calabria, took me away. I sang the arms [*The Aeneid*], the herds [*The Georgics*], the fields [*The Eclogues*]." In two lines we get an account of his whole life.

After their birthplace-driven exchange, Sordello and Virgil embrace, a demonstration of the reciprocity of affections across time. This embrace, this existential encounter, is insubstantial, however, because they can't really embrace. They're spirits, after all, so this moment becomes another failure after the one that we saw with Casella in Canto 2 of *Purgatorio*. That failure triggers Dante's political invective against Italy, having awakened his civic sense of responsibility.

So, Dante begins his incredible vituperation, his attack against his homeland: "Ah, servile Italy, hostel of grief, ship without pilot in great tempest, no mistress of provinces, but brothel! So eager was that noble soul, only at the sweet name of his city, to give glad welcome there to his fellow-citizen—and now in you your living abide not without war, and of those whom one wall and one moat shut in, one gnaws at the other!"[5] Here we get a much grimmer version of the reciprocity seen between Virgil and Sordello. Earlier one embraced the other, now one gnaws at the other. The new exchange is an exchange that always turns on itself. It reverses and denies the reciprocity indicated by the previous phrase.

Another detail worth emphasizing here is the idea of community that Dante simultaneously establishes and dismantles. The word *community* etymologically comes from the Latin for "wall," *moenia*. Community thus stems from a concept of sharing walls, houses, piling them together and building one on top of the other. The shared walls of the city are here viewed as separating one person from another. This separation will continue as a motif in this diatribe, with mentions of the lack of laws and divided families, including the Montagues and Capulets. Things are falling apart.

Dante concludes this rant with a return to his birthplace in the form of bitter satire: "O my Florence, you may indeed rejoice at this digression which does not touch you, thanks to your people who are so resourceful."[6] Dante talks about Italy but then, with the invocation of Florence, turns back to *Inferno* 6. He calls this invective a digression, which literally means that it does not belong in the poem, that Dante is stepping out of the economy of the poem and talking in his own voice. But the meaning of this digression is made clear when he says, "which does not touch you." How ironic. Of course he's literally saying that Florence is so much better than all these other towns, but the irony is that Florence is truly no better, so the digression doesn't concern it. The line can also be understood in another, far more tragic and sinister way. This digression does not touch you, that is, my language will not affect you. The whole statement in all its ambiguity becomes a reflection on the impotence of poetic language to affect the unfolding of history and the ordering of the city. It is as if Dante were saying that the relationship between the voice of the poet and the political order is one of inevitable rupture. Dante tries to bring about improvement and change, that's clearly the thrust of the passage, but the invective also declares his powerlessness in doing so.

Dante then begins to discuss where the first night of *Purgatorio* will take place. He and Virgil take refuge in the so-called Valley of the Princes, where a new garden is going to be described, which in many ways fulfills the garden of Limbo in Canto 4 of *Inferno*. Dante brings in motifs that keep reappearing, and here not only in the sense of the natural beauty of the place. There are precious stones here, implying that though Purgatory is the world of transition for transient souls, there is something abiding about this realm. And yet Dante the pilgrim is taken with nostalgia for his hometown. It is a pilgrimage of desire and a poem of desire, desire for God, desire for Beatrice, and now desire for the comfort and shelter of the home he has lost. The Latin hymn whose opening words follow gives a sense that the night is dangerous, fraught with phantasms of the past that will intrude on the powers of judgment of various souls, including Dante's.

The movement forward to Canto 9 of *Purgatorio*, as with every Canto 9 of the *Comedy,* marks the rupture from a particular area of the canticle to another. Remember Canto 9 of *Inferno* and the failed encounter with Medusa, the passage into the city of Dis? Now, with this ninth canto, Dante moves into Purgatory proper. How is this purgatorial purification going to take place? The seven deadly sins are arranged by starting with spiritual sins, with pride as the root of all sin, to lust at the end. In every representation of sin in Purgatory, Dante precedes it with a representation of its opposite virtue, so we have humility in Canto 10, and then punished pride in Canto 11. It is as if Dante has to learn intellectually that which he's going to witness a little later. The incredible quality of the structure of the poem is that Dante wants us to see experiences of evil in *Inferno* first, so that when we get to *Purgatorio* and *Paradiso,* we really have a chance to appreciate what the good is and what the absence of the good may be, what evil generates and engenders. In *Purgatorio,* he starts instead with the representation of the virtue and then follows with the sin. In a sense, *Purgatorio* presents an absolute reversal of the economy of *Inferno.*

The idea of having the virtues before the vices seems to cast *Purgatorio* as a variant of a medieval poetic form called *psychomachia,* which means "a battle of thoughts." The whole poetic mode of *Purgatorio,* unlike that of *Inferno,* is played out through the imagination, art images, memories, phantasms. In other words, we are really in a world that is in between that of bodies and souls, a world of art, and a world of the middle ground of the imagination and all its warring thoughts.

To enter more specifically into Canto 10, we turn to a bit of etymology. The word "pride" in Italian is *superbia.* The word "humility" in Italian is *umiltà.* The latter word comes from the ground, the sense of being down, of having one's feet on the ground, as it were. This is, of course, the very opposite of *superbia,* which implies an immoderate flight away, a sense of being a superman. It's the idea that someone wants to transcend the limitations of this world and of being human. In fact, the word *humility* and the word *human* have the same etymology, coming from the Latin *homo,* or "man." We are called human beings because we come from the earth, are close to the earth, and return to the earth. The idea of humility carries the same notion.

So, how are humility and pride represented in the next few cantos? Canto 10 begins, "When we were within the threshold of the gate which the souls' wrong love disuses, making the crooked way seem straight, I heard by its resounding that it was closed again; and if I had turned my eyes to it, what would have been a fitting excuse for my fault?"[7] Purgatory is a sequence of variations on love; that's the moral law of the land. All sins here are because we give love to the wrong object, we love too much, or we love too little. These are the three general subdivisions of Purgatory, laid out along the steep slopes of a mountain, which has an abyss underneath it, an invitation to be prudent on the way up.

As a result, "this made our steps so scant that the waning orb of the moon had regained its bed to sink to rest before we came forth from that needle's eye. But when we were free and out in the open above, where the mountain draws back, I weary and each of us uncertain of our way, we stopped on a level place more solitary than roads through deserts. From its edge, bordering the void, to the foot of the high bank which rises sheer, a human body would measure in three lengths; and as far as my eye could make its flight, now on the left and now on the right, such this terrace there seemed to me."[8] Dante is measuring the purgatorial landscape in terms of the measure of a human being. He's asking if we are the measure of creation, which is exactly the point of the canto, because pride means an inordinate love and a belief in our own excellence. Pride means that we do not think that we can be measured by others or that we belong where others may think we belong. Instead we want to become the measure for others. We are always proud with those who endanger our sense of our own measure. And this scene is only the first sign that measurement will become a crucial metaphor in *Purgatorio*.

Then, on the side of the cliff, Dante notices sculptures embodying examples of humility, a representation of virtue through the language of art. He studies these images made of white marble, "such carvings that not only Polycletus but Nature herself would there be put to shame."[9] The metaphor points to measure and order and emphasizes that these are works of art produced directly by the hand of God. God is an artist so skilled that nature, the daughter of God and the mother of the arts, and also a famous artist, the Greek sculptor Polycletus, would be put to shame by His talents. Already there is a sense of rivalry within the pattern of generating the arts.

The first of His images that we see here is of the angel Gabriel, the messenger who came to earth. That's certainly an image of humility, since he descends from on high, becoming low, while the prideful human beings who are low want to think of themselves as very high. God's art is so clear and effective that the stone angel "seemed not a silent image: one would have sworn that he was saying, 'Ave'"—the first words of the angel Gabriel during the Annunciation.[10] The Annunciation is a true story of humility, in which, albeit obliquely, God becomes man. Not only does it describe the humility of Mary in accepting the mandate, but it offers up yet another idea of descent.

And Mary, too, appears among the statues in this part of Purgatory: "She was imaged who turned the key to open the supreme love, and these words were imprinted in her attitude: '*Ecce ancilla Dei.*'"[11] Mary acknowledges her ancillary role. She is a servant ("Here is the handmaid of God"), and she considers herself a servant. Her image is the central model of humility for those who climb this mountain.

Like the lost souls, Dante has to learn what humility is. There is a need for an ethical education, and there is an aesthetic education occurring simultaneously. After all, Dante is looking at art. The question thus becomes, what is the relationship between virtue and art? How can the two be brought together? To give you an idea of how complicated the problem is, in the next canto Dante meets many painters, including Giotto and Cimabue, who are emblems of people who invest their productions with an inordinate sense of their value. Then Dante compares his friends Guido Cavalcanti and Guido Guinizelli, acknowledges that one Guido outdid the other in terms of fame, and suggests that he himself will probably rout both of them. His proud statement suggests that artists are always prone to inordinate ideas of who they are and what their value may be. The problem, then, is that art can be a source of pride even as it teaches its audience humility.

As for the aesthetic education, Virgil is telling Dante how to look, which is really the most complicated task of the student of art. How do we look at something? What do the eyes reveal to us? Virgil's advice: "'Do not keep your mind on one part only,' said the sweet master, who had me on the side where people have their heart; wherefore I moved my eyes and saw beyond Mary, on the same side as was he who prompted me, another story set in the rock."[12] We must not give into the temptation to lose sight of the totality of things, to take one part for the whole. Dante has to learn how to look and what he's looking at here are stories. But the word *story* is etymologically tied to *history,* so in a certain sense what he sees is also an allegory of history. We begin with the New Testament, the story of Mary, then we get a picture from the Old Testament, David dancing in front of the ark, and then an episode of Trajan, the emperor who is an example of humility. The point is that the whole of history can be read as an allegory of humility, and that is God's art. That's what Dante has God represent for us.

The next scene, then, comes from the Old Testament: "There, carved in the same marble, were the cart and oxen drawing the holy ark, because of which men fear an office not given in charge. In front appeared people, and all the company, divided into seven choirs, made two of my senses say, the one, 'No,' the other, 'Yes, they are singing.' In like manner, by the smoke of the incense that was imaged there my eyes and nose were made discordant with *yes* and *no.* There preceding the blessed vessel, dancing girt up, was the humble Psalmist"—David—"and on that occasion he was both more and less than king. Opposite, figured at the window of a great palace, was Michal looking on, like a woman vexed and scornful."[13] This story is told in Samuel, in the Bible, but Dante's reinterpreting it for us. First of all, David is humbling himself. He's dancing. He lifts up his ephod, his dress, and starts dancing out of joy. It's an episode that is used as one of the many cases of so-called ludic theology, playful theology. In the plan of salvation there is always the presence of comedy, and David embodies that. Then there's this telling little phrase that appears so often in this canto: "more and less." In a canto where measure is a central issue, it becomes impossible to determine a precise position.

One thing is clear: opposite to David sits his wife, Michal, whose window-side seat offers her a different perspective. This is art, this question of her perspective and what she sees. She is so angry with David because by dancing in front of the ark, he humiliates himself. He's losing his stature as king. But the fact is that, for Dante, Michal is completely missing the point. It is a stance of someone who thinks that she's superior, of someone who's sitting in her great palace and will not have anything to do with what's below her. We are truly entering the domain of what pride may be, what's wrong with pride, and why pride may really be a sin. Pride is not sinful simply because we want to reach higher than we are. That's probably okay in itself. What makes pride a sin is that we tend to have contempt for what we think is below us. That displacement blinds us. So, pride is tied to perspective because it sets my view of myself at odds with my reality. Certainly, this is the case with Michal.

The third episode depicted in this canto is, I think, even more interesting, and comes from secular Roman history. "There storied," Dante writes, "was the high glory of the Roman prince whose worth moved Gregory to his great victory: I mean the emperor Trajan. And a poor widow was at his bridle in attitude of weeping and of grief. Round about him appeared a trampling and throng of horsemen, and above them the eagles in gold moved visibly in the wind. Among all these the poor woman seemed to say: 'My lord, do me vengeance for my son who is slain, wherefore my heart is pierced.' And he seemed to answer her, 'Wait now till I return' "—he's going to Romania, Dacia, and the column of Trajan in Rome today is the monument of that expedition. "And she, 'My lord,' like one whose grief is urgent, 'if you do not return?' And he, 'He who shall be in my place will do it for you.' "[14] It's the story of an emperor who gets off his high horse and levels with a little widow, the diminutive added by Dante. The language is humble, as Trajan administers and gives this woman justice because, for Dante, the perfect emperor must possess the attributes of mercy and justice. As such, the final lesson in humility in this canto is made clear by Dante's representation of a Roman emperor.

So, Dante has seen and understood these images and their meaning, but a bit of drama follows in their wake. "While I was taking delight," Dante explains, "in gazing on the images of humilities so great"—a deliberate oxymoron—"and for their Craftsman's sake precious to behold, 'Lo, here are many people,' murmured the poet [Virgil], 'but they come with slow step: they will direct us on to the high stairs.'" Virgil has prompted Dante to turn away, to abandon his appreciation of God's art, but in so doing he leads to Dante's drama: "My eyes, which were content to behold novelties whereof they are fain, were not slow in turning towards him." Dante yields to the temptations of the eye. The three temptations include the pride of life, the pride of the eyes or curiosity, and the pride of the heart, and all three temptations are present here. But instead of addressing his own weaknesses, Dante chastises the reader in an apostrophe: "But, reader, I would not have you turned from good resolution for hearing how God wills the debt shall be paid. Heed not the form."[15] He's telling us not to care about the images as such. He is making a preemptive strike, and asking us not to worry about the peculiar form of the art, but rather to look at its meaning. A certain hypocrisy prevails.

Dante follows Virgil's instructions, but admits that "what I see moving towards us does not seem to me persons, but what it is I do not know, my sight wanders so."[16] What an incredible contrast! What Dante had seen with God's images was all clear to him, but now that he's seeing some human beings who are doubled under massive boulders (because that's the punishment inflicted on the proud, to be pressed against the earth), he does not recognize them. It is as if his aesthetic education has been for nothing; his ethical education, for nothing. He had no difficulty in deciphering God's art, which is so clear and luminous, but now he does not want to identify with what he sees. He resembles Michal, who from on high does not want to have anything to do with David. He had no problem with Gabriel, and his descent; he had no problem with Trajan; but he himself is unwilling to identify with those whom he believes are beneath him.

Virgil explains to Dante that these bent and tormented figures are humans like Dante. Dante launches into another apostrophe, to all Christians this time, questioning, "O proud Christians, wretched and weary, who, sick in mental vision, put trust in backward steps: are you not aware that we are worms, born to form the angelic butterfly?"[17] I want to stress this shift in pronouns. I begin with "are *you* not aware" because it shows that Dante is literally taking the higher ground. He is the one who knows, and he's preaching to the rest of us. But then with a subsequent pronoun—"*we* are worms"—Dante erases the distance between himself and the readers, between himself and other Christians. He places himself on the same ground as everyone else. That's the quality of the double voice of Dante, systematically punctuating this text, as a claim of a transcendent superior perspective, because after all, he really has seen the whole unfolding of God's cosmos, but at the same time, he descends and is part of a common plight.

This line is also an allusion to the fact that you would often see a butterfly imprinted on ancient Roman sarcophagi because the Greek word for "butterfly" is *psyche*. The Greeks use the same word for the soul, and this emblem of the butterfly indicated that at death the soul would finally be capable of flying off toward the light and the Creator. Finally, this apostrophe includes the language of a metamorphosis. Dante reminds us that we are always in the process of making ourselves, both while alive and in the penitential world of Purgatory.

Dante concludes this introduction to the spirits of Purgatory with an iconographic motif that recapitulates the iconographic aspect of the entire tenth canto: "As for corbel to support a ceiling or a roof, sometimes a figure is seen to join the knees to the breast—which, unreal, begets real distress in one who sees it—so fashioned did I see these when I gave good heed. They were truly more or less contracted according as they had more and less upon their backs; and he who showed the most suffering in his looks, seemed to say, weeping, 'I can no more.'"[18] Dante has just warned us not to pay attention to the form and to look at the meaning of the particular message, and yet here he returns to a focus on form. What he's describing are the so-called caryatids, decorative human forms that appear to be buttressing buildings. Dante is telling us that form matters after all. By picking up the sculptural motif of the canto, he reveals that we cannot truly arrive at the ultimate meaning by bypassing the form.

What is Dante's understanding of art, then? It's potentially dangerous, but there is an important role that art can play in altering our moral perception. In effect, form becomes a way to understand the moral world and the moral terms of your existence. This relationship between ethics and aesthetics is at the heart of Purgatory, and we'll see this idea resurface many times in the cantos ahead. For now, Dante is giving examples of art and humility, of his mistakes, of his confused perception.

And it is his perspective on perspective that brings together these myriad concerns. Perspective is connected with the representation of art, and it means that I see the world according to the position that I occupy in it, and the position that I occupy in it reveals things to me that are unique and irreducible. For Dante, perspective is connected to an inner world. What is my perspective of myself? What is my sense of the measure of things? A misperception like that of Michal can lead one to pride, the primary sin in these cantos and the spiritual root of all evils. No wonder Dante makes such a big deal of this question of perspective. It means everything when it comes to Dante's simultaneous aesthetic and ethical education in *Purgatorio*.

CHAPTER 12

Purgatorio 11–17

Dante's problem in Canto 10 of *Purgatorio* stems from the fact that he is initially a spectator of works of art, which he seems to have no difficulty understanding. He's witnessing what he calls visible speech, synesthesia, *visibile parlare* in Italian, but this is God's art and it has a precise meaning that Dante has no trouble comprehending or enjoying. But then he has to be involved. He has to show at least some compassion to and some self-recognition in the penitent souls who are under these huge weights that they carry. But he cannot do it. He still has to learn what grief is and how to connect to the images that he sees.

In *The Confessions,* St. Augustine also speaks of the experience of being a spectator. The real pleasure of going to the theater, he claims, is in images of grief. They don't really touch us. We are not expected to jump on the stage to relieve the characters who were involved in a sad situation. Augustine criticizes the disengaged spectator and the limits of the theater, the limits of that kind of aesthetic experience. I think that Dante is picking up exactly from what Augustine says in this chapter, and he's showing how unavoidably one has to be involved. In the measure in which we think that we are not touched by somebody else's grief, we're really admitting the overpowering quality of that experience.

Dante has learned something, then: he has learned that there is no such a thing as a safe perspective. Dante realizes and admits that he may be no different from Michal in his disclaimer that he does not know and does not see any of these penitents who disfigure the human form. He refuses to acknowledge that they are like him. These admissions are true signs that some of this aesthetic education has sunk in. Cantos 11 and 12 will further this new understanding.

Canto 11 begins with the penitents, who now reverse their perspective. They remain just as close to the ground, but now they are looking up, and they recite the Lord's Prayer, or rather Dante's recasting of the canonical prayer: "Our Father, who art in heaven, not circumscribed, but through the greater love Thou hast for Thy first works on high, praisèd be Thy name and Thy worth by every creature, as it is meet to render thanks to Thy sweet effluence. May the peace of Thy kingdom come to us, for we cannot reach it of ourselves, if it come not, for all our striving. As Thine angels make sacrifice to Thee of their will, singing Hosanna, so let men make of theirs. Give us this day our daily manna, without which he backward goes through this harsh desert who most labors to advance. And as we forgive everyone the wrong we have suffered, even do Thou in loving-kindness pardon, and regard not our desert."[1] The change that Dante makes is to emphasize that God is not in space, not circumscribed, and therefore He is really everywhere. He is free. The formula he is using is a traditional one in medieval thinking, whereby God is said to be an infinite sphere whose center is everywhere and whose circumference is nowhere. God is not in a place; God does not have a perspective. Indirectly there is a critique of the inadequacy of perspective here.

Another change that he's making is to add a Neoplatonic element to the Lord's Prayer. He literally places "give us this day our daily manna, without which he backward goes" into the prayer, which turns it into the prayer of the exiles in the desert. These souls are like the Jews in the wilderness, who ask for and receive their manna. This is another metaphorical element that casts Purgatory as a journey through the desert between the bondage of Egypt and Jerusalem.

Additionally, we know that there is a reversal of perspective here, but what kind of a perspective is Dante gaining now? I think I would call it a Franciscan perspective, even from that first line, "Praisèd be Thy name and Thy worthy by every creature." This line is an echo of the first poem of the Italian poetic tradition, a poem written by St. Francis called the "Canticle of Creatures," which is an anaphoric sequence of praises: praised be Thy name, praised be the water, and so on. The point of that poem is that it begins with human beings looking up to the highest, and it ends with the idea of humility. Francis tells us that we are not the center of creation, that we are just like everything else valuable in the created world. That's the thrust of the poem, and the only way in which you can truly understand that creation is to look from the bottom up and not from the top down. This is the perspective that Francis describes and that Dante subsequently adopts.

The rest of the canto is about the connection between art and pride, not surprising considering that the whole of Canto 10 was a reflection on these same premises. Dante illustrates this link by referring to painters and poets who surpass each other. Of Cimabue and Giotto he writes, "O empty glory of human powers! how briefly lasts the green upon the top, if it is not followed by barbarous times! Cimabue thought to hold the field in painting, and now Giotto has the cry, so that the other's fame is dim." And then of the poets, Guido Cavalcanti and Guido Guinizelli: "So has the one Guido taken from the other the glory of our tongue—and he perchance is born that shall chase the one and the other from the nest"—meaning Dante himself.[2] The idea of fame, which is what the proud souls may be seeking, is here dismissed as having the inconsistency of the wind, vanishing as quickly as a breath of fresh air. This is Dante's new moral understanding of pride and humility.

In Canto 12, Dante explains the punishments of the prideful, and in doing so he deploys a peculiar rhetorical artifice that merits further consideration. Here the images that Dante sees are on the ground, so he has to look down to view them. They are images of the proud souls who have been punished in this part of Purgatory, souls like Nimrod, Niobe, Saul, Arachne, Sennacherib. And Dante concludes his description of the setting with a final tercet: "I saw Troy in ashes and in caverns: O Ilion, how cast down and vile it showed you—the sculpture which is there discerned!"[3] These are all figurations of pride that has been humiliated. And their presentation in the Italian involves a form of visible speech. We are in the presence of a so-called acrostic; if you read the first letters of each tercet from the top down, it spells out V-O-M and then repeats. The letter is V, but in Italian it's also the U, so that we get the first part of the word *uomo,* or "man."

This part of the poem is about the fall of man. To illustrate that point, Dante is using an artifice that you can only understand if you *read* the text. If you have to hear it, you can't quite get to it. In other words, he's using God's own art as a model for himself. This seems like pride—excessive love of one's excellence. But what Dante is really telling us is that pride is not a sin in this case. He is, in a sense, redefining the ethical language of the Middle Ages and the ethical language of his own text. He's saying that in the measure in which you love what is *above* you, that is not a sin. Pride is a sin only in the measure in which you have contempt for those you think are *below* you. We have, thanks to the world of art, a reevaluation of moral language, the first and most important textual example of what will be happening throughout Purgatory.

With that in mind, let's dive into the center of the world of Purgatory. In Canto 15, Dante explores the sin of envy and contrasts it with charity, a virtue he defines with an image of light and reflection. He writes, "Because you still set your mind on earthly things, you gather darkness from true light." We tend to think in terms of the light that is available to us, but that light does not necessarily produce more light; rather, it can dim our understanding about the way things really are. The metaphor continues: "That infinite and ineffable Good that is there above speeds to love as a ray of light comes to a bright body. So much it gives of itself as it finds of ardor, so that how far soever love extends, the more does the Eternal Goodness increase upon it; and the more souls there are that are enamored there above, the more there are for loving well, and the more love is there, and like a mirror one reflects to the other."[4] This image of the mirror is a Platonic image of the notion in *The Celestial Hierarchy* by Pseudo-Dionysius, a mystical theologian whom Dante mentions in *Paradiso*. Pseudo-Dionysius thinks of all creation as a hall of mirrors, where everything is reflected one in the other in a number of reflections that all produce the light of God in different ways. He thinks of the divine in terms of light that is refracted and reflected throughout all the orders and ranks of creation. This reciprocity is how we arrive at mercy and charity.

This image thus leads us to the generative idea of charity, that is to say the idea that charity produces more charity. It has the power to generate itself and multiply itself. This is the principle of mercy for Dante. The whole of creation is sending back light, without any loss of its original light. This is the metaphysics of Dante's mirror. The world exists, therefore, on the basis of mercy, and not from the point of view of envy, from which we do not even see the light in the first place. Charity completely allows for a God who creates without envy and with generosity. Dante reveals this system of exchanges, this interconnectivity and reflexivity of all things, and then he moves into the true center of his text.

In Canto 16, Dante meets a famous magnanimous figure, Marco Lombardo, with whom he has a discussion about the issue of human degradation and degeneracy. The scene takes place in the biblical cloud of anger, a world deprived of any light, possessed by a kind of madness. Anger is thus understood as that which violates the clarity and light of reason. Dante is led through the gloom by Virgil, "as a blind man goes behind his guide that he may not stray or knock against what might injure or perhaps kill him."

Within this context, in this background of cloudiness and near invisibility of the world around him (which has been carried over from the sin of envy, a sin, as you know, that is all about being blind), Dante hears a voice and asks of it one question, namely if the "world is indeed as utterly deserted by every virtue as you declare to me, and pregnant and overspread with iniquity, but I beg you to point out to me the cause, so that I may see it and show it to men, for one places it in the heavens and another here below."[5] In other words, is there such a thing as free will? What is the cause of all our deeds? Is it, as the astrologers say, in the planets and therefore a matter of determination by forces that transcend us, over which we have no control? This interpretation results in a severe limitation of the meaning of choice and the possibility of choice, and therefore of merits and demerits. If we have no choices, then we cannot be praised or blamed for what we do. The other option is that what we do originates within us. With this question Dante is revisiting an ancient debate about the relationship between free will and God's foreknowledge, a debate that Boethius had famously confronted in *The Consolation of Philosophy.*

Lombardo salutes Dante as "Brother," the typical form of salutation in *Purgatorio,* before he begins his discourse. We already saw "Our Father" in Canto 11, with this idea of a human family, and therefore a brother is the appropriate form of interlocution and address among the souls and Dante. At any rate, Lombardo explains: "The world is blind, and truly you come from it! You who are living refer every cause up to the heavens alone, as if they of necessity moved all things with them. If it were so, free will would be destroyed in you, and there would be no justice in happiness for good or grief for evil. The heavens initiate your movements: I do not say all of them, but supposing I did say so, a light is given you to know good and evil, and free will, which if it endure fatigue in its first battles with the heavens, afterwards, if it is well nurtured, it conquers completely. You lie subject, in your freedom, to a greater power and to a better nature."[6] The text is fairly clear, but there is a distinction between choice and will that ought to be elucidated somewhat. The difference is that a choice is an intellectual problem, we choose thanks to what we know, while free will implies that the will is never in bondage and it's possible to attain a moment where we will freely. And yet, so many theologians ask whether free will means that the will can be moved by an act of choice that follows on the prior knowledge. This is not the only seeming paradox here. Lombardo also says that we are free subjects, and you can likely perceive the contradiction in those two terms. Only later will this all make full sense, when Dante shifts the argument to the law (16.93–98), which he says is precisely the metaphor that will make us understand what it means to be free and subject at the same time, where limitations are going to be posited and within those limitations we can be free. That's the argument he's trying to make.

The next thing that Dante does is give a sense of creation, positing human freedom in the act of the creation of the soul. He writes, "From His hands, who fondly loves it before it exists, comes forth after the fashion of a child that sports, now weeping, now laughing, the simple little soul, which knows nothing."[7] This alludes to a famous Latin poem by the emperor Hadrian about a little, childish soul that goes wandering around (St. Thomas Aquinas, too, refers to the soul as originally simple, a *tabula rasa*). Dante reinterprets it not as the soul that is lost in the world, but rather as a soul that is playing. For Dante creation is a playful act, both in the sense of the innocence of the experience and in the sense of being free. When one is at play, one has all the attributes of spontaneity and liberty that go with it. This concept is the basis of what I call the playful theology of Dante: God creates the world in an act, in a moment of freedom, and that freedom becomes the foundation for positing our own human freedom. It's because we were born free that we can go on believing that there is such a freedom for us, that it was not an act of necessity. Such a need would be the opposite of Dante's vision of creation as spontaneous and ludic.

Canto 16 proceeds from these theological arguments to extraordinary political and legal arguments. From human freedom Dante moves to political freedom: "Rome, which made the world good, was wont to have two Suns, which made visible both the one road and the other, that of the world and that of God. The one has quenched the other, and the sword is joined to the crook: and the one together with the other must perforce go ill—since, joined, the one does not fear the other."[8] What is he talking about? Rome had two suns? This passage deliberately mistranslates a line in Genesis where it is said that God gave mankind two luminaries, the sun and the moon, but in such a way that we could really see both in the daytime and at night. This image from Genesis was used by the so-called hierocrats, the canon lawyers of the Middle Ages, as the emblem for the Empire and the Church. The sun, having the greater light, the hierocrats would claim, was the light of the Church, and the moon, having a reflected light, was the light of the Empire. They would use this gloss as a way of explaining the superiority of the Church over the Empire—the latter had to take its light and its direction from the former. Dante is purposefully violating that idea of the sun and the moon, instead equating them by saying "the two Suns," all in order to convey his conviction that the two institutions God provides for the guidance of human beings, the Church and the Empire, are equal. By questioning the legality of systems posited by lawyers at the University of Bologna working for the pope, Dante shines light on the ways in which we may make claims of being free, even when we are also subjects, as discussed in Canto 16 (78 ff.).

And with that, we turn to Canto 17, which is numerically the center of the *Divine Comedy*. The canto begins with an apostrophe to the reader's memory: "Recall, reader, if ever in the mountains a mist has caught you, through which you could not see except as moles do through the skin"— the difficulty of seeing is highlighted again—"how, when the moist dense vapors begin to dissipate, the sphere of the sun enters feebly through them, and your fancy will quickly come to see how, at first, I saw the sun again, which was now at its setting. So, matching mine to the trusty steps of my master, I came forth from such a fog to the rays which were already dead on the low shores."[9] It's a twilight landscape. There are a number of reversals, along with the contrast between the blind mole that burrows underneath the earth and the alpine scenery that also makes vision impossible. Dante is simultaneously evoking the highest heights and the lowest possible point of sight. The sun is setting, and the night is approaching. It is as if the solidity of the world around him is vanishing before his eyes. At the same time, he's appealing to the memory and the imagination of the reader. When the world outside seems to be failing us, Dante suggests that we have an inner light, this possibility of recollecting or imagining the world as it disappears. Even in the darkness, even rendered blind, we can see with the light within us.

He's also preparing a remarkable second apostrophe, this one to the imagination. We are approaching the center of this poetic universe, and Dante wants to remind us that this is a work of the imagination. He says, "O imagination, that do sometimes so snatch us from outward things that we give no heed, though a thousand trumpets sound around us, who moves you if the sense affords you naught?"[10] It's the same question he had been asking earlier: where do our choices come from? Why do we do what we do? Is it because a power from the outside moves us, or is there something within us that does it? Here, though, this question is asked in slightly different terms, in terms of the imagination, which is a power that removes us from the outside world. It's not just, as Aristotle posited, that the imagination translates sensory experiences into images for the benefit of our rational judgment, acting as the middle ground between the work of perception and the work of reason. This is a standard triadic pattern that Dante could certainly have found in Aquinas, who, in turn, found it in Aristotle. But Dante is talking about a different conception of the imagination, one that needs nothing of the world of perception. It's a faculty that is completely free from our external reality, a power that we have within us to imagine worlds that don't even exist. As Dante is approaching the center of his world, we are shown the power of the imagination as a visionary faculty. It encompasses the real world and yet is almost prophetic, for it eschews contact with that reality. These combatting ideas of the imagination will both play a role in Canto 17.

But first Dante spends some time describing the laws of Purgatory. How is this realm constructed and run? Unsurprisingly, it is built, as Singleton made clear, upon a fabric of love and an architecture of love. At the very center of the *Divine Comedy,* lines 91, 92, and 93 of Canto 17 of *Purgatorio,* Virgil says, "Neither Creator nor creature, my son, was ever without love, either natural or of the mind. . . . The natural is always without error; but the other may err either through an evil object, or through too much or too little vigor."[11] He's distinguishing here between two types of love but emphasizing that the instinctual impulse of love is never prone to sinfulness. It's a natural impulse, a natural desire. What *is* sinful instead is a love where choice is involved. Whenever we make a choice, we may either not love the right object or we may love it too much or too little, as previously mentioned. This triadic division in terms of love defines Purgatory's topography. Everything here is a problem of love, but then there are varieties that organize the realm's subdivisions.

The question thus becomes how to understand this love of choice. What is it, really? Does it depend on my particular perception of the world? If so, and that perception makes me see whatever I encounter as beautiful and desirable, where is my fault? Once again, Dante repeats the same problems of will and fate that were raised in Canto 15. This time Dante will explain the conundrum in terms of love, and yet we are going to be brought back to the world of perception, for our perception of what we love becomes crucial to our responsibilities for it. Love is problematic. Dante's theory of love is a rational one, one that brings us to knowledge and organization, and yet love is one of those experiences exactly like the imagination, the powers of which always seem to be transgressing whatever rational limitations we want to impose on it.

At the center of the poem, then, Dante seems to be oscillating between two ideas. On the one hand, there is the notion of a real world in which we have responsibilities for love and for everything that we do, and on the other hand, there's our imagination, which is completely disengaged from the world of reality and cannot be constrained by it. Suspended between these two possibilities, how can Dante bring them together? If the world of the imagination is free and disengaged from reality, how am I going to be held accountable for what I do to the world around me?

One resolution is that the imagination does not exclude rationality; it simply surpasses it. Dante claims that the imagination cannot be held in check, but his poem is designed with a precise principle of order in mind. Thematically, it's about order, too: ordering the appetites, ordering the will. And yet, the text is complex, and some elements are left out of the fabric that Dante is weaving. In spite of his careful construction, there are still loose ends. Fortunately, Dante's poem is only nourished by these contradictions, its beauty enhanced as it moves back and forth between love and the imagination, the fossae at the poem's core.

CHAPTER 13

Purgatorio 18–22

Dante has finished one stage in his movement toward self-knowledge and knowledge of the world, and in Canto 18, we're moving into a different moral realm, toward what Dante and medieval theorists of vices call *acedia*. *Acedia* is a Latin term, which in English we can describe as a sort of despondency, indecisiveness, sluggishness, or sloth. In a sense it's a parody or inversion of contemplation, tied to a sense of loss of the outside world. It describes the condition of the mind that has found itself indifferent to objects of desire, which have lost their consistency, their attractiveness, their luster. It's the so-called noonday devil, the temptation that the monks experienced in their cloisters when they no longer found the idea of turning their minds toward the divine appealing in that moment. It's the indifference to anything outside of oneself and indicates an equally intellectual and dreamy state of mind.

Canto 18 is the most intellectual canto in *Purgatorio*. Dante faces theoretical issues that flow out of the problems that we saw in Canto 17 with an imagination that is somehow vagabond. It breaks out of any particular confines and dislodges us, taking the ground out of our own certainties about the way we see the world. Dante has the same problem in Canto 18, which begins with a question that he asks of Virgil regarding the theory of love proposed in Canto 17: "Master, my sight is so quickened in your light that I discern clearly all that your discourse distinguishes or declares; wherefore, dear and gentle father, I pray that you expound love to me, to which you reduce every good action and its opposite."[1] In other words, what you told me before is not enough. So Virgil explains the very philosophical theory of perceptions. Your perception takes from outward reality an impression and unfolds it within you, so it makes the mind turn to it. Love is simply the unfolding of one such perception.

He goes on to criticize the belief that all love is inherently good. He's attacking the view of the Epicureans, who believe that every pleasure, without any particular judgment attached to the object of pleasure, is praiseworthy. Instead, according to Dante's mouthpiece, Virgil, we have to exercise some moral judgment. We have to create distinctions. We have to discriminate between good and bad love, "because perhaps its matter appears always to be good: but not every imprint is good, although the wax be good."[2] I would go so far as to say that when Dante says this through Virgil, he's really thinking of his friend Guido Cavalcanti and Guido's Epicurean leanings. Cavalcanti's Epicurean ethics, the idea that pleasure is the only object worthy of any pursuit, is so hedonistic that Dante has to renounce it.

Dante responds confusedly: "Your discourse and my understanding which has followed it . . . have revealed love to me; but that has made me more full of doubt; for if love is offered to us from without, and if the soul walks with no other foot, it has no merit whether it go straight or crooked." So now you're telling me that everything is love and the love that I have depends on my experience of images, but how am I deserving of my fate for choosing well or not choosing well, since at the basis of the imagination, we have perceptions? What I perceive may look good to me and not look good to you, so the issue is displaced from the world of imagination to the world of perception. Virgil will have to explain a Scholastic theory that indeed we do incline to the good, but within us we still have the faculty of choice, "the faculty that counsels and that ought to hold the threshold of assent."[3] He's talking about free will once again. But then he admits his limitations on this point and says that other issues about free will have to be explained to Dante by Beatrice. We see a distinction between the knowledge of Virgil and that of Beatrice.

Beatrice will never actually discuss this problem, however. And yet, in a sense, Beatrice represents the explanation that Dante is seeking, because Beatrice, for Dante, stands for a visionary form of love, not just a love that can be reduced to a question of mechanics or the physics of perception. Ultimately, then, Canto 18 responds to, enlarges, and at the same time brings us right back to the very predicament that Canto 17 had posed for us. It only seems like Dante is moving forward, when in fact another impasse has been reached.

With this in mind, we turn to what Dante unavoidably has to do next, namely try to translate all of these issues of love, imagination, and choice from the theoretical into the autobiographical or existential dimension. This is done in an erotic dream that Dante relates at the beginning of Canto 19. Before I turn to that canto, though, let's look at Dante's introduction to the dream, which comes at the end of Canto 18: "Then when those shades were so far parted from us that they could no more be seen, a new thought arose within me, from which others many and diverse were born; and I so rambled from one to another that, wandering thus, I closed my eyes, and transmuted my musing into a dream."[4] The line is very interesting because it presents a connection between thinking and dreaming. And at this point Dante favors dreaming over thinking.

We shouldn't be surprised that Dante is doing this. *The Romance of the Rose* tells of a dream. Chaucer's "Book of the Duchess" is the story of a dream. The *Vita nuova* is full of dreams. Much later there's Keats's great poem "Sleep and Poetry." Poets love sleeping because sleep and dreams introduce the possibility of a knowledge that is not willed. You can have some revelations within yourself, which are not what you would normally have if you were awake, so this is why poets give great privilege to dreams. Still, are the writers of the Middle Ages really conscious of this dimension? Yes. There is a text by an author called Macrobius, who writes on "The Dream of Scipio," Cicero's figure in *The Republic*. It's an encyclopedia of dreams based on Artemidorus, and it makes distinctions between oracles, fantasies, insomnia, deliriums, and so on. The text was well known, so these writers were very conscious of the sort of power and revelations that can, as the Bible has it, come through dreams.

What is Dante's specific dream about? It's definitely grounded in the world of *acedia* that we discussed earlier. The dream is really a means of highlighting the autobiographical dimension of all the problems we have been discussing in the last several cantos. Dante has to give these theories of love and free will and the imagination a personal shape and to investigate the kind of importance that they may have for him. And so we get this account:

> At the hour when the day's heat, overcome by Earth and at times by Saturn, can no more warm the cold of the moon—when the geomancers see their *Fortuna Major* rise in the East before dawn by a path which does not long stay dark for it—there came to me in a dream a woman, stammering, with eyes asquint and crooked on her feet, with maimed hands, and of sallow hue. I gazed upon her: and even as the sun revives cold limbs be-

numbed by night, so my look made ready her tongue, and then in but little time set her full straight, and colored her pallid face even as love requires. When she had her speech thus unloosed, she began to sing so that it would have been hard for me to turn my attention from her. "I am," she sang, "I am the sweet Siren who leads sailors astray in mid-sea, so full am I of pleasantness to hear. Ulysses, eager to journey on, I turned aside to my song; and whosoever abides with me rarely departs, so wholly do I satisfy him." Her mouth was not yet shut when a lady, holy and alert, appeared close beside me to put her to confusion. "O Virgil, Virgil, who is this?" she said sternly; and he came on with his eyes fixed only on that honest one. He seized the other and laid her bare in front, rending her garments and showing me her belly: this waked me with the stench that issued therefrom. I turned my eyes, and the good master said, "I have called you at least three times: arise and come, let us find the opening by which you may enter."[5]

It's a dream that happens at dawn, and a dream at dawn was believed to be prophetic. It can be understood as an allegory because it's about rending a veil, tearing clothes. There is something hidden underneath it all, a truth-value, so it's not a mere fable. Notably, Dante is evoking the planet Saturn, and when Dante mentions planets, he joins them to the various liberal arts. When he talks about the moon, Dante is also discussing grammar. When he talks about Mars, the planet of war, and he is talking about music as well. Jupiter is associated with justice, and Saturn with astronomy but also contemplation. I think he's hinting that sloth is the obverse side, the parody, of contemplation, which is just a different type of self-absorption rather than a way of reaching within in order to break out of oneself and reach a space outside of time. Here it's solely an inward movement. Dante continues with this language of astronomy and divination, divining signs, a different type of rational knowledge, and this is the context in which the dream is set.

The first thing that I have to point out to you about the dream itself is that within it the dreamer is an object. The dream comes to him. Clearly, it is not willed, it's not something that he decides or wants for himself. One is the object of some apparitions, or signs and images that descend into oneself without one's own dominion being involved. Dante thus places himself in a condition of passivity, that is, the passivity of sloth. Being awake, and therefore vigilant, and capable of making judgments about what's happening to him is bracketed for the time being.

What is this dream about, though? Well, it's a dream of two women, two modes of being, two choices. It involves the mythography of Hercules at the crossroads, forced to choose between vice and virtue, but Hercules has an easy time because he's always going to go right. In mythography, if you go to the right then you are aiming toward virtue, as we have previously discussed. Rather than a simple left-right choice, though, here there are two women, which complicates matters. Fortunately, the language of the poem distinguishes very carefully between them. One is a *femmina,* a word for which there is materiality and even a kind of animal sense, and when the other woman appears, she's called a *donna*—which comes from *domina*—*santa e presta,* a holy and alert lady. The choice becomes clearer on these terms.

The first woman crystallizes what we could call an aesthetic of ugliness. We're always talking about beauty and the idea that beauty brings about a revelation of love and pleasure. As a result, the conventional way of thinking about aesthetics is to imagine beautiful proportionate forms. Here, Dante is providing exactly the opposite, an aesthetic of the ugly, but an ugliness that is not static, that somehow experiences a metamorphosis. In fact, at the outset she is "stammering, with eyes asquint and crooked on her feet," a veritable anti-Beatrice, but then the dreamer becomes a subject for the first time and changes her. His desires transform her image and invest it with attributes of attractiveness as love prompts.

But we still don't understand who she is. The temptation that she offers Dante comes in her song. This is primarily a poetic temptation, a certain way of understanding a meretricious form of poetry. Of course, she brings to center stage the myth of Ulysses, which is, as you know by now, a steady source of temptation for Dante. It's the point of reference: to what extent is my own journey, which I believe to be taking place under the aegis of divine providence, actually a transgression? Is it a way of going beyond boundaries, of breaking down all limits, because after all, that's what Ulysses did in Canto 26 of *Inferno*? And Dante knows where he has placed the Ithacan wanderer, but he cannot get Ulysses out of his mind because Ulysses stands for something powerful. What he represents is the idea that there is no knowledge worth having that is not connected to transgressions. The great temptation for Dante is thus to believe that his journey reenacts that of Ulysses, which is exactly what the siren is telling Dante here, that she can make him happy just as she did Ulysses. It's a lie, of course, because Ulysses never stopped at the island of Capri, in whose grotto the siren is said to reside. He did listen to her song, but he was bound to the mast of the ship, so she never bought him any pleasure. There is a transgression and a binding going on at the same time. The siren is making false promises, claiming to be the end of all Dante desires, urging him to conclude his journey and stay with her.

But then we have another figure that emerges, a woman who is clearly the antagonist of the siren. We don't know who she is, but we'll find out very quickly, in Cantos 30 and 31, because the same scene will be reenacted with the arrival of Beatrice. We already have reason to imagine that here too she is Beatrice. Identity aside, what is the difference between these two women? They are two different forms of poetry. Now we understand why Dante has been talking about the imagination all along—because it is what will introduce him to the stakes in claiming to be a poet. He's been talking about his faculty as a poet, and the cantos that come next constitute the most important segment of the poem in terms of ways of understanding literary history and the place of originality within that particular history. We are going to enter the world of poetry more directly. At any rate, these women speak in two markedly different voices: one sweet, meretricious, and false, the other one very harsh but true. One forecloses Dante's journey, encouraging him to be like Ulysses and call it quits. The other one claims exactly the opposite: the journey has to continue. The song of the siren seems sweet but also has the stench of death attached to it. The more austere voice instead insists that the true language of sweetness is that of love as an ongoing quest. So, we encounter two forms of love, two forms of poetry, two types of women.

Which of the two is better? Is there an objective criterion by which we can say that Beatrice is actually better than the siren? Yes, and the criterion is going to be very simple: the necessary avoidance of death. The siren stands for death. Underneath the pleasures of her language, she reeks of decomposition. Dante thus recognizes the danger of making the here and now, and the limitations of the here and now, and the limitations of that song in particular, the end of his journey. This is the only way in which you can objectively assert that there is a hierarchy established between these two loves and between these two women.

There are certain parallels between this scene and the scene of Casella in Canto 2. It's the reappearance, under different guises, of the same temptation, how the beautiful or aesthetic can gather people around itself. As in the story of Casella, the song collects individuals and drives them to forgetfulness of whatever purposes they are supposed to entertain and carry out. The difference here is that we have entered as deep as we can into Dante's unconscious mind. This is a moment of amazing *self*-revelation, whereas the story of Casella had the ring of a public discourse, of poetry as a public act.

Fittingly, we now move into a segment of the poem that has poetry as its central subject matter. Dante begins with the classical tradition, and a critical encounter takes place in the purgatorial realms of avarice and prodigality, the encounter between Statius and Virgil. Statius views himself as a disciple of Virgil, but in many ways he challenges Virgil's thought. Virgil presents us with Aeneas, a hero who is so divided against himself and yet always manages to find his way around, albeit by following a zigzag, erratic path. Statius counters this tendency in *The Thebaid,* which makes a conjunction between tragedy and the epic and focuses on the impossible monstrosity of that world, casting it as nightmarish. It's indubitably the most psychological of these epics—Greek and Latin—because it focuses on the wars that happen in the mind, and this idea of the horror of human fate and human desires.

These are the two worlds that Dante now wants to bring together in this little *epyllion,* a Greek word meaning a "little epic," a transcription of two epic texts into one text in a lyrical form. This is a tough task because what he wants to show is the possibility of harmonizing the two of them, demonstrating how they can be seen to talk as friends across time. Statius lived around A.D. 70, and Virgil died in the year 19, but the poetry of Virgil has made them friends. And Statius can be considered a classical version of Dante himself. Dante is the disciple of Virgil, and so was Statius, so Dante tries to bring them together.

But it's not just a question of making their two different visions agree, which in and of itself would not be all that difficult. For instance, Statius is very skeptical about the empire, while Virgil is not all that skeptical. There is certainly a lot of ambiguity in the way in which Virgil talks about Augustus and the empire in *The Aeneid,* but he's basically writing an epic that justifies the ideology of empire. These kind of thematic differences can be reconciled, though. The real difficulty in bringing them together is that Dante has to try to adjust Statius's vision of monstrosity to some idea of the sacred. How do we understand the sacred in Statius? Is it possible to see in these texts of Statius the seeds of something good? How can we build anything good out of this vision of heroes who fornicate with their own fantasies, who cannot really get out of their minds, who discover their own unchanging submission to a force that transcends them to fate? It's really absolutely a different worldview from that of Virgil, and Dante will truly have to grapple with the gap between them.

Dante begins Canto 21 with an allusion to the natural thirst for knowledge. It's very much an entry into the Aristotelian world of the *Convivio*. Then the figure called Statius appears, and in the same moment the natural world starts mysteriously shaking. There's an earthquake, we discover, because every time that a soul gets liberated from the purgatorial experience of expiation, this purification and expiation, then the mountain trembles. In this case, it is Statius who can go up to the Garden of Eden: "I, who have lain in this pain five hundred years and more, only now felt free volition for a better threshold. Therefore you felt the earthquake and heard the pious spirits about the mountain give praises to that Lord."[6] His resurrection has taken place.

Statius's next task is to describe himself. He evokes the time of the destruction of the temple in Jerusalem when the good emperor Titus, with God's help, enacted divine justice for the crimes of Judas. Statius was a pagan at this time, but he became a born-again Christian. He was drawn to Rome by the pull of desire, and there he wrote of Thebes and began a second text about Achilles that he failed to finish. Finally, he explains the process that produced his poetry: "The sparks which warmed me from the divine flame whereby more than a thousand have been kindled were the seeds of my poetic fire: I mean the *Aeneid,* which in poetry was both mother and nurse to me—without it I had achieved little of worth; and to have lived yonder when Virgil lived I would consent to one sun more than I owe to my coming forth from exile."[7]

There are two metaphors for poetry here. One is that of sparks, so that poetry is invested with the power to light a fire in its readers, and the second one is that of nourishing the inner hunger, of mother and nurse. The latter constitutes a great acknowledgment of a master, without his knowledge that it is Virgil to whom he is speaking. And then Dante reveals Virgil's identity to Statius, and the two of them try to embrace, though Virgil quickly calls a halt to the futile gesture: "'Brother do not so, for you are a shade and a shade you see.' And he, rising, 'Now you may comprehend the measure of the love that burns in me for you, when I forget our emptiness and treat shades as solid things.'"[8] This is a mistake that has been made before, a mistake meant to convey the claims or illusions of poets to believe that there is a solidity to them, and not just to their poetry. But there is no solidity to them. Rather, there is a kind of emptiness and a distance between the poets and their works. Perhaps for this reason, works of art are going to be the focal point of Canto 22.

The two poets start to converse, and Virgil asks Statius to explain why this moral blight existed in him, this sin of avarice: "Wherefore, from the hour when Juvenal descended among us in the Limbo of Hell and made your affection known to me, my good will toward you has been such as never yet did bind to an unseen person, so that these stairs will now seem short to me. But tell me—and as a friend pardon me if too great confidence slackens my rein, and talk with me now as with a friend—how could avarice find place in your breast, amid wisdom so great as that wherewith you were filled by your zeal?"[9] This is a passage of some importance. First of all, we get the claim of friendship between Virgil and Statius. Friendship is an ethical virtue in Aristotle's *Ethics* and also for Cicero, who writes a treatise called *On Friendship,* which Dante mentions at the beginning of the *Convivio,* his philosophical text, in the belief that friendship is really the other term for philosophy. The friend and the philosopher are interchangeable because there is a love of truth in both cases. Still, there is some exaggeration on the part of Virgil because friendship implies some degree of equality. It's often said that tyrants and slaves are not capable of love or friendship with each other because one is the inversion of the other, and the slave is, by definition, inferior to the tyrant. So, here there's a rhetorical exaggeration of Statius and Virgil's relationship because Statius sees himself as a disciple and therefore views Virgil as superior from a poetic point of view, while from a theological point of view Statius is superior to Virgil. Statius is going on to Paradise, and Virgil is going to go back to Limbo. In other words, there is perhaps a push in the direction of wishful thinking on the part of Virgil when he calls them friends.

I must also add that Dante may be aware that friendship was never really thought of as a Christian virtue. It's a classical and pagan virtue, and it confuses Christian ethics with the idea that a friend is always part of one's soul. It's a truly earthbound concept and experience, so by and large it was held that friendship could distract the mind from an ascent to higher and superior ends, paradisiac ecstasies and pleasures. Dante has to know that there were efforts to Christianize this idea.

Nonetheless, it brings the conversation between the two souls back to the earth, and they talk as if they were truly two friends meeting in the forum, in the agora, chatting about their moral failings or their own poetic crafts and visions. But the question remains: how could you be so avaricious, when you are quite enlightened in so many other ways? Statius responds that he's not avaricious and spends a great deal of time talking about the fact that he is actually prodigal. You may remember from Canto 7 of *Inferno* that prodigality was a violation of the economy of goods by devaluing them, not holding onto them, while avarice means overvaluing the goods and trying to amass larger quantities of them.

Statius defends this classification of his sin at length before explaining his moral conversion, which is the first thing he mentions about just what poetry can do: "Know that avarice was too far parted from me, and this want of measure thousands of courses of the moon have punished; and were it not that I set right my care, when I gave heed to the lines where you exclaim, angered as it were against human nature, 'To what do you not drive the appetite of mortals, O accursèd hunger of gold?' at the rolling I should feel the grievous jousts."[10] What Statius is saying here is that he read a passage in book 3 of *The Aeneid,* the story of Polydorus, who had been killed because they wanted to rob him of his gold, and as a result of this reading he was converted. This account exemplifies how we actually read, for we dismember the integrity of the text. We take out of a book, or a passage of a book, that which we find relevant to us. In this case, he takes some lines from *The Aeneid* and alters their meaning. The original text of Virgil's is the opposite of Statius's interpretation of it. The word *sacred* is used, which can mean either "sacred" or "cursed," as the English translator uses here. It's a most ambiguous term semantically speaking because it can describe both the holy and the profane. It joins them together, so that there's no longer a clear-cut distinction between them. So, the poetic text of Virgil has a moral power over and against Virgil's own intentions. We can understand now, retrospectively, why Dante has to distinguish between poets and their works. We can read the works regardless of the intentions of the authors and we can select or take out of those texts whatever we think that they are saying to us.

From there, Virgil questions Statius's poetic and spiritual growth. Dante purposefully refers to Virgil here as the author of a pastoral poem, *The Eclogues,* in which rivalries are always placated. Pastoral poems are always about rivalry, a rivalry between two shepherds, but there's never any tragic outcome. There's some uneasiness and anxiety running through the debate between the poets, but it's not a serious rivalry. That's really the difference that Dante is highlighting. At any rate, Virgil the pastoral poet says, "It does not appear, from that which Clio touches with you there, without which good works suffice not, had yet made you faithful. If that is so, then what sun or what candles dispelled your darkness, so that thereafter you set your sails to follow the fisherman?"[11] What he's really asking about, in a general way, is the relationship between poetry and faith. How did Statius find faith after his conversion? Can poetry reveal and lead us on to the world of faith or not?

Statius responds, "You it was who first sent me toward Parnassus"— the mountain of poetry, suggesting that the poetic apprenticeship is the preamble to the experience of faith—"to drink in its caves"—a metaphor that picks up the natural thirst of the previous canto—"and you who first did light me on to God. You were like one who goes by night and carries the light behind him and profits not himself, but makes those wise who follow him, when you said, 'The ages are renewed; Justice returns and the first age of man, and a new progeny descends from heaven.'"[12] Virgil is a prophetic voice, using language that benefits those who follow him though he himself remains in the dark. The cited passage is from the famous fourth eclogue of Virgil, where Virgil is celebrating the birth of a child, Pollio, and also talking about the rejuvenation of the world. Pollio's birth is an emblem for this Pythagorean vision that he has, a vision whereby the world goes through 360,000 years of the Golden Age, the Silver Age, and so on, and then degrades itself and goes right back to where it started. Interestingly, this also crystallizes Virgil's concern with birth, his belief that being born has within itself the potential to renew the world.

Then Statius talks about how the world outside only buttressed the message of faith that he had found in the fourth eclogue. The fourth eclogue is thus seen as a messianic eclogue and a mechanism for the transition from poetry to faith. As Statius proclaims to Virgil, "Through you I was a poet, through you a Christian."[13] This crucial line requires some close reading. First of all, it contains an anaphora, which gives continuity to the movement of the line from poetry to faith: "through you . . . through you," "per te . . . per te." Nonetheless, if you read this line carefully, you see that there is also a caesura, a break in the middle. The line has a mobility that seems to promise the transition from poetry to faith, but at the same time technically, it forces you to stop as if they were two discontinuous experiences. You cannot quite go directly from the world of poetry to the world of faith, but you can still go from one world of poetry to the other. That ambiguity of poetry and its power is exactly what Dante aims to replicate here.

Ultimately, the differences between the two poets are largely overridden by the links between their poetry, but an insurmountable divide remains. Statius deals with the tragedy of birth, while Virgil treats it optimistically, talking about the history-making quality of a birth. At the same time, Virgil's stance indicates a desire to establish a sense of what the sacred is, while Statius has come to know the sacred by taking advice from Virgil that Virgil was unable to apply to himself. In a way, then, their poetry is imbued with the ambiguous sense of the word *sacred* that we discussed earlier, containing both the profane and the holy within it. It's a hybrid art, a hybridity that allows Dante to assimilate Statius's contradictory vision to his own understanding of history and the sacred. In sum, Dante writes powerful, ambiguous poetry precisely to demonstrate poetry's powerful ambiguity.

CHAPTER 14

Purgatorio 24–26

The encounter with Dante's own friend Forese Donati among the gluttonous sinners in Canto 23 signals a shift in the articulation of the literary segment that had begun with the recognition of Statius and Virgil. Poetry will continue to figure centrally, but Dante brackets the classical paradigm of literary history (Virgil/Statius). Virgil's conception of the "generosity" of poetry will remain a standard against which modern versions will be measured, but the focus shifts to Dante's own role and place in contemporary poetic history and takes on an autobiographical coloring. The moral landscape of *Purgatorio* 24 is characterized by the expiation of gluttony, and both sin and punishment (an ascetic purification of gluttony) shed light on the specifically poetic confrontation dramatized between Dante and a poet of an earlier generation, Bonagiunta da Lucca.

Over the conversation with Forese Donati—who was a brother to Piccarda Donati and was related to the family of Dante's wife, Gemma Donati—there hangs the memory of a series of violent, vituperative sonnets the two had exchanged in life. The tone between them now is one of reconciliation: the follies and abuses of their satirical poems are set aside, and their urbane mode foreshadows the more sustained, demanding encounter with Bonagiunta of Lucca. A reference to the moral virtues of a woman who had been kind to Dante, Gentucca, gives way to a number of pressing questions about Dante's identity, the novelty of his poetic style, and Dante's own construction (through the mask of Bonagiunta) of the poetic school known as the *dolce stil novo,* or "sweet new style."

Bonagiunta states, "'But tell me if I see here him who brought forth the new rhymes, beginning: "Ladies that have intelligence of love"?' And I said to him, 'I am one who, when Love inspires me, takes note, and goes setting it forth after the fashion which he dictates within me.' 'O brother,' he said, 'now I see the knot which kept the Notary, and Guittone, and me, short of the sweet new style that I hear. Clearly I see how your pens follow close after him who dictates, which certainly befell not with ours—and he who sets himself to seek farther can see no other difference between the one style and the other.' And, as if satisfied, he was silent."[1] The passage is replete with allusions and echoes of long-drawn debates, of texts and concerns that have been the object of intense critical controversy. Bonagiunta, in a manner that seems to test Dante's likely proud claims about his art, cites the opening line of Dante's song from the *Vita nuova*, "Ladies that have intelligence of love." In the *Vita nuova* Dante had self-consciously introduced the poem as if it marked a radical shift in Dante's understanding of love and of poetry. He had related how one day he was walking down the banks of the river (the Arno), and the words came spontaneously to him, with the natural ease, one infers, of the smooth waters of the stream.

But the conceptual thrust of the song proceeds from a sharp polemical source. In one of the most famous of Guido Cavalcanti's lyrical-philosophical reflections on love and poetry, the poem "A Lady begs me . . . ," Guido makes a stark statement: namely, that no relation exists between love and knowledge. Love is born not of intellect but of a violence that darkens and shatters the mind. Dante's song, to which Bonagiunta makes a reference, counters Guido's shadowy imaginings. By a radical break with his own lyrical tradition (that assumed the existence of a closed circle of poets), Dante evokes a circle of women, the "ladies who have the intellect of love," who are cast as the privileged audience for grasping the intellectual essence of love. In short, he challenges Guido's philosophical presuppositions and holds that love and intellect can go together as they do in a philosophical discourse. Dante's argument is based on the principle that a passion can become a virtue, and that the rhetoric of praise—a mode that resonates with religious *laudes*—constitutes the distinctiveness of a new amorous discourse that the *Vita nuova* pursues.

In another work of his, the *De vulgari eloquentia*, Dante had distanced himself polemically from Bonagiunta's (and other Tuscan poets') practices exactly in terms of their style: style, which Dante understands as a perspective, as a mode of seeing the world. The style of the earlier generation, to which Bonagiunta belongs, evoked a narrow, "municipal" focus: it is a style that relies on prefabricated, abstract technical language of the Scholastics, and thus it misses the radical openness of poetic language that

Dante enacts. The question of a different style that Dante (along with Guido Guinizelli and Guido Cavalcanti) had inaugurated presents to us the question of Dante's historical consciousness, his realization that he and the two Guidos live in a "modern world," although elsewhere the notion of "modernity" is seen by Dante as synonymous with precariousness and the transitoriness of time (as we remarked in our reading of Canto 11 of *Purgatorio*).

In what way, then, is Dante's implicit recognition of a gap between Bonagiunta's poetic values and his own values to be understood? Let me restate that the new poetry Dante has in mind is the poetry that Guido Guinizelli and he, among others, practiced: the poetry of the "sweet new style." The two adjectives are highly problematical. "Sweet" evokes the *dulcedo,* which describes the musical quality of the lyrical language they deploy. In the context of gluttony—a word that resonates with the tavern songs of the so-called goliardic poets (the poets who sing the pleasures of banquets, dice, and women in the tavern)—"sweetness" alludes also to the refinements of a new "taste." The adjective "new," on the other hand, conveys the sense of modern, young, and fresh, and so it casts Bonagiunta, Guittone, and the Sicilian poets (such as the Notary) as attached to past and unalterable modes of composition. But the genuine sense of Dante's claim of the novelty of his poetry emerges from the rhetoric he deploys in his self-definition: "I am one who, when Love inspires me, takes note, and goes setting it forth after the fashion which he dictates within me."

In this account of his poetic inspiration, of a poetry born under the inspiration of love, Dante submits to the authority of the "him who dictates," or the dictator: a term designating the inner voice of Love as the absolute Master, a figure whose powers are supreme and who governs, like an inner political authority, the mind of the love servant. More precisely, the poet casts himself as a scribe of the dictator: he is one who takes notes and writes down what he has heard. The word *noto* ("I note down") resonates, furthermore, with the title used to identify the Sicilian poet "the Notary," Jacopo da Lentini, who at the court of Frederick II held the office of a scrivener: he would draw up legal papers and administer oaths. Dante's metaphorical activity of "noting" highlights his sense of poetry as the activity dramatizing what can be called the law of love, a new code of love that replaces that of the Provençal and Sicilian schools.

Unavoidably, this sort of claim must be seen through the prism of contemporary literary history, of a modern poetic tradition, that would be parallel to the classical tradition of Virgil and Statius in Cantos 21 and 22 of *Purgatorio. Purgatorio* 26, where Dante meets the poet he identifies as his poetic father, Guido Guinizelli, who in turn points out to him the great poet of love, the Provençal Arnaut Daniel, raises this sort of concern with the tradition of the "new." The poets in *Purgatorio* 26 are sinners of lust, and their moral condition raises the more traditional topic of poetry and desire. In a sense, the encounter with Guinizelli deliberately recalls the canto of Francesca (*Inferno* 5) as well as the first canto of the sodomites (Canto 15). I stress this detail not simply because Brunetto's sin is now rethought: the sin of Guinizelli lacks the tragic finality that distinguished Brunetto's punishment.

Before considering the sense of the encounter with Guinizelli, mention must be made of *Purgatorio* 25, which, on the face of it, is constructed as a mere digression from the poetic rhetoric of the surrounding cantos. In reality, appearances to the contrary, *Purgatorio* 25 raises highly generalized intellectual issues, which obliquely shed light on the questions debated in *Purgatorio* 24 and 26. I repeat that *Purgatorio* 25 comes through as a highly technical, doctrinal exposition of the "ontological status of the shades" (the phrase is Étienne Gilson's). As we have seen, the substance of the explicitly literary cantos, from 21 to 26, ranges from problems of literary hermeneutics, such as the hidden sense of Virgil's texts, to the violence of interpretation, to the "intention" of the literary author as well as the sense of literary modernity. In *Purgatorio* 25, Statius explains to Dante how it can be that the shades, who have no bodies, can suffer their punishments. The reason for their suffering lies in their aerial bodies, and to prove his contention Statius gives a sophisticated lecture on the relationship between bodies and souls, embryology and theology.

He begins by dismissing Averroes' doctrine of the separate existence of substances, such as the possible intellect as a separate faculty, as well as the notion of a metaphysical discontinuity between the vegetative-sensitive powers of the soul. The soul is marked by the coexistence of a threefold activity, and its creation is directed by the "First Mover." The Prime Mover, so we are told, "turns to it with joy over such art of nature, and breathes into it a new spirit replete with virtue, which absorbs that which is active there into its own substance, and makes one single soul which lives and feels and circles on itself."[2] God's activity is clearly described thus in order to recall the "spiration of love" in the process of poetic creation advanced in *Purgatorio* 24. Retrospectively, then, the language about the creation of the soul draws on Dante's definition of his poetic practice as an analogy to the economy of God's own production of souls.

Another link holds together Cantos 25 and 26 of *Purgatorio*. Statius will provide an account for the origin of the soul: its genetic process is described from the sperm of the father to its incarnation, and its life is finally viewed in the eschatological context of the Resurrection. In *Purgatorio* 26, in short, Dante transposes the doctrine of the process of creation of the soul from its point of origin, the father's blood, to a genetic perspective whereby he can explain the question of literary generation: the relationship between Dante and Guinizelli is expressed in terms of the organic metaphor of the father-son relationship: "I hear name himself the father of me and of others my betters who ever used sweet and gracious rhymes of love."[3]

The literary-theological coherence of this sequence of cantos in what we have called an extended literary segment in *Purgatorio* does not, however, explain other aspects of *Purgatorio* 26. As in the two other parallel Cantos 26—those in *Inferno* and *Paradiso*—here again Dante raises the issue of language, specifically of foreign languages: in *Inferno* 26, Ulysses' rhetorical performance is said to take place in Greek, which he speaks with Virgil. In *Paradiso* 26 Dante meets the first poet of the human race, Adam. The conversation between them focuses on Hebrew, and the changes in the Hebrew names of God. In *Purgatorio* 26 Dante has Arnaut Daniel, a love poet whose sestina Dante much admired in his *De vulgari eloquentia,* speak using Dante's tercets but in his native Provençal: "*Tan m'abellis vostre cortes deman.*"[4]

In short, poetry comes through as the imaginative world of intimacy, one in which, much like in the world of Limbo, different epochs and different voices are bound together. At the same time, however, the poetic experience described over six cantos evokes a heterogeneous space where the unbound and the unbindable counter the bonds of affection and influence the poet. The ambiguous light of these cantos takes the pilgrim and the two poets flanking him, Statius and Virgil, to the edge of the Garden of Eden, where Dante will come face to face with his own history as well as the history of mankind, both of which demand a widening of his theological vision.

CHAPTER 15

Purgatorio 27–33

With Canto 26, the purgation of the pilgrim is complete. He has been going through the various stages of Purgatory, from pride to lust. In Canto 27, he crosses a wall of fire, so that he can be cleansed completely of all the stains that may be residual on his soul and thereby approach and enter the Garden of Eden. Canto 27 comes to a close with a passage that contains what are the last words that Virgil will speak. In fact, until Beatrice begins guiding him, the pilgrim will be morally on his own, and there is a very personal moment that stems from this attainment of self-mastery. Virgil says, "The temporal fire and the eternal you have seen"—meaning Hell and Purgatory—"my son, and are come to a part where I of myself I discern no farther onward."[1] This is the limitation of Virgil's vision. From now on the geometry of their relationship and the arrangement of their journey will be completely reversed.

Virgil continues: "Take henceforth your own pleasure for your guide."[2] What an extraordinary line! This is the poem of desire in the sense that what pushes the pilgrim to proceed and impels him to this journey of discovery and self-discovery is really desire. Desire is the moving force in him, but now the language changes. The first part of the journey is over and pleasure can become the only guide; he can go after what he likes. In a sense, it's an adumbration of free will. And the relationship between pleasure and happiness will be repeatedly dramatized in *Paradiso.* Then we get a description of the natural delights near the earthly paradise. It is as if Dante, simply by taking his own pleasure as his guide, has already reached an edenic place. Virgil speaks of a land spontaneously producing vegetation as a metaphor for the pilgrim, who is now capable of spontaneous action and spontaneous decisions. And Virgil is also recapitulating the first part of Dante's journey, which began in the wilderness and ended in a garden.

But then Dante must choose his own adventure, offered a choice by Virgil: "You may sit or go among them."[3] Is Dante going to make the journey to the Garden of Eden, which is a journey forward, but also a journey back in time? The Garden of Eden is behind all of us and yet lies ahead of us. The past is really the future. Is Dante going to think that the journey is the journey to the complacencies and beauty of the garden, to idleness? Or is he going to turn into an antipastoral poet, that is to say a poet who is always questioning the sense of arrival and moving on to new departures? *Paradiso* tells us that the latter is a more accurate assessment, but for now Virgil is just telling him the options he has. He can stay where he is, where Virgil will remain, or he can go farther. There's a peculiar language that resonates behind this moral dilemma placed before the pilgrim. It's called *felix culpa,* the idea that the fall of man was actually a happy fall because it allowed human beings to go beyond their previous state. So, Dante may sit and turn into an Adam figure, returning to the beauty and innocence of the garden, or he can surpass even that.

Finally, the teaching of Virgil has been completed, so he leaves Dante to himself: "Free, upright, and whole is your will, and it would be wrong not to act according to its pleasure; wherefore I crown and miter you over yourself."[4] This is the moment of the attainment of free will, so that the whole of *Purgatorio* moves between two poles: the pole of liberty, which was the object of Cato's quest through the wilderness of the Libyan desert, and now the pole of free will, which allows the pilgrim to view it not just as a point of arrival, but as the necessary precondition for moral life. You can only have an autonomous moral life in the measure in which you think you have free will. Now the pilgrim is his own responsibility. Ultimately, then, this is a kind of secular coronation ceremony. Virgil acts as a kind of lay priest, consecrating the attainment of self-mastery on Dante's part (Dante the poet, careful to use Virgil as an intermediary figure in this process of transferring power to the pilgrim).

Of course, once he's under the guidance of Beatrice, especially when it comes to *Paradiso,* aesthetics takes over. It's no longer an ethical problem. You may have heard about recent philosophers who think that life or knowledge is arranged according to stages: the aesthetic, the ethical, and then the theological. Dante reverses this order, so that the point that seems to be the most mature is the aesthetic one, which others may view as superficial or elementary, the one where perceptions are going to be engaged even before it is possible to get involved and mature in ethical experiences. Once you are in Paradise, you can only enjoy and get to know the world, so all the problems there are intellectual concerns, not moral issues.

We're not quite there yet, though. From Canto 28 to Canto 33, which is the end of *Purgatorio,* we come to a fragmentary area. We have a literary segment that we could call a pastoral oasis. It's also a representation of what in classical literature is called a *locus amoenus.* You may recall adumbrations of this phenomenon from Limbo. A lovely spot outside of the world of history where relaxation can take place, Dante also combines it with a biblical *hortus,* or enclosed garden, as found in the Song of Songs, for instance, or, more obviously, the Garden of Eden. The interesting thing about Dante's representation of the *locus amoenus* is that it's never really outside of history. The general assumption with this trope is that you have the garden and the city, and whenever life becomes unbearable in the city, you can take off for a villa in the garden and find aesthetic relief from the hustle and bustle of the city. Dante instead combines the two worlds. There's no easy position between them here, in the sense that the Garden of Eden is going to be a very problematical place in the poem, a place where the pilgrim is engaged in a self-confrontation and where he experiences some terrifying moments.

Let's examine how this representation is carried out, starting at the outset of Canto 28: "Eager now to search within and round about the divine forest green and dense, which tempered the new day to my eyes, without waiting longer I left the bank, taking the level ground very slowly over the soil that everywhere gives forth fragrance. A sweet breeze that had no variation in itself was striking on my brow with the force only of a gentle wind, by which the fluttering boughs all bent freely toward the quarter where the holy mountain casts its first shadow; yet were they not so deflected from their upright state that the little birds among the tops ceased practicing all their arts, but singing they greeted the morning hours with full joy among the leaves, which kept such burden to their rhymes as gathers from branch to branch through the pine forest on Chiassi's shore when Aeolus lets forth Sirocco."[5] A veritable warehouse of the pastoral tradition is on display here: a fragrance, a running brook, deep shade, birds that seem to rival human beings, introducing songs, a plenitude of the natural order and its innocence. An exception to that unblemished state is present, however, for Dante arrives, and though he has gone through the wall of fire in order to purify himself further, he is not a new Adam. He carries with him the stains of experience and of history, so there is desire that acts in him. An interesting element to this imperfect pastoral scene, one that carries with it the poignancy of autobiography, is that Dante is imagining the Garden of Eden as the pine wood near Ravenna, where he would take morning walks among pine trees on the way to the sea. And that, to him, was the garden: this mixture of the ordinary and the great sublime imagination.

His next few lines in the garden provoke a shock of recognition. He writes, "Now my slow steps had carried me on into the ancient wood so far that I could not see back to where I had entered it, when lo, a stream took from me further progress, which with its little waves was bending leftwards the grass that grew on its bank."[6] These lines are clearly meant to remind us of the very beginning of *Inferno*. The Garden of Eden is a different version of the wilderness that we saw before and left behind. We're just seeing it from a different perspective, which means that the supernatural world is just the natural world with a different lens. This reenactment of the drama of *Inferno* 1 is no shipwreck, though. The mountain has been climbed this time, and a new departure is going to take place. Dante stakes his claim as an antipastoral poet, as he dismisses, refuses, and repudiates all the temptations of gardens, of premature halting and self-enclosure in their luxurious fiction.

But something, or rather someone, does stop Dante in his tracks. Her name is Matelda, a woman who appears on the scene dancing, singing, and gathering flowers. She embodies a true aesthetic fascination for him. In this moment Dante becomes a practitioner of a form of traditional Provençal poetry called the *pastourelle*. The *pastourelle* involves a knight who goes to the woods or a meadow and meets a shepherdess, gets off his steed, and woos the young woman. Such a poem usually ends with a pun on the promises of the ecstasies of paradise, so it's an erotic kind of song. And the other principal Florentine practitioner of this genre was Dante's good friend Guido Cavalcanti. Dante is using the mode of Cavalcanti but definitively taking his distance from him. There's nothing of the overtones of erotic violence that Guido Cavalcanti had celebrated in his own version of the *pastourelle*. This is simply a love scene.

Now Dante has just come out of the circle of lust. He has cleansed himself, but there is a lingering trace of his history, his body, and his humanity. Thus he goes through the Garden of Eden as a fallen man who is not quite redeemed, certainly not reinstated into the innocence of the prelapsarian garden. As such, it's no surprise that he finds the fair lady to be so distracting. He explains his perceptions of her and the obstacle she represents through a series of three mythological images. First he says to her,

"You make me recall where and what Proserpine was at the time her mother"—Ceres—"lost her, and she the spring." He thinks of her as Proserpine, or Persephone, the young woman who was picking flowers on the plains of Enna in Sicily when death came and snatched her away. In other words, loving another human being can be a kind of death itself. The second mythological image is more telling: "I do not believe that so great a light shone forth under the lids of Venus, transfixed by her son against all his custom." It's the story of Venus wounded by the arrows of Cupid and falling in love with him. It's more telling because it's Dante's way of casting, without going into a full psychoanalytical explanation, the Garden of Eden as a representation of the desire to return to the state of infancy, of the child with the mother. But he understands that this fantasy would lead him nowhere. Finally, the third image is also erotic, but now with distance involved: "The river kept us three paces apart, but Hellespont where Xerxes passed it—ever a curb on all human pride—did not suffer more hatred from Leander for its swelling waters between Sestos and Abydos than that from me because it did not open then."[7] So, an insurmountable barrier exists between Matelda and the pilgrim, which is to say between Dante and his fantasy of what the Garden of Eden could be. And Dante has no choice but to continue.

He goes on to explain the mechanics of the Garden of Eden and then the canto ends with a more accessible fantasy represented by this *locus amoenus*. Dante writes, " 'They who in olden times sang of the Age of Gold and its happy state perhaps in Parnassus dreamed of this place. Here the root of mankind was innocent; here is always spring, and every fruit; this is the nectar of which each tells.' I turned then right round to my poets, and saw that with a smile they had heard these last words."[8] From Dante's point of view, the perplexity that he feels is also the perplexity of Virgil and the perplexity of Statius. They know no more than he does now. The burden of this passage is that Dante is clearly alluding to the bucolic quality of this place, but also suggesting that the ancient poets prefigured the Garden of Eden in their fabulous visions of the Golden Age. He's establishing a link between their poetic visions and this encounter that he has in the Garden of Eden, which becomes a bucolic fantasy of poets and Parnassus, all of which are projections of Dante's poetic imagination.

From the distraction of Matelda, however, we move to Canto 30 and the introduction of a far more crucial female figure, Beatrice. Beatrice is linked to the number three, so it makes sense that Canto 30 is where Beatrice arrives. And for those of you who are lovers of the symmetry in the poem, Canto 30 of *Paradiso* is the canto where Beatrice will disappear. Her residence in the poem lasts for exactly 33 cantos. Her name is three times the good. She's linked to three (in the form of nine, which is the square of three) in the *Vita nuova.* It's a reference to the arcane significance of her presence in the pilgrim's life.

Canto 30 describes a double drama, though: the arrival of Beatrice but also the disappearance of Virgil, a changing of the guard, as it were. As a result, there are two contrasting moods, one of elegy for the loss of Virgil and the other of sacred terror at the appearance of Beatrice. The canto begins with singing—"*Veni, sponsa, de Libano*"—that echoes the Song of Songs, a sublime love poem, extending the erotics of previous cantos in anticipation of Beatrice's presence. Dante continues, "As the blessed at the last Trump will rise ready each from his tomb, singing Hallelujah with re-clad voice, so upon the divine chariot, *ad vocem tanti senis*, rose up a hundred ministers and messengers of life eternal, who all cried: '*Benedictus qui venis.*'"[9] This cry is an allusion to the greetings of Jesus when he comes to Jerusalem. Beatrice is coming into Dante's story the way that Jesus came into history. Beatrice will come into the soul of the lover wrapped in an aura of Christological language, and she will become grace or the way that one can experience grace in the world through direct love aimed at oneself. And then we get further Latin phrases, including one image taken straight out of *The Aeneid,* in homage to Virgil, who is about to disappear. The Latin citations demonstrate the interwoven nature of Dante's interpersonal dramas, revealing both the meaning of Beatrice in the life of the pilgrim and the meaning of the loss of Virgil as a poet and as Dante's guide.

The fragment from *The Aeneid* refers to the premature death that Virgil celebrates in a very elegiac way in book 6, when Aeneas goes down into Hades in order to see the whole of history. This is the descent to see his father Anchises, from whom the future of Aeneas and of all mankind is going to stem. At one point Anchises indicates to Aeneas the shade of a young man named Marcellus, who sits off to the side and who died too young, and he says that all throw lilies with open hands, the lily being a funereal symbol like chrysanthemums. This image of premature death is linked to Beatrice, who also died prematurely, and to Virgil, because it's an anticipation of the loss of the poet-guide. It is as if Virgil's vision was under the aegis of mortality and finitude because his song is limited to the world of death.

And so Virgil is lost and a new guide found. She arrives in elegant dress that resembles the Italian flag: "Olive-crowned over a white veil a lady appeared to me, clad, under a green mantle, with hue of living flame; and my spirit, which now for so long a time trembling with awe in her presence had not been overcome, without having more knowledge by the eyes, through occult virtue that proceeded from her, felt old love's great power."[10] This is a rewriting of the early autobiographical work of Dante, the *Vita nuova*. He's experiencing the presence of Beatrice through the effects that she has on him: the courtly love, the sweet new style, the trembling, the inability to speak.

In response, Dante turns to Virgil for succor, but Virgil is gone, suddenly vanished: "As soon as on my sight the lofty virtue smote which already had pierced me before I was out of my boyhood, I turned to the left with the confidence of a little child that runs to his mother when he is frightened or in distress, to say to Virgil, 'Not a drop of blood is left in me that does not tremble: I know the tokens of the ancient flame.' But Virgil had left us bereft of himself."[11] Dante is scared and seeking guidance, about to say he knows "the token of the ancient flame," a translation of the words Dido uses when she meets Aeneas in Hades, another image of death and mortality taken from *The Aeneid*. Dante clearly links Virgil with that kind of metaphor of the limitation of passion. No matter their sentiments and shared experience, Dante is alone now, and Virgil is a part of his past.

Beatrice, sensing Dante's distress at this turn of events, speaks her first words in the *Comedy*: "'Dante, because Virgil leaves you, do not weep yet, for you must weep for another sword!' Like an admiral who goes to stern and bow to see the men that are serving on the other ships, and to encourage them to do well, so on the left side of the chariot—when I turned at the sound of my name, which of necessity is registered here—I saw the lady, who first appeared to me veiled under the angelic festival, direct her eyes to me beyond the stream. Although the veil that fell from her head, encircled with Minerva's leaves, did not let her be seen distinctly, royally and ever stern in her mien, she continued, like one who speaks and keeps back the hottest words till the last, 'Look at me well: indeed I am, indeed I am Beatrice! How did you deign to climb the mountain? Did you not know that here man is happy?'"[12] This is the first, and only, time in the poem that Dante's name is heard. She will never call him Dante again, and he has never been called Dante before. In other words, this is the point where the poem, from the epic that it has been—the epic of desire, the epic of hope, memory, and justice—now becomes an autobiography. With the loss of Virgil, the epic poet, we shift in genre, and the poem is now about the specificity and irreducibility of Dante's own experience.

Furthermore, Dante emphasizes the necessity of including his name here. What necessity? Why would one go on speaking of oneself? One speaks of oneself because one wants to be exemplary to others. One believes that what one has experienced is crucial for somebody else's knowledge and experience, or one wants to exempt one's own name from vituperation. In the philosophical text the *Convivio,* Dante claims that there are two people who have spoken about themselves in exemplary ways: one is Augustine in *The Confessions,* and the other is Boethius in *The Consolation of Philosophy.* Dante is alluding to these two autobiographical texts, both of which render talking about oneself a necessity, as he states in this passage.

Canto 31 continues the story of Dante's failures when Beatrice died, as told first in the *Vita nuova,* when he sought out someone who could replace Beatrice. Dante indulges in a confession, an Augustinian moment, another part of the autobiographical shift, but his first attempt is a stuttering, speechless one. Beatrice, in an inversion of the roles in Canto 5 of *Inferno,* asks Dante to resume his temporarily blocked admission, as if it were the same sort of confession of a failing that Francesca offered up in Hell. And Dante does resume: "After drawing a bitter sigh, I barely had the voice to make answer, and my lips shaped it with difficulty. Weeping, I said, 'The present things, with their false pleasure, turned my steps aside, as soon as your countenance was hidden.'" He finally alludes to his change of heart as soon as Beatrice died, and so Beatrice may proceed with her first act of guidance: "Still, that you may now bear shame for your error, and another time, hearing the Sirens, may be stronger, lay aside the seed of tears and listen: so shall you hear how in opposite direction my buried flesh ought to have moved thee."[13] She is preparing to teach Dante an ethical lesson.

What makes this passage so extraordinary, though, is how it helps us to gloss retrospectively what was a fairly mysterious allegory in *Purgatorio.* You may remember when Dante met the siren in his dreams and then a lady appeared. The siren was an allegory of a temptation, specifically an erotic temptation. Then an enigmatic woman arrives and manages to send away the siren. She wakes up the pilgrim and allows the journey to continue. Now we know for sure that the mystery woman was none other than Beatrice.

So, she is now glossing the scene of the siren that appeared in Canto 19, but there is more to her words. There is a little phrase that Beatrice uses, "another time," which suggests that the encounter with the siren is not just an event that happened in the past. It can happen all over again. And since it can still happen in the future, Dante's conversion, which the poem has been telling us—especially now that it has attained a kind of autobiographical quality—is not over and has to be understood as an ongoing journey. The future is just as fraught with temptations as the past was. Thus, what Dante changes is the Augustinian idea of a conversion that takes place once and for all. In other words, once again, we witness the antipastoral imagination of the poet. Do not believe that you can ever stop on the way, Dante warns the reader. Do not ever believe that there are truths that are going to be unchallenged or untested in time. Dante is irresistibly drawn to the idea that the future is still part of his experience.

And in keeping with that future-oriented outlook, after Cantos 31 and 32, that respectively deal with the pilgrim's confession and the with the allegory of Church history, we come to Canto 33, the end of *Purgatorio*, where I really want to focus on one passage in particular, a prophecy that Beatrice makes. Beatrice promises a deliverer who will come. The argument is no longer about Dante himself; now it's about history. Is there a deliverance for history? Is it possible for the whole human family to return to a place that is, if not in the Garden of Eden as such, then at least among the towers of the true city, as Dante calls it in his political tract the *Monarchia*? The prophecy refers to a figure that may enter human history, but only at the end of time, so that the whole poem is literally poised at the outer edge of time.

Beatrice speaks as a tough teacher while she delivers her prophecy to Dante:

> From fear and from shame I wish that you henceforth divest yourself, so that you may no more speak like one who is dreaming. Know that the vessel which the serpent broke was, and is not: but let him whose fault it is believe that God's vengeance fears no hindrance. Not for all time shall be without an heir the eagle [probably the eagle of the empire] that left its feathers on the chariot, whereby it became a monster and then a prey: for I see surely, and therefore I tell of it, stars already close at hand, secure from all check and hindrance, that shall bring us a time wherein a Five Hundred, Ten, and Five, sent by God, shall slay the thievish woman, with that giant who sins with her. And perhaps my prophecy, obscure as Themis and Sphinx, persuades you less because, after their fashion, it darkens your mind; but soon the facts shall be the Naiads that will solve this hard enigma, without loss of flocks or of harvest.[14]

With some criticism of Dante, Beatrice offers up an enigmatic vision of the future. It's not quite clear, and the lack of clarity only adds, I think, to the fear and the speculations about what this all means.

At its heart is a numerical symbol, which is written five hundred, ten, and five: 515. Medieval numerical symbolism views numbers as containing the essence of the secret of creation. Thinkers like Isidore of Seville claimed that to take the number away from things will result in those things falling apart. Some of the speculations as to the meaning of this specific number are utterly hilarious. There were some who believed that it refers to the year 1315, since 800 was the year of Charlemagne's declaring the Holy Roman Empire and adding 515 gives you 1315. Therefore, Dante was thinking about an imminent event in his own time. But there's nothing in the text that would allow us to see this idea as credible.

Another ridiculous interpretation revolves around a rearrangement of the roman numerals DXV, 515, to spell DUX, or "Duce" in Italian, a common nickname for Mussolini. Yes, some have actually said Dante was making a prophecy of the eventual rise of Mussolini. Absurd.

So, what *does* it mean? For the best solution, I turn to two historians, who found an explanation in medieval illustrations of the Roman Catholic mass. There's a moment in the mass where there's a so-called antiphonal prayer, the idea that Christ is coming sacramentally; it says, "it is truly right and just." In Latin the phrase is "vere dignum et justum est," and the letter V at the beginning of the phrase is brought into contact with an X, in the form of a cross that joins the human (also V, or U, *uomo*) and the divine (D for *Dio*). Thus the enigma of Beatrice evokes the apocalyptic end of time, the eschatological time when Christ will return to the earth. First he came as a human being signaled by the number five, but he will come a second time in the splendor of his divinity, and the humanity and divinity are joined by the X of the cross. This interpretation, by R. E. Kaske and G. R. Sarolli, is a great discovery, but it too is not without its problems.

If Dante believes in some kind of imminent end of time and this is to be understood as an apocalyptic symbol of an imminent end of time, Dante would be what is called a Joachist. In *Paradiso* we'll encounter a man by the name of Joachim of Flora who had a theory of history in a kind of tripartite structure. The idea is that history is patterned on the Trinity, so there is an age of the father, which roughly goes from creation to the time of the biblical patriarchs. Then there is the age of the son, which goes from the time of the Incarnation to roughly 1260, Joachim's time. Finally, there's the age of the spirit, which goes from 1260 to a time when, thanks to the fraternal orders, all structures and institutions will disappear, and mankind will experience a time of brotherhood and chastity. There will be no marriages, no state, nothing. If Dante were a Joachist, though, that would create a number of problems because what I have just been describing was viewed as a most heretical vision of history. Why was it heretical? With this idea of an age of the father, an age of the son, and an age of the spirit, Joachim of Flora was in effect undoing the unity of the Trinity. He was dividing the Trinity into three distinct parts, and no less a great theologian of Dante's own time than Bonaventure—whom Dante will encounter very soon in Paradise, and with whom he will discuss this very Joachim of Flora—declares Joachim of Flora heretical. So if this very powerful explanation that Dante's really alluding to the second coming when Christ will return to earth to restore the Messianic advent is accurate, is Dante therefore a heretical, apocalyptic writer?

I am doubtful because there's no poet I know who cares more about institutions and believes that they *are* history. Of course he attacks them insomuch as he thinks that they need to be revitalized, refreshed, and improved. But you cannot go on attacking these institutions without believing in their vital importance in history. He talks about the empire, the Church, the law, the family, all institutions that preserve their enduring importance.

But if he's not an apocalyptic writer, what is he? I think that this allusion is indeed to the second coming, but that Dante has removed all of the Joachist paraphernalia that generally accompanied such a prophecy. His version doesn't refer to the "now" of history; it refers instead to a time that nobody can really fathom, nothing imminent or within the scope of linear history. These logical complications are a necessary addition to an excellent explanation of the prophetic image, which would otherwise be too neat and simple.

It is with this prophecy of the end of times that *Purgatorio* climaxes. After it, Dante has to be ritually immersed in two rivers—the river Lethe, the river of forgetfulness, and the river Eunoè, the river of good memories—a ritual that ought to remind you of the ritual actions at the beginning of Canto 1, when Dante washed his face and had to gird his loins with the reed that was growing spontaneously on the shore of the sea. As Dante explains, the two rivers, Lethe and Eunoe, flow out of the same source, and like two friends who are fond of each other, they depart from each other only very lazily. The two continue to be intertwined, so that there's no erasure that is not at the same time a memory. Each—memory and forgetfulness—contains the other.

Finally, the whole of *Purgatorio* ends with a line that obviously recalls the end of *Inferno:* "I came forth from the most holy waves, renovated even as new trees renewed with new foliage, pure and ready to rise to the stars."[15] Dante is once again ready for the journey to continue. Now, he is at the top of Mount Purgatory, and he will soon fly on, like lightning, to the moon. There he commences the planetary, cosmological epic that is *Paradiso.*

CHAPTER 16

Paradiso 1–2

Now we move beyond the earthly paradise into *Paradiso*. As we read the third canticle, we find that Dante uses a Ptolemaic structure of the cosmos. For him, as for Ptolemy, the earth is at the center of the universe—unmoved, immobile—and there are seven planets that circle around it: the moon is thought of as a planet, Mercury, the sun (also thought of as a planet), Venus, Mars, Jupiter, and Saturn. Beyond that there is the heaven of the so-called fixed stars, the Prime Mover in the ninth sphere, and beyond that the Empyrean, the heaven of fire. From the Prime Mover all motion begins, from it time starts. Out there at the edge is really where the roots of time are found, stretching out into the finite world; so that we find ourselves in the shadows of the leaves of time, which are always falling and being re-placed. Such is the layout of Dante's Ptolemaic cosmos.

Another thing we have to keep in mind in Paradise is that Dante links each of the planets with one of the liberal arts, a propensity of his mentioned previously. He begins with grammar in the moon, and so you have to expect that you will find there the language of grammarians and a very wide definition of what grammar can be. It includes poetry. It includes history. It even includes some rhetorical tropes. And then there's the heaven of Mercury, tied to dialectic (which means logic here), and so you find the language of dialectic deployed throughout the canto. The heaven of Venus is linked with rhetoric, probably the least surprising connection, that of eros and rhetoric. They have an old kinship, and they seem to entail each other. Then Dante couples the heaven of Mars, the god of war, with music, in the persuasion that music is a harmony made of discordant parts. As a result, there is a kind of simultaneous attraction and strife within this heaven. Then there's geometry, linked with the temperateness of Jupiter, and then astronomy and Saturn. The heaven of the fixed stars, at least in *Convivio,* is tied to physics and metaphysics, and the Prime Mover is associated with ethics. Finally, the heaven of the Empyrean is the heaven of metaphysics and theology, a sign that Dante has changed his mind since writing the *Convivio,* where he had claimed that ethics was the first and most important of the arts, the discipline to which all other arts are subordinated and toward which they all point. When Dante writes *Paradiso,* he acknowledges that you cannot quite separate ethics from a metaphysical theory about the being of the world. Dante will go on back and forth in reconfiguring the relation of those two disciplines.

The other thing that I should mention before we go on is that much of *Paradiso* is going to come across as a way of teaching. It's already implied that this should be the thrust of *Paradiso* by the very idea that there is the disposition of the arts and sciences throughout the canticle. Dante's interplanetary journey is an educational voyage: he goes through grammar, rhetoric, dialectic, and so on until he reaches metaphysics and theology. This pedagogical structure is carried out by the focus on teaching that Beatrice will deliver.

In fact, it must also be noted that Dante's teacher in *Paradiso*—and this is an innovative, imaginative, and highly unusual move on the part of a poet—is not some kind of abstract matron called Dame Philosophy. It's not an allegory of nature. You do find some didactic allegories where nature appears as a disheveled woman, wounded, because nature has fallen, teaching the pilgrim about the secrets and the wealth of nature. But there is a far more personal education taking place here. Dante learns from his beloved, to be sure, someone who replaces all the other likely candidates for his instruction, like Aquinas, Boethius, Bonaventure, all figures whom he meets. And yet, it's a mistake to believe, as some great scholars of Dante have said in the past, that *Paradiso* is ultimately a journey to be like Beatrice. Why? Because Beatrice will disappear. She will still be within view up to a point in Paradise, but her role ends with Canto 30, after which a historical figure, a mystic by the name of Bernard of Clairvaux, will take charge of Dante's education.

Some of you may claim that, in spite of the absence of abstract allegory, *Paradiso* is meant to be an account of a mystical experience, that Dante goes beyond his own self, beyond any idea of a rational understanding of the world. He surrenders his own subjectivity to an insight into the whole of being. But I don't think that this is what's happening here. Dante does preserve his rationality and his sense of separation from some kind of cosmological absolute. There *is* a way in which Dante deploys the language of the mystics, but this is not to be read as a transcription of a mystical experience so that the text then goes on in an approximation of what the mystic "saw" and becomes ineffable. Dante occasionally uses the language of ineffability, but it remains a poetic construction, an imaginative projection into the absolute unknown, into a space no other imagination had really traveled. Those who have traveled there never came back to tell us about it. Dante will play with that. His language battles against the threatening boundaries of silence. Of course, from a Christian point of view, Dante's defeat at the hands of silence would be a victory, but Dante is suspended between those two poles.

Ultimately, this third and final canticle is a poem about beauty, in the sense that here Dante will try to understand what beauty really is. Plotinus says that it's the visibility of being, that the whole of life becomes visible only because we have perceptions and images of it. Dante's trying to see that, but he is also exploring what it is that lies beyond what we see. He knows beauty is not skin-deep, although one of the dangers of focusing on beauty is that it can be seen as no more than the surface of things. Dante will inhabit a space between appearances and the idea that there are essences lying beyond them.

With that introduction to *Paradiso* in mind, let's get into Canto 1. It begins, "The glory of the All-Mover penetrates through the universe and reglows in one part more, and in another less."[1] The rhythm and even the syntactical structure of the poem shifts here. At the beginning of the other canticles, the poet immediately casts himself in the role of the agent: "in the middle of the journey of my life I found myself" (*Inferno*) and "to course over better waters the boat of my genius now goes and I will sing" (*Purgatorio*). Not so in *Paradiso*. Here the first tercet seeks to bracket the idea of the self and subjectivity. It emphasizes instead the question of God, who becomes the agent here. So God is the one who moves all, and all then becomes one, "the universe" in the next line. The tercet presents God through a circumlocution, not a God who is visible through His effects but a God who appears as a cause.

But we also see the effects in the form of the glory that is his light. Dante ushers in a change in the history of the word *glory*. That's what poets do; they invent and reinvent language. "Glory," in the classical era and all the way down to the Renaissance and the Romantic age, means fame. It's the power we have to survive, to have a posthumous life because of whatever noble deeds heroes may have achieved. For Dante, though, glory means light, which is now linked to two verbs, *penetrates* and *reglows*. So, the first tercet presents God in a cosmological role that is double: one of motion and one of light, a combination of an Aristotelian idea of God as the Prime Mover, and a Neoplatonic idea of God as the principle of light. In both cases, God participates in, is part of, creation, and the natural world is part of the supernatural world. There is not just a causality that begins all things and then somehow retreats into a sort of invisible and unknown nonspace of its soul.

The other element of this first tercet that I want to emphasize is the principle of hierarchy. Light shines "more and less." This is really a great problem for Dante in other parts of the poem. Differences are very crucial for Dante because they allow us to know things that can be known only through differences. That's the value of hierarchy. It is a structure that unifies all differences according to the principle of degree and yet keeps individualities intact. And here God is diffused throughout the entirety of the hierarchy.

However, as I said in the last chapter, Dante is not a mystic. Subjectivity is not erased. So now, Dante introduces the subject, saying, "*I* have been in the heaven that most receives of His light"—that is to say that Dante is in the Empyrean, as close to God as he could possibly be—"and have seen things which who so descends from up there has neither the knowledge nor the power to relate."[2] And no sooner does Dante introduce his subjectivity and this intimacy with the beatific vision than he also has to cast himself as a visionary, for he "had seen things." All of *Paradiso* is about the refinement of sight. Dante has an internal vision, not like Homer, who is blind and therefore sees everything with his inner eye, but in the sense that Dante can see things as a whole. That's the difference between the ear, which only allows you to hear in a linear way so that things can come from all sides but you only catch one thing at a time, and the eye, the organ that gives you the chance to see totalities. The expansiveness of Dante's vision enables the infinite scope of his poem.

He goes on to explain the status of his poetic language vis-à-vis this vision: "As it draws near to its desire, our intellect enters so deep that memory cannot go back upon the track." The intellect longs for the objects that it desires, but forgetfulness intervenes; so, Dante may have intuition and insight into things, but cannot quite recall them. "Nevertheless," he continues, "so much of the holy kingdom as I could treasure up in my mind shall now be matter of my song."[3] Whatever he's going to tell us is literally a shadow of things he manages to remember. It makes sense that he should not remember because one of the paradoxes of this poetic construction is the impossibility of retaining in his mind a finite sight of the infinite. How could that be rendered poetically if not through vestiges and shadows? How can memory, a metaphor of time by definition, hold that which is without time? *Paradiso* becomes a poem of paradox from its outset.

But with his next breath, Dante turns to the god of poets, Apollo, and casts himself in a passive mode, as a vessel, one who receives. It's the language of restraint. In a sense it's the classical commonplace of asking the muse to breathe through us. Specifically, Dante requests that Apollo "for this last labor make me such a vessel of your worth as you require for granting your beloved laurel."[4] He recalls the story of the god chasing Daphne, the object of his desire whom he cannot truly have. He can only obtain the young maiden in the form of a metaphor, the laurel crown. So the possession of the object becomes dislocated, not quite what the god himself wanted, and this introduces an idea of Dante's own journey in *Paradiso*.

And yet, Dante will shortly contrast this passivity with an image of violence. Although in humble language, he says, "Thus far the one peak of Parnassus has sufficed me, but now I have need of both, as I enter the arena that remains." There's a struggle now. In the arena battles are fought, a reality emphasized by Dante's next demand: "Enter into my breast and breathe there as when you drew Marsyas from the sheath of his limbs"—an echo of the struggle between the poet and the god. Dante does not actually want to be like Marsyas, because the latter, out of presumption—so that you will soon understand Dante's language of restraint and withholding—had tried to outdo Apollo, who defeated and flayed him. This passage is about the fear of the battle for the description of Paradise, the fear that he may be usurping God's role, the fear that he may be transgressing and violating that which is the sovereign claim of the divinity. This fear of blaspheming is on full display as he continues: "O divine Power, if you do so lend yourself to me that I may show forth the image of the blessed realm which is imprinted in my mind, you shall see me come to your beloved tree"—of laurel—"and crown me with those leaves of which the matter and you shall make me worthy. So rarely, father, are they gathered, for triumph of caesar or of poet—fault and shame of human wills—that the Peneian frond ought to beget gladness in the glad Delphic deity whenever it causes anyone to long for it. A great flame follows a little spark."[5] Dante is struggling to be able to describe the heavens fittingly, but he is constantly aware of and aiming to prevent the possibility of hubris in such an attempt.

Throughout, Dante is moving. He thinks he's on earth but he soon discovers that he's actually in the heaven of the moon. Here he describes a self-transformation that occurs as a result of this motion: "Beatrice was standing with her eyes all fixed upon the eternal wheels, and I fixed mine on her, withdrawn from there above. Gazing upon her I became within me such as Glaucus became on tasting of the grass that made him sea-fellow of the other gods."[6] It's a story of the pilgrim shifting into another level of experience and being. Dante references another Ovidian account, this time of Glaucus who becomes immortal and lives in the sea after tasting some magical herbs. Dante indicates that a similar change has occurred in his case, placing emphasis on its internal nature with that little preposition "within." The transformation occurs from within himself, not in some external fashion.

Then Dante will have another encounter with the divine. He writes, "Whether I was but that part of me which Thou didst create last, O Love that rulest the heavens, Thou knowest, who with Thy light didst lift me."[7] This is a reference to the Second Letter to the Corinthians, where St. Paul tells the story of his being rapt to the third heaven. What happens to Paul there? In the Middle Ages, what was meant by the third heaven was the third mode of vision. There are levels of vision that they emphasized: a literal, worldly level, an imaginative level, and the ecstatic level that Paul experienced. Paul went to the third heaven and had a beatific vision, and when he returned, he could not speak about it because what he saw had to be kept wrapped in silence. The whole of *Paradiso* is about limits and the impossibility of establishing clear limits, so Dante will do what Paul himself could not do. Paul believed that the silence was the proper language of his sublime experience, but Dante will go on speaking until he really has forgotten everything that he has seen. Dante is establishing his own poetic powers somewhere between two different modalities: he doesn't want to go as presumptuously far as Marsyas did, but he also does not want to retreat as Paul did.

To truly understand Dante's perception of his poetic powers, however, we will step briefly outside of the poem. While living in Ravenna, Dante decides to send the first ten cantos of *Paradiso* to the so-called Cangrande, the "great dog" of Verona, who had been his patron for a number of years, and he introduces those ten cantos with a letter now referred to as the "Letter to Cangrande." In this letter Dante references Aristotle, Ezekiel, Richard of St. Victor, Bernard of Clairvaux, and Daniel in order to justify his possibly transgressive descriptions of a visionary experience in *Paradiso*.

The poem, like the letter, invokes a number of models in the contemplative philosophical tradition. Again, Dante is not a student of the prophetic tradition, but he makes the prophets and the philosophers agree here. Readers of the Bible may argue, he notes, that there is no necessary link in the Bible between the mystics, those who have visions, and prophets. But for Dante these are not different experiences or different states. Dante thinks that the two go hand in hand. You have to have vision in order to speak, and that's the sense of poetry that Dante invokes here at the beginning of *Paradiso.*

Less abstractly, Dante is still trying to find out what is happening to him. He thought he was on earth, in the earthly paradise, but now he seems to be on another planet. Beatrice dismisses some fantasies of his about these strange circumstances: "You make yourself dull with false imagining, so that you do not see what you would see had you cast it off. You are not on earth, as you believe; but lightning, fleeing its proper site, never darted so fast as you are returning to yours." Dante has been traveling at the speed of light to go from the earthly paradise to the moon, so quickly that it was beyond perception. But the questions do not end with this explanation. "If by these brief words which she smiled to me I was freed from my perplexity," Dante says, "within a new one I became the more enmeshed; and I said: 'I was already content concerning one great wonder; but now I marvel how it can be that I should pass through these light bodies.'"[8] *Paradiso* unfolds via a narrative economy in which the pilgrim experiences perplexities and doubts that Beatrice clarifies, and in turn those responses go on triggering new doubts. It's an unending process of the mind enlarging itself, though it always remains filled with wonder.

What is this wonder? It is, first of all, a definition of the aesthetics of *Paradiso.* "Wonder" is a translation of the Latin *admiratio,* a term that in the Middle Ages meant nothing less than the sublime. It's a Greek notion of indicating that the mind is overwhelmed with the spectacle of things that dwarf it. Those things that the mind cannot quite comprehend, they are the sublime. They can be the sublime in nature; they can be the sublime in art; they can be other forms of the sublime. Dante's mode of Paradise thus involves an oscillation of a mind that is opening up, full of doubts, subjective, critical, and then the experience of the sublime overwhelming that open mind.

This idea of the sublime introduces the way in which Beatrice will deliver an image of the universe to Dante. With a sigh and a glance that labels Dante as akin to a misguided child, Beatrice offers Dante his first picture of the universe. We will find that this picture is subsequently refined in a number of ways, but this initial image is what he can understand now.

Beatrice tells him that "all things have order among themselves, and this is the form that makes the universe like God."[9] The picture that Beatrice evokes for Dante is one of beauty, which in turn implies vision, because beauty is defined as that which is seen giving one pleasure, at least according to Aquinas. Here Beatrice steps beyond the subjective immediacy of Aquinas's conception of beauty and thinks, as Aquinas also does with his notion of beauty as a transcendental, of an objective order of the world. Beauty usually implies a self, a personal taste, a very rich medieval understanding of the aesthetic experience, but there is also an objective idea of the whole universe laid out in order, shape, and clarity. These proportions and arrangements are the attributes of this cosmological beauty, so perfect that the universe even resembles God! This seems to be such a nice way of thinking about the universe, but if you really think about it, it could easily be seen as a heretical proposition. If the universe is like God, what are we to make of the evil that there is in the universe? Is there continuity between God's transcendence and God's immanence? Fortunately, Beatrice will soon clarify this stance.

This talk of how the universe resembles God is only the beginning of Beatrice's discourse on the natural order of things. She continues: "The high creatures behold the imprint of the Eternal Worth, which is the end wherefore the aforesaid ordinance is made. In the order whereof I speak all natures are inclined by different lots." We all have our own specific gravity. We're all drawn by our desires. There's a kind of natural instinct, a natural movement, in the way in which a stone, if you drop it, always falls to the ground because of its specific gravity, and the fire, if you light a candle, always moves upward. This specific gravity is also a spiritual gravity, enacting movement on the soul, for "not only does this bow shoot those creatures that lack intelligence, but also those that have intellect and love"—meaning humanity, in an expansion of his earlier great poem about "women who have intellect and love." But we are not necessarily always guided by this instinct. Beatrice explains, "To be sure, even as a shape often does not accord with the intention of the art, because the material is deaf to respond, so the creature sometimes departs from this course, having the power, thus impelled, to swerve toward some other part; and even as the fire from a cloud may be seen to fall downwards"—lightning, for instance, is fire moving downward rather than upward—"so the primal impulse, diverted by false pleasure, is turned toward earth."[10] In other words, within her description of the order of the cosmos, Beatrice goes on to say that human beings are the odd figures, who somehow have the power to deviate from this pattern of order. We can undo. We have a paradoxical freedom that allows us either to stay within a particular idea of what God may have meant for us or to breach that particular order. Human beings are the absurd elements in this otherwise ordered portrait of the universe, and with this statement of freedom, Dante eschews a deterministic idea of the cosmos, which would render the text heretical.

Having thus explored the bigger picture, in Canto 2 Dante can examine his new surroundings more closely. He begins by discussing a commonly known fable of the moon and its spots. There was a medieval legend explaining why, if you look at a full moon, you see dark spots. The legend was that Cain, riding away from the knowledge of the murder of his brother, had actually, with the help of God, been removed from the earth. He had taken refuge on the moon, and whatever we see there is thus the imprint of Cain. Dante dismisses this fable and engages in a scientific discourse with Beatrice. Do we see shadows on the moon simply because there's a density of matter? Or is it because light has a way of going through this matter of the moon? Or is it because there's a different way in which light is distributed here? The solution that Dante gives through Beatrice is that we see the shadows on the moon simply because there is a different source of light. But in broader terms, he is saying that the natural cosmos has to be understood according to its metaphysics as well. The physics can only be understood in terms of the metaphysics, so that Dante always sees the natural and the supernatural as going hand in hand. They are not two separate dimensions. They are simply two different ways of looking at the same thing.

Dante's own sense of this new realm and how far he has come spurs him to address the readers who have accompanied him on this journey. He says, "O you that are in your little bark, eager to hear, following behind my ship that singing makes her way, turn back to see again your shores. Do not commit yourselves to the open sea, for perchance, if you lost me, you would remain astray. The water which I take was never coursed before."[11] This message gives poignancy to the little bark in spite of the fact that the language of humility is now suspect in the face of the trope of sublimity that Dante has brought into focus in this canticle. It's a little bark that is doing something so mighty; Dante is aboard it on a magnificent, extraordinary adventure.

So he's urging his readers to turn back, but then he limits the agents that he is addressing: "You other few who lifted up your necks." He makes a reductive apostrophe, aimed at only the crème de la crème of his readership, a select group who are truly interested in the mysteries of the most esoteric, arcane sciences that he's going to navigate now. In full, he says, "You other few who lifted up your necks betimes for bread of angels"—for knowledge—"on which men here subsist but never become sated of it, you may indeed commit your vessel to the deep brine, holding my furrow ahead of the water that turns smooth again. Those glorious ones who crossed the sea to Colchis, when they saw Jason turned plowman, were not as amazed"—once again the language of admiration and the sublime—"as you shall be."[12] The metaphor of the journey by water to describe an aerial journey indicates that Dante is clearly thinking of a similar metaphoric compression that we saw with Ulysses. The sailing that became a mad flight is now a flight that becomes a sailing. Dante recognizes that he is guiding us, so he feels a sense of responsibility to turn us back, unlike Ulysses, who led his companions astray. But we dispose of that mythic resonance fairly quickly, for what he's really saying is that the journey we're undertaking, which is the reading of this book, can become extraordinarily dangerous as he travels over water that leaves no wake behind it. This is what I would call the danger of seafaring. In seafaring, you have no preestablished routes. There is no way, no road, no path that can be fixed and easily found, so although Dante is inviting us to keep very close to him, we might still lose him.

Then finally, he alludes to Jason, the hero of the Argonauts, who goes looking for the Golden Fleece. It's an image that also appears at the end of *Paradiso* 33, where Dante has the god Neptune from the depths wondering at the extraordinary power of the human imagination and the human will as expressed by the heroics of Jason. Neptune can't quite believe what he sees. It's an allusion to what Dante himself is going to do by seeing God face to face and then returning to the earth. However, in Canto 18 of *Inferno*, we find Jason punished among the flatters and seducers because he is famous for seducing Hypsiphyle and then abandoning her. Thus Dante is positing an interesting distinction between the ethical judgment of Jason, who is suffering in Hell, and the imaginative aesthetic value of the adventure itself. Is he saying therefore that the good and the beautiful are really two distinct things? He's warning us about the dangers of conflating them, and we'll see his ideas on the value of images versus the ethics of images play out over the course of *Paradiso*.

CHAPTER 17

Paradiso 3–10

In *Paradiso* 3, Dante meets two women, the empress Constance (the irony of the name is a little bit obvious among the inconstant spirits) and Piccarda, who had joined a cloister and taken the name of Sister Constance, as well. She was later forced to leave the cloister on account of her brother Corso Donati's political maneuvers, however. He wanted her married to an ally of his.

In Canto 4, Dante returns to this issue, which is really the issue of the will. What is the will? How can somebody else's force on me compel me to do things for which I am subsequently held accountable? The other primary question in Canto 4 has to do with Dante's wonder about the souls in the various stars. They are arranged among the various planets, and he considers whether they may be in Plato's paradise. Was Plato right to believe that at death souls return to the stars, to the place of origin?

I will try to explain how the two questions are related, for their juxtaposition is far from arbitrary. There is a sort of link between these concerns. Canto 4 begins with a rather strange formulation about the nature of the will and the freedom of the will. Dante has to clarify what the will is, so he starts with a statement that seems to suggest that the will is inert. The will, given the opportunity to choose between two contradictory objects of desire, can't quite move one way or the other. You need the intellect, the argument that forces the will to make a decision. As Dante explains, "Between two foods, distant and appetizing in equal measure, a free man would die of hunger before he would bring one of them to his teeth. So would a lamb stand between two cravings of fierce wolves, in equal fear of both; so would a hound stand still between two hinds. Wherefore, if I was silent, urged in equal measure by my doubts, I neither blame nor commend myself, since it was of necessity. I was silent, but my desire was depicted on my face, and my questioning with it, in warmer colors far than by distinct speech."[1] There seems to be a kind of will that joins human beings and animals, such that choices paralyze the will. Thus it is possible that when we speak about the freedom of the will we are really speaking about the freedom of the will in the intellect. The multiple metaphors here introduce Dante's own doubts and perplexities, since he has two questions; each of them seems more compelling than the other, so he does not know which to ask first. Dante is indeed talking about the limitations of his own will from an Averroist position, a radical interpretation of Aristotle, in order to make broader statements about free will in general. Namely, he establishes a hierarchy of the intellect over the will.

Beatrice gets to the heart of Dante's conundrum: How can it be that Piccarda, who was forced to act by somebody else's will, appears in the lowest berth of beatitude, on the moon? Why should she be so undeserving of a closer intimacy to God? That's actually Dante's question, according to Beatrice, along with the equally pressing perplexity "that the souls appear to return to the stars, in accordance with Plato's teaching." Beatrice's solution: "I will first treat that which has the most venom."[2] Interestingly, the language of venom or poison, this idea of which is the more dangerous of the two questions, is not applied to the question about the will. The question that Beatrice deems more precarious is the question that deals with representation. What is the mode of appearance of the souls in heaven? Do the souls inhabit the stars? Is it a fiction, pyrotechnics if you wish, wherein once the night is over, then the souls return to the proper abode, which or may not be visible to the pilgrim? Is this a theatrical performance, and if so, why should that be a question that has more poison in it? What's so dangerous about representation?

It is the poetics of *Paradiso*, by the way, that confronts us with these questions. What is the mode of Dante's representation in *Paradiso*? Beatrice tries to shed further light on the matter: "Of the Seraphim he who is most in God, Moses, Samuel, and whichever John you will—I say, even Mary—have not their seats in any other heaven than these spirits which have now appeared to you, nor have they more or fewer years for their existence; but all make the first circle beautiful, and have sweet life in different measure, by feeling more and less the eternal breath. These showed themselves here, not because this sphere is allotted to them, but to afford sign of the celestial grade that is least exalted."[3] In other words, these souls enjoy a lower degree of beatitude than the other souls, so they appear here for the benefit of your understanding. Thus, the whole of Paradise, its representation here, is fictional, and once the pilgrim disappears so too will the souls. They will return to the bosom of Abraham, according to biblical accounts.

Dante goes on to explain why this allegorization is needed: "It is needful to speak thus to your faculty, since only through sense perception does it apprehend that which it afterwards makes fit for the intellect."[4] *Paradiso* is literally an accommodation of varieties, of realities that far exceed the powers of our mind and therefore must condescend to it. The souls deign to show themselves in a way that makes sense to us. Dante had been talking about the limitations of the will, and now he's talking about the limitations of the intellect, so the two issues are brought together in Canto 4, and each seems to need the other and be made stronger in the light of the other.

Dante further elucidates this mode of representation, which he says is true not only for *Paradiso,* but also for the Scripture, for all the iconography of the churches. It's necessary to speak in a way that accommodates itself to our limited faculties, that "condescends to your capacity, and attributes hands and feet to God, having other meaning," which is the very definition of allegory.[5] The Bible includes this anthropomorphic trope, though God has neither feet nor hands, and these body parts mean something else. They refer to the power and majesty of God. The sequence of examples is meant to suggest that there is a language of representation even in the Bible, and the idea legitimizes and authorizes Dante's own presentation of Paradise.

Now we move to the distinction between the biblical allegory just presented and the Platonic metaphor. Dante writes, "What Timaeus argues about the souls is not like this which is seen here, for seemingly he holds what he says for the truth." That's already one basic difference: what for the Bible is a metaphor becomes true in the context of Timaeus. Then we get a description of Plato's view on these concerns: "He [Plato] says the soul returns to its own star, believing it to have been severed thence when nature gave it a form. But perhaps his opinion is other than his words sound, and may be of a meaning not to be derided. If he means that the honor of their influence and the blame returns to these wheels"—if by returning to the stars he implies that at the fall of the souls, the souls are touched by the various stains of the planets and then return to the planets from which they originated—"perhaps his bow hits some truth. This principle, ill-understood, once misled almost the entire world, so that it ran astray in naming Jove and Mercury and Mars."[6] With this, Beatrice has resolved the first question for the pilgrim and for us. She's distinguishing between biblical theology and philosophical allegory, the language of metaphor in the Bible and the language of metaphor and truth in Plato. Dante is clearly legitimizing his own use of metaphor, for the whole poem we read is indeed a metaphorical journey whereby Dante is simultaneously both biblical and philosophical. He's locating the common ground, the metaphorical language that both the Bible and Plato will use, and then applying it in his own work.

But why is representation considered so dangerous in the first place? Representation has the power to erase the world of references that it represents. Representation has the power to make appearances and simulacra the only reality that we manage to see. By virtue of the representation, we may end up in the predicament of believing that that's all that there is. We may make the mistake Dante made of believing that these souls actually live on the moon and, therefore, that we are in a Platonic otherworld where the souls go back to this planet. The journey of Dante is the journey between images themselves and testing what these images may mean, finding out whether behind these images there is some kind of substance, essence, or reality. Dante moves between the two worlds and tries to join them. Hence, representation is a key issue here.

Furthermore and finally, this discourse of allegory gives us an idea why Dante has labeled this the heaven of grammar. You may recall that each planet seems to deploy one of the liberal arts, and the heaven of the moon is associated with grammar, according to Dante's schema. This is how Dante can connect grammar and the moon in the text: allegorical discourse is a grammatical issue.

The other problem that Dante raises in Canto 4, the less poisonous one, is the question of the will. Beatrice explains why it is less problematic: "The other perplexity that troubles you has less of poison, for its malice could not lead you away from me elsewhere. For our justice to seem unjust in mortal eyes is an argument of faith."[7] It's an easier issue for Dante because he distinguishes between a conditional will—what we will whenever we are beset by circumstances that force resolutions upon us—and an absolute will—the will of martyrs, for instance, of those who are unwavering and unfaltering in their confrontation with particular experiences. The souls of Piccarda and Constance were really exercising their own conditional will, not their absolute will, and thus their heavenly status. It's an interesting distinction, but like Dante, we'll leave it at that.

We move now instead to the heaven of Canto 6, the heaven of dialectics, Mercury. Why is Mercury the god tied to dialectics or logic, which are not exactly the same thing, though Dante does use them interchangeably?

Mercury, or Hermes, is the psychopomp, the god who brings messages to the realm of shades and who carries the souls to Hades. He is also the deity of laws, the bearer of messages of the gods to human beings, and the god of the marketplace, though this last role may have less of a particular resonance in this canto. Ultimately, Mercury seems to relate more to logic than dialectics, but Dante has the planet fulfill this heavenly role all the same.

What is dialectics, exactly? It's one of the arts of the classical trivium, and it is the art that provides a method to distinguish between truth and falsehoods. If dialectics is the science of the power to distinguish between falsehood and truth, it's also a rational discipline, the discipline that follows the rule of reason by means of which one can go on making such distinctions. Interestingly enough, Dante is really talking about laws here, so perhaps that's the tie to Mercury, and actually here he meets the great theorist, the emperor Justinian, who is usually acknowledged as the one who favored the real organization of Roman law in Byzantium, where he lived. Dante not only meets Justinian, but the emperor also tells the story of Rome, so it's a canto about history. The question is: what is the rationality of Roman history, if there is rationality to it? What kind of justice was there in its laws?

The canto begins with the story of Constantine, who is famous for the Donation of Constantine, about which we already know a few things. It's the famous alienation of imperial property to the Church as Constantine's token of gratitude to Pope Sylvester, who had cured him of leprosy. This alleged transaction gave rise to a famous debate, and Dante dismisses the donation, views it as no less transgressive, no less tragic and disruptive of the order of the world, than Adam's sin. It's of the same cosmic proportion because it mixes together the sacred and the profane. It makes the pope a temporal ruler, and doing so is the ultimate degradation of the exercise of moral authority from Dante's viewpoint.

So, he alludes to the donation again, but the reference to Constantine has a slightly different sense in this case. "After Constantine," Justinian says, "turned back the Eagle counter to the course of the heavens which it had followed behind the ancient who took Lavinia to wife, a hundred and a hundred years and more the bird of God"—the eagle, the emblem of the empire—"abode on Europe's limit, near to the mountains from which it had first issued; and there it governed the world beneath the shadow of its sacred wings, from hand to hand, until by succeeding change it came into mine. I was Caesar, and am Justinian"—here, once again, the use of that shift of verbs from the past to the present—"who, by will of the Primal Love which I feel, removed from among the laws what was superfluous and vain."[8] This is really a definition of dialectics, making the distinction between what was "superfluous and vain" and what was essential.

The first allusion here is to Constantine's moving the seat of the empire from Rome to the east, Byzantium. This is seen as the violation of a metaphor of history, a paradigm of history, which was called *translatio imperii.* In the Middle Ages people spoke constantly of translation, the translation of studies, the translation of the empire. They had an idea that the whole of history is patterned on the movement of the sun from east to west, and thus when the empire reaches the westernmost point of the map, that's going to be the end of history, history's sunset. Constantine, by turning back this translation, this movement, actually delays the apocalyptic denouement, the end of time and the end of the day, and for Dante this is a major violation of the economy of history.

The other allusion in the passage is to Aeneas with whom the empire had started to move westward after the fall of Troy. He, the husband of Lavinia, had begun the process that Constantine reverses. This is one of the first times that Dante starts using geographical coordinates, a geographical description of Europe. He has really not done that in *Inferno* and *Purgatorio.* He's asking what kind of messages can come from this historical Europe that are still valid today. He does distinguish, however, between Rome and Europe, in the sense that the history of Rome, he will say in the *Monarchia,* is different from the history of Europe. The emblem for Rome's distinctiveness is to be found in Aeneas's experience of marrying three wives. He marries Creusa, as we read in *The Aeneid;* he marries Dido, though it's a marriage of convenience, so to speak; and then he marries Lavinia. Dante explains that the three wives Aeneas marries are from Asia, from Africa, and from Europe, respectively, so Aeneas's whole experience encompasses what at the time was thought of as universality, the three known continents. And yet there is a European context, for from Justinian we have what seems to be a celebration of the Roman Empire. This is Canto 6, after all, and like Canto 6 of *Inferno* and Canto 6 of *Purgatorio* before it, the canto's focus is political, but this time the politics are not just those of the city or of Italy, but those of the whole empire.

However, what begins as a celebration of the Roman Empire in effect becomes also a critique of the ideology of empire. Dante follows two models here, and they are two models that contradict each other. We have the Virgilian model, which is really a commendation of the empire's origins with Aeneas, the account told in *The Aeneid,* and a vision of what is to come. But then there is Augustine's *City of God,* a fierce condemnation of the empire. The empire has fallen by the time Augustine writes, the claims of the eternity of the empire turn out to be false, and to Augustine the empire is nothing more than another episode in a long history of predatory politics of imperial possessions and violence. The Roman Empire as an empire is no better than all the other empires that have long since vanished, vanquished. Clearly, the two models are markedly opposed, and Dante oscillates between them throughout the canto.

The very language that Dante uses is Augustinian. At one point Dante says, "You know that it [the eagle] made its stay in Alba for three hundred years and more, till at the end, when the three fought against the three for it still"—a reference to the Curatii and Horatii, two sets of three brothers who fought each other in a duel. "And you know what it did, through seven kings, from the wrong of the Sabine women down to the woe of Lucretia, conquering the neighboring peoples round about."[9] These are all phrases that come straight out of Augustine's *City of God*. They are used by Dante as cases of exemplifying the libido and power of Rome. They are stories of erotic violence: Lucretia, who has been raped; and the Sabine women, who have been kidnapped by the bands of Romulus and Remus. All these references point to the idea that the empire was born under outlaws.

Dante is using the perspective of Augustine on the aberrant policies of the empire, but at the same time, all the rest of what he says in Canto 6 is really Virgilian. This is the moment when Virgil and Augustine are shown to disagree quite strongly with one another. Why does Dante do this? What is his reason for bringing together two contradictory sources of historical thought? Is he in favor of the empire or is he against it? One thing is clear, that Augustine, who loves Virgil, still decides that the empire is an abhorrent reality in his own history. It's already falling apart, and he has no use for this decay. In his theological vision, the question that he raises is: what do I care who governs me, provided that they do not make me sin? Reality is internalized, found in the interior life of all of us, and what are empires, if not great thefts?

But we still must ask ourselves where Dante stands between these two poles. He makes a shift in focus that holds the answer. Toward the end of the canto, he writes, "Now you may judge of such as I accused but now, and of their offenses, which are the cause of all your ills. The one opposes to the public standard the yellow lilies, and the other claims it for a party, so that it is hard to see which offends the most. Let the Ghibellines, let them practice their art under another ensign, for this one he ever follows ill who cleaves justice from it. And let not this new Charles strike it down with his

Guelphs, but let him fear talons which have stripped the hide from a greater lion. Many a time ere now the sons have wept for the sin of the father; and let him not believe that God will change arms for his lilies."[10] The canto all of a sudden seems to turn into a replica of *Inferno* 6 with its discussion of the civil war between Guelphs and Ghibellines. The civil war is the perspective from which Dante can take his double view on the history of the empire, standing up both to the stance of Augustine and to that of Virgil. What he really seems to be saying is, yes, Augustine you are right, the empire has been a negative force in history, and reality is, as you say, an internalized reality of our own peace and the internal will that we can placate. At the same time, he says to Virgil, but you're also right in your valorization of the empire because the empire has brought order and laws into the world. Against Augustine he says, if there were no laws of the empire, then there would be no way of sheltering each and every unrest in cases of civil war. What makes the argument for the necessity of the empire is the reality of the civil war, which demands the presence of a transcendent institution that will manage to contain the violence of human beings. So, he agrees with Augustine and disagrees with Augustine. He agrees with Virgil and disagrees with Virgil. Virgil leaves no room for the inner experiences of Christians. Augustine leaves no room for the necessity of an outside structure that could order the appetites of human beings. On these terms Dante establishes his middle ground.

The canto comes to an end with a little bit of semi-autobiographical poetry, involving an emperor who praised a counselor who has now fallen into disgrace: "Within this present pearl shines the light of Romeo"—Romeo Villeneuve, a Provençal courtier who held the role of counselor for the prince—"whose noble and beautiful work was ill rewarded; but the Provençals who wrought against him have not the laugh, and indeed he takes an ill path who makes harm for himself of another's good work. Raymond Berenger had four daughters, each of them a queen, and Romeo, a man of lowly birth and a pilgrim, did this for him. And then crooked words moved him to demand a reckoning of this just man, who had rendered him seven and five for ten. Thereon he departed, poor and old, and if the world but knew the heart he had while begging his bread morsel by morsel, much as it praises him would praise him more."[11] It is an oblique representation of Dante himself, who also ends up begging in poverty for a morsel, as a result, he believes, of the selfishness of political powers.

The final question raised here is one that I think underlies this whole canto: what is the relationship between dialectics and history? Why in the

heaven of logic does Dante have to talk about history? I think that the idea
is that history itself is an encomium that ends up being not quite mitigated.
There is a reason for the empire, and yet this reason doesn't quite justify all
that the empire perpetrated in history. From this perspective Dante is also
forcing on us some perplexities about the nature of logic as an instrument
of power, as one that could justify all possible powers. So, there is also a
critique of dialectics as much as there is a critique of history.

Here we omit a discussion of the heaven of Venus and we move to the
heaven of the sun, which is the heaven of arithmetic and numbers. In this
section Dante talks about a model of the Trinity that I will describe to you
in a moment. Here he encounters two wheels of saints, two garlands of wise
old men who hold each other's hands, dancing around the sun. It is the
dance of wisdom. You can also refer to this heaven as a reorganization of
the encyclopedia. I used this metaphor at the beginning of the book, this
idea that the *Divine Comedy* tries to repropose a new circle of knowledge, a
way in which things can really be known, and the encyclopedia represents
the journey of education, which is circular because the mind moves through
the various arts and sciences, and then returns to what it already knew
from a different viewpoint. That's how you learn, and that's what we find
in the heaven of the sun.

Dante begins Canto 10 with a Trinitarian representation, the Father
and the Son joined together by the breath of love: "Looking upon His Son
with the Love which the One and the Other eternally breathe forth, the primal and ineffable Power made everything that revolves through the mind or
through space with such order that he who contemplates it cannot but taste
of Him." That was the idea of the Trinity, as a unity, an arithmetical paradox of theological fecundity. God is an image of love generative of itself,
within His own unity. Then Dante turns to his readers for the last time and
tells us to be stargazers. He urges our eyes upward: "Lift then your sight
with me, reader, to the lofty wheels, straight to that part where the one motion strikes the other; amorously there begin to gaze upon that Master's art
who within Himself so loves it that His eye never turns from it. See how
from there the oblique circle which bears the planets branches off, to satisfy
the world which calls on them."[12] He directs our eyes to an intersection, the
cosmic equator and the ecliptic, a term that describes the diurnal and an-
nual movement of the sun. With this astrological crossroads in our sights,
Dante asks the reader to ponder his description of the Trinity.

But why does Dante think of the Trinity in the heaven of the sun
in the first place? For a potential answer, we turn to a passage from

Pseudo-Dionysius, a mystic whom Dante mentions. Pseudo-Dionysius wrote on the mystical hierarchy of divine names, including a semimystical idea of the Trinity, an idea that knowledge has to be love, which Dante will take up. His is a solar theology, a theology that has to be understood as the life of the sun itself. In *The Divine Names,* he says:

> Think of how it is with our sun. It exercises no rational process, no act of choice, and yet by the very fact of its existence it gives light to whatever is able to partake of its light, in its own way. So it is with the Good. Existing far above the sun, an archetype far superior to its dull image, it sends the rays of its undivided goodness to everything with the capacity, such as this may be, to receive it. . . . Such beings owe their presence and their uneclipsed and undiminished lives to these rays. . . . They abide in the goodness of God and draw from it the foundation of what they are, their coherence, their vigilance, their home. Their longing for the Good makes them what they are and confers on them their wellbeing. Shaped by what they yearn for, they exemplify goodness and, as the Law of God requires of them, they share with those below them the good gifts which have come their way.[13]

God, or the Trinity as a given, is depicted as a fountain here, eschewing the Aristotelian or Thomistic idea of causality. We think of God as the one who imparts a cause or a motion to things, and then there is a teleology, there is an effect. The idea of the Trinity here, on the contrary, is one of an inexhaustible source that keeps giving to all, and we're all part of this gift. Dante is getting this solar theology from Pseudo-Dionysius, who appears as one who behind the rationalist facade of his thinking is aware of depths and other ways of thinking that are not those of the rational mind.

Next Dante sees these two garlands of saints and meets Aquinas, who will give an encyclopedic list of the names of the sages around him. He says,

> I was of the lambs of the holy flock which Dominic leads on the path where there is good fattening if they do not stray. He that is next beside me on the right was my brother and my master, and he is Albert of Cologne, and I Thomas of Aquino. If thus of all the rest you would be informed, come, following my speech with your sight, going round the blessed wreath. That next flam-

ing comes from the smile of Gratian who served the one and the other court so well that it pleases in Paradise. The other who next adorns our choir was that Peter who, like the poor widow, offered his treasure to Holy Church. The fifth light, which is the most beautiful among us, breathes with such love that all the world there below thirsts to know tidings of it. Within it is the lofty mind to which was given wisdom so deep that, if truth be true, there never rose a second of such full vision.[14]

That fifth light is Solomon, described through a circumlocution. In numerical symbolism, five is the natural number for the things of the earth, which is to say that Dante presents a very difficult, dangerous proposition: namely, the idea of Solomon as naturally perfect, as having a perfection of the intellect. The intellectual virtue of Solomon consists in the fact that he knew what to ask for when he had to govern his people. He was the perfect king for this reason. Why would this be a dangerous idea? If you believe that there is a perfection of the intellect within the natural immanence and order, then it means that there's no need for the Revelation. There is no need for intermediaries or Redemption. If the natural intellect is capable of ascending as is claimed here for Solomon, then the whole redemptive apparatus will collapse. Dante himself does not believe in this perfection, and Aquinas will step back dramatically from this position in Canto 13.

For now, though, Aquinas continues his list: "At its side behold the light of that candle which, below in the flesh, saw deepest into the angelic nature and its ministry"—Augustine—"the body from which it was driven lies down below in Cieldauro"—Boethius—"and he came from martyrdom and exile to this peace. See, flaming beyond, the glowing breath of Isidore, of Bede, and of Richard [of St. Victor] who in contemplation was more than man." The word Dante uses in the Italian (*considerar*) is not actually *contemplation,* but rather *consideration,* and it's a key word for Dante, since its etymology means "moving with the stars." The mind is at its most perfect when it imitates the circulation and circularity of the stars. And finally, "this one from whom your look returns to me is the light of a spirit to whom, in his grave thoughts, it seemed that death came slow. It is the eternal light of Siger who, lecturing in Straw Street, demonstrated invidious truths."[15] The last one whom Aquinas points out in this circulation of wise spirits is a so-called heretic by the name of Siger of Brabant, an Averroist condemned for his Averroism. Whatever canonized knowledge we may have of these figures, Dante places in heaven individuals who have been

judged unworthy of knowledge or heretical or wrong, and now are redeemed. The idea of knowledge is one that keeps changing. The canon of
knowledge is always expanding, growing to include voices that had previously been rejected.

How does Dante go about justifying the salvation of an alleged heretic, though? Canto 10, from this point of view, is retrospectively one that
sheds light on Canto 10 of *Inferno,* where we also saw, you may remember,
the Averroists and the Epicureans, like Guido Cavalcanti, those who believed that love and knowledge never interact with each other, that rationality is darkened and dimmed by the infusions of passions, and that the
mind is one that receives ideas from the outside, the notion of both the in-
ertia of the will and the divisions within the mind itself. Dante is now cor-
recting some of those views. He gives the address of this man, the Street of
Straw in Paris, the Rue de Fouarre (now known as the Rue Dante, a sign
that Parisians are mindful of this passage), and tells us that Siger lectured,
a word that had a certain value in the university lexicon of the time. Lecturing was an activity that implied glossing of texts. Dante sets Siger on the
road by giving us his address, informing us that Siger's thinking, which
produces his lectures, takes place while he is on the road. Philosophy always understands itself as a journey, a method, an exodus, to reach the ultimate truths about God. Dante is a poet on the way to theological certainty,
theological truth, and theological knowledge, and Siger "demonstrated invidious truths" to him.

What are these invidious truths? Dante indulges in etymology by calling the truth that Siger pursued "invidious," which etymologically means
those truths that cannot be demonstrated or seen. Philosophy appears as an
art of speculation that takes us on the path to a truth that it cannot quite
access. In the specific case of Siger of Brabant, these truths include the immortality of the soul, about which Aristotle was very doubtful. He also
tried to determine the origin of the world. Siger believed the universe to be
eternal, an argument that engaged many medieval thinkers and theologians, with Averroism on one side and on the other those like Aquinas, who
maintains that philosophically you can show that the universe is eternal,
but out of faith you continue believing in creation, that things have a beginning. If you don't think that things have a beginning, then there's never a
possibility of rooting the idea of your freedom, your innovations, the possibility that things can be different for you from what they were before.
These are ideas Siger was challenging with his invidious truths.

The reason why Dante rescues Siger of Brabant is to make a statement that whatever we believe is knowledge is never definite. We are literally on the way, rethinking things and making them an object of our own self-critique. This is not the only place where Dante is rethinking himself. Very soon, around the notion of the Trinity, Bonaventure will have to change his mind about a man we've mentioned before, Joachim of Flora. We are going to have Canto 11 balancing off Canto 10. For now, however, the canto ends, "Then, like a clock"—mechanical clocks were a recent technological invention in the late thirteenth century—"which calls us at the hour when the Bride of God rises to sing her matins to her Bridegroom, that he may love her, in which the one part draws or drives the other, sounding *ting! ting!* with notes so sweet that the well-disposed spirit swells with love, so did I see the glorious wheel move and render voice to voice with harmony and sweetness that cannot be known except there where joy is everlasting."[16] Dante is describing the songs of the eternal blessed souls in erotic terms, so that what seems to be a canto of pure knowledge ultimately becomes a love song too, and this is the whole trajectory of Canto 10.

In Canto 10 a poetic break takes place. Dante literally moves us beyond the sunlight, the ordinary natural daylight, into a world that is his own, where he starts raising the issue of knowledge, as if to say that a new way of thinking is now necessary. Once you move beyond the ordinary boundaries of the universe you have to start asking yourself what kind of knowledge you need there. He's rethinking, therefore, the whole relationship between heresies and knowledge, the canonical certainties that Aquinas seems to possess, though he now makes a mistake about the fate of Solomon, in opposition to the alleged heresy of Siger of Brabant. Dante is forcing on us a different way of thinking that begins with a redefinition of nothing less than the Trinity. It would be inconceivable that something as imponderable as the Trinity could just have one formula to account for it, but Dante adds onto it that first definition of the Trinity as a unity of love, which I think is a mystical definition. Love and learning, philosophy and theology, are all brought together as Dante redefines himself, his world, his knowledge, and his poem in Canto 10.

CHAPTER 18

Paradiso 11–12

Canto 10, discussed in the last chapter, leads quite naturally into Cantos 11 and 12. To begin to explore these latter two cantos, let's look at the end of Canto 12, where we meet Bonaventure, who is a Franciscan, a member of one of the orders of Francis. One trait that theologically distinguishes the Franciscans is that they believe in the priority of will and love in the act of knowledge. The Dominicans, by contrast, or neo-Aristotelians like Aquinas believe in the priority of the intellect in the apprehension of the world. The Dominicans were founded with the explicit mandate to teach in universities, where they thought heresies abounded, and therefore they had to block off the routes of these heresies. The Franciscans were instead witnessing in the world. But both orders are shaped by a belief in poverty that we will soon examine because we need to understand what it means.

At any rate, Bonaventure is a Franciscan, and by the end of Canto 12, he has chronicled the life of Dominic. This is sort of another case of Dante's own extraordinary openness, a view of these characters in the sense that the Franciscans and Dominicans were historically at odds with each other, in terms both of their theologies and of their premises—intellectual premises above all. Here, Dante has a Franciscan tell the life of Dominic, just as earlier in Canto 11 a Dominican, Aquinas, tells the life of Francis. The two cantos are controlled by a chiasmus that permits an intersection of voices and a sense of the interdependence of the two perspectives.

The last words of Canto 12, though, function as a counterweight to the description of the encyclopedia that Aquinas had given at the conclusion of Canto 10, ending with Siger of Brabant. Bonaventure says, "I am the living soul of Bonaventura of Bagnorea, who in the great offices always put the left-hand care behind. Illuminato and Augustine are here, who were of the first unshod poor brethren that with the cord made themselves God's friends." Then there's a theorist of medieval encyclopedias, Hugh of St. Victor, a Parisian friar who wrote the *Didascalicon,* a text about the stages of education and how the mind comes to the knowledge of God, starting with small elements in outer life, the material world, and proceeding on to the interior lights before reaching God's supreme light. Then we see Peter the bookworm, Peter the Spaniard, another theorist of medieval logic; then Nathan the prophet, who is known as being David's bad conscience, or good conscience, the one pricking him to think about his moral life. After him, there's Chrysostom, the Metropolitan, meaning the man with the golden mouth, the one who possesses the flower of eloquence. And Anselm, another theologian who writes about the reasons for the Incarnation, why God became a man. And Donatus, a Roman grammarian. And Rabanus, a historian. And finally "beside me shines the Calabrian abbot Joachim, who was endowed with prophetic spirit. The glowing courtesy and the well-judged discourse of Brother Thomas has moved me to celebrate so great a paladin, and with me has moved this company."[1] Bonaventure ends with a tip of the hat in the direction of Aquinas, whose example he has followed, an example, once again, of a dialogue and openness between the two orders that are separate but also somehow interdependent.

The presence of Abbot Joachim is another counterweight to Siger of Brabant in Canto 10. This is not our first encounter with Joachim, since I mentioned his name to you in glossing the apocalyptic prophecy of DXV in *Purgatorio* 33. The Joachistic interpretation of that symbol successfully introduces the idea of the end of time, but I also asked you to reject the implications of that prophecy. The Joachistic prophecy was viewed as heretical for a number of reasons. It expresses an impatience with regard to history. That is to say, it really believes, first of all, in the imminent closure of history, the idea that the end is close at hand, and this end of history implies the coming into being of a utopia of the spirit, the third age of the spirit, when finally all institutions and barriers are torn down. The problem is that it always begs for a closure that we cannot really fathom, a closure of the world of historical occurrences. And it was actually Bonaventure himself who asked that Joachim's views be anathematized, and now, here in *Paradiso,* he is writing a sort of palinode. Dante allows him to make amends for the previous condemnation.

Bonaventure found the ideas of Joachim of Flora objectionable because Joachim was de facto dissolving the whole notion of the unity of the

Trinitarian life. His tripartite idea of history was based on the three persons of the Trinity: the age of the Father, the Son, and the Holy Spirit. Each person of the Trinity becomes a separate entity, and that view, for Bonaventure, was heretical, but now he acknowledges that Abbot Joachim was in fact endowed with a spiritual prophecy. What seemed to be heretical, in other words, was only prophetic; an intellectual question of thoughts and opinions now appears as divination about things to come, not specified any further. Retrospectively, Dante is legitimizing Joachim and therefore also legitimizing his own position in Canto 33 of *Purgatorio*. Dante shares Joachim's view of the apocalyptic denouement of history, but he rejects the idea that it's possible to establish a date for such an occurrence. So it is that Joachim appears now as a visionary among saints and grammarians.

The other figure that I would like to say something about is Nathan the prophet. Namely, I have to explain why Dante would include Nathan at all. Dante could have chosen so many other figures to place among these wise spirits. He could have chosen someone whose works are canonical in the Bible, but he doesn't. The idea is, I think, a little bit of an autobiographical pun about Dante himself because the name Nathan means "he who gives." And that's what the name Dante means, as well. So perhaps, in the canto where the Franciscan sense of giving is dramatized, Dante saw his own name in the name of Nathan, and it pleases him. Nathan becomes a kind of mask for Dante himself. It is as if he were saying that with another life or a posthumous life in the heavenly apotheosis, that's where he would like to end up.

Now what is so peculiar about this encyclopedic ordering of the arts and the sciences? It doesn't really differ very much from Aquinas, but it's interesting that it's Bonaventure who articulates and celebrates all these names and arts because Bonaventure is himself a theorist of the encyclopedia, very much in the wake of Hugh of St. Victor. But he has one crucial reflection at the beginning of his encyclopedia. He says that the activity of knowing and learning is like going up and down a ladder. It's the metaphor of the ladder of Jacob in the Bible, which is where Bonaventure probably found it, and the ladder of Plato. The idea is that the mind ascends when we learn something, when we get educated, and it actually can go down, too. The interesting thing about Bonaventure is that he says that in a ladder the lowest rungs are always more important than the higher ones, because without those none of us would be able to climb up the ladder. His is a theory of knowledge as a proliferation of lights, internal and external lights, the lights of the senses, the lights that come to us from books, and the light of God. It is a process of enlightenment. But as we are enlightened, the lowest lights are self-sufficient; there are those who may not be capable of ascending much higher than the first few rungs, but there is already a self-sufficient knowledge that even those individuals can acquire. There is no hierarchy, since the lower elements are as crucial as the higher elements, and that's what really sets Bonaventure apart.

With this image, as with the inclusion of Joachim, we are getting into the erasure of strict barriers and boundaries between what is heretical and what is canonical. Dante's openness reverberates with the lessons of Francis and Dominic in these two cantos. Keep in mind that we are still in the heaven of the sun here, and the sun is such a fundamental symbol of divine generosity. It always gives of itself without ever asking anything back, so it stands for pure munificence. Cantos 11 and 12 are all about this kind of out-reach and openness.

For instance, Canto 11 starts with an apostrophe against logical, legal forms of knowledge, the kind of knowledge that tries to define the world in formulas. Dante begins in his own voice, declaring, "O insensate care of mortals! how false are the reasonings that make you beat your wings in downward flight. One was following after the laws, another after the *Aphorisms,* one was pursuing priesthood, and one dominion by force or craft, and another plunder, and another civil business, one was moiling, caught in the pleasures of the flesh, and another was giving himself to idleness, the while, free from all these things, I was high in heaven with Beatrice, thus gloriously received."[2] I think it's an interesting counterpoint between these icons of power that derive from the study of law and logic, and then Dante's reference to himself as free from all of these concerns. This idea of freedom will be a dominant theme of Canto 11.

Dante continues with a little prayer and the introduction of Dominic and Francis: "The Providence that governs the world with that counsel in which every created vision is vanquished before it reaches the bottom, in order that the Bride of Him who, with loud cries, espoused her with the blessed blood, might go to her Delight, secure within herself and also more faithful to Him, ordained on her behalf two princes, who on this side and that might be her guides. The one was all seraphic in ardor"—Francis—"the other, for wisdom, was on earth a splendor of cherubic light"—Dominic. "I shall speak of one, because in praising one, whichever be taken, both are spoken of, for their labors were to one same end."[3] That's the formula that seals the sense of interdependence of intellect and will, of love and knowledge, of two seemingly competing voices.

What follows is what we call a hagiography or a legend, the life of a saint, specifically that of Francis, as told by the Dominican Aquinas. First of all, he tells us, "Between the Topino and the stream that falls from the hill chosen by the blessed Ubaldo, a fertile slope hangs from a lofty mountain wherefrom Perugia feels cold and heat through Porta Sole, while behind it Nocera and Gualdo grieve under a heavy yoke."[4] It's an extraordinarily localized representation of Francis's origin. It's a topography. St. Francis was born in Assisi, but it's almost as if Aquinas were locating him in a more specific place, near the gate called Porta Sole, which is where the the road to Perugia leads.

Then we go from the toponymic, the name of a place, the gate of the sun, to a metaphor for Francis as the sun. So we are in the heaven of the sun, and now Dante invests Francis with all the attributes of this solarity, this continuous, steady giving of oneself as the sun does in the mystical Neoplatonic imagery of Pseudo-Dionysus. Also, as soon as Dante has mentioned the specific place of Francis's birth, the geographic coordinates completely change. We go from the specific and local to the global, the world of the Ganges, the Orient, something vaster. As if he were the sun, Francis really acts between the concrete and local and the widest possible reference. As Dante puts it, "Therefore let him who talks of this place not say *Ascesi*"—which means "I rise," though it's also an obvious punning with Assisi—"which would be to speak short, but *Orient,* if he would name it rightly." It's an extraordinary image of two astronomical terms—the sun and the Orient—for Francis. Francis appears just as the sun does, as one who orients us. What Dante is implying, I think, is that for those who go on the face of the earth and lose their way, Francis becomes the person who can tell them how to find their way back to wherever they are going. For those who do not know their way at all, have never known the way, they are rendered capable of discovering it through him. Francis is providing a light, continuing the metaphorics of the sun, and "he began to make the earth feel, from his great virtue, a certain strengthening."[5] And with that glowing description, Aquinas now gives the story of Francis's life.

Before delving into that biography, however, I want to tell you that Dante knew of Francis also as a great poet. He is actually considered the first poet in the Italian vernacular. A few stanzas from his "Canticle of Brother Sun and Sister Moon" ought to demonstrate how Dante's own poetics here derive straight from this Franciscan vision of spirituality. The "Canticle" is a prayer that praises the Lord in all His aspects, all his connections to the natural world. Francis goes through all four elements, and part of the suggestiveness of this poem is that it's a song of praise to God, clearly enough, but we never know if Francis is thinking of these elements as the medium through which he can praise or as the cause of his praise, for the Italian is very ambiguous. Furthermore, we can finally understand the rhetoric of praise that is running through this poem. But we also saw the rhetoric of praise in Dante's *Vita nuova*, when he finds out that the best way of writing about Beatrice is to write praise poems, which he distinguishes from flattery by suggesting that poems of praise reject all sense of ownership. He realizes that the fact that one may know the world doesn't mean that one owns it, so that not knowing Beatrice is not just a wish to own her, and his praise of her is as disinterested and as free a mode of acknowledgment of Beatrice herself as possible. Francis is clearly a source for these ideas in Dante's oeuvre, and this whole poetic vision of Francis continues throughout Canto 11.

Dante goes on recounting the life of Francis, and he catches Francis in what I would call, using the language of anthropology, a liminal stage. The word *liminal* comes from the Latin *limen*, which means "threshold" or "limit." These are two concepts that are, in many ways, very contradictory, but the threshold may be a limit or it may be an opportunity to cross beyond a limit. At any rate, Dante places Francis in a liminal position betwixt and between two different orders: on the one hand, the world, and on the other hand, some kind of utopian idea that would be the order that he goes on to institute, a general vision of what the world ought to be.

So, that's where Dante catches Francis as he begins a biographical account modeled on a number of biographies that existed at the time:

> For, while still a youth, he rushed into strife against his father for such a lady, to whom, as to death, none willingly unlocks the door; and before his spiritual court *et coram patre* [a Latin phrase that has the value of a legal formula, which is to say that he marries this as yet unknown woman in the presence of his own father, thus giving legitimacy to his act of marriage] he was joined to her, and thereafter, from day to day, he loved her ever more ardently. She, bereft of her first husband [Christ], for eleven hundred years and more, despised and obscure, remained unwooed till he came; nor had it availed to hear that he who caused fear to all the world found her undisturbed with Amyclas at the sound of his voice; nor had it availed to have been constant and undaunted so that, where Mary remained below,

she wept with Christ upon the cross. But, lest I should proceed too darkly, take now Francis and Poverty for these lovers in all that I have said. Their harmony and joyous semblance made love and wonder and tender looks the cause of holy thoughts; so that the venerable Bernard first bared his feet, following such great peace, and running, it seemed to him that he was slow. Oh wealth unknown, oh fertile good![6]

There is clearly a reversal. Francis marries Poverty, and in this liminal position, Francis is shown as he is turning upside down all the values that the world holds dear. He wants to marry nothing, for to marry Poverty is really to marry nothing. He embraces owning nothing, but that "union" is conducted as if it were a sacramental act, so he is clearly making fun of marriage.

Not to imply any blasphemy here, but he's parodying the sacrament of marriage. He's parodying the law, because he's marrying Poverty in the presence of his own father. He's parodying social values as he divests himself of all his clothes, which in the Middle Ages, as much as now, stood for some symbolic social status. We are in the presence of a parody of legal language, of sacramental language, even the language of love, for the phrase "none willingly unlocks the door" refers to the door of pleasure. "Their harmony and joyous semblance" is another parody of the language of the amorous discourse of medieval love poetry. Even sexuality, which is certainly a value of the world, Francis will turn on its head. This is a radical critique of the value system of the world, which could be called a prophetic mode of abandoning the idols of the world in favor of some kind of utopia or unexpected vision of how the world ought to be. Ultimately, though, it's an extraordinary nonvalue, because that's what poverty is, something that questions all values.

What did Francis mean by all of this? A little detail that I should tell you is that Francis, in Italian, is Francesco, meaning "free" or "frank." Francis, true to his name, is now absolutely free in his poverty. There's no bondage to anything, nothing that holds him to anything in the world, so this is one important ethical extension of poverty. Dante certainly seems to have stressed the idea of poverty as a very material, corporeal, physical experience. I call it prophetic in the sense that what distinguishes the biblical prophets from other prophets is that they usually choose to bear on their flesh the signs that they utter against the world. This is part of what Francis is doing with this idea that he's *living* his poverty. Poverty is not just an allegorical representation; it is something lived in the flesh. The literal and the allegorical are now compressed. Dante, I repeat, thinks about the material idea of poverty, a way of opposing avarice and prodigality, but poverty to Franciscans also means poverty of language. Even that poem we saw before was repetitive, full of the same simple formulaic expressions. Even in their language they acknowledge that we cannot own the world, that the world is a world of gifts, and that the more you give and the less you have for yourself, the more you are free and the more productive your own acts can become, as was the case for Francis.

Are we supposed to also associate Dante's own fate as a poor, exiled beggar with this idea of poverty? Of course! For poverty means several things for Dante. Bonaventure will ponder the poverty of language and the poverty of philosophy, but all of these writers also understand poverty in a very literal way. All of them understand that this kind of poverty is really a description of the human condition to begin with. We are all poor, we are all born defective and in need, and some of us go on being needy. The other side of that shared lack is that it's actually a blessing because it permits our universal state of freedom. Is it a consolatory note for Dante to believe that he's not alone in his deprivation? Yes, since Dante, unlike Petrarch, who died one of the wealthiest men of his time by virtue of being a poet, never attained any material success on account of his writing.

But poverty is not all that Dante will discuss with regard to Francis. Francis will try to receive a seal of approval from the popes about the fraternity or order that he organized: "After the poor folk had increased behind him, whose wondrous life were better sung in Heaven's glory, then was the holy will of this chief shepherd circled with a second crown by the Eternal Spirit through Honorius." Pope Honorius agrees to recognize this new order, "and when, in thirst for martyrdom, he, in the proud presence of the Sultan, had preached Christ and them that followed him, and, finding the people too unripe for conversion and in order not to stay in vain, had returned to the harvest of the Italian fields, then on the harsh rock between Tiber and Arno he received from Christ the last seal, which his limbs bore for two years."[7] Dante is alluding to the famous story of the stigmata that Francis received, his body becoming a sign. It's the story of the stigmata, but it's also the story of Francis trying to go and convert the sultan. He fails to produce a convincing theological argument, and the two men separate, each along his own way, and that's it. It's a story that can be understood as an apparent failure of Francis's message. At the same time, it is an extraordinary hermeneutical turn that has taken place in Dante's thinking, a turn to celebrations of the Crusades. Here we have an encounter between Christians and Muslims in peaceful language, where the two exponents of these belief systems can come together and discuss their ideas. The sultan denies Christian thought, ultimately, but this is an extraordinary change in the dissemination of violence that had been at the center of so much previous theological discourse. Dante is following Francis on a different route, allowing for an important change in the historical understanding of the relationship between Christians and Muslims and their interpretations of the Crusades.

Furthermore, geographic coordinates here and elsewhere in this canto begin to paint a picture of a wide, wide world. We have just read about Francis's trip to Egypt to see the sultan. A little earlier Dante referred to the birthplace of Francis by talking about the Ganges. In other words, Dante is obviously aware that there is a Christian, European world, but there are at least two other places on the map: one a Hindu world of the Ganges, and the other the Muslim world of the Egyptians. Dante is obliquely acknowledging a concern that will prove crucial to Bonaventure.

In 1273 Bonaventure, the man whom Dante will highlight in Canto 12, traveled to Paris to give a number of lectures at the University of Paris. A number of these lectures debate the question of the relationship between what he sees as three distinct cultures: Hindu, Christian, and Muslim. He tries to see in what way they can be harmonized. He connects the Hindu religion with Joachism, in the sense that Joachim's third age, his own age, the age of the Spirit, implies the elimination of all institutions, so that the Spirit is now everywhere and there is no need for any hierarchy or order. Bonaventure claims that this is identical to the world of the Hindus, who believe that God is everywhere. Then he talks about the Muslims as having a theology of an impassable distance, a transcendence that nothing can really bridge, between a God who remains invisible and the world of every man here. Of course, Christianity provides the mediation between the two worlds because it contains a simultaneous transcendence and immanence of God. Dante is, I think, echoing this text and these problems in the canto of Francis, so he places Francis between the Ganges and Egypt, as one who is carving a new space, the space that he calls that of poverty, which means freedom and love as a way of coming to the knowledge of God.

Dante is clearly talking from a Christian standpoint; there's no question about this. To be fair, however, the underlying spirituality of Dante is what I call the "spirituality of the desert." Dante is truly the "poet of the desert," in the sense that in the desert you have modes of a quest such that where everyone is really going is to the absolute. Whatever journey we may take is always the same journey as everyone else's, and so the spirituality of the quest at least tempers this idea of Dante being unyieldingly strict and firm in this universe of degrees and distinctions that he sets up.

To return to the text, though, the description of Dominic as told by Bonaventure in Canto 12 really rewrites the previous canto. There, Francis represented a parodic, anarchic marriage to the absence of all worldly values. Here, we have a different marriage, between Dominic and faith, or between knowledge and theology if we want to put it at a very general level. The hagiography of Dominic begins: "In that region where sweet Zephyr rises to open the new leaves wherewith Europe sees herself reclad, not far from the smiting of the waves, behind which the sun, after his long course, sometimes hides himself from every man, sits fortunate Calaroga."[8] Dante is talking about the birthplace of Dominic and places him, rightly, in the western part of Spain, where the sun sets. Dominic thereby becomes the counter to Francis, who was born where the sun rises. Between the two of them the whole movement of the sun, the *translatio,* the translation of faith and culture this time rather than empires, seems to be encompassed. The movement of the sun from east to west on account of them seems to have its own quickness, its own rhythm.

Bonaventure continues, "Therein was born the ardent lover of the Christian faith, the holy athlete, benignant to his own and harsh to his foes. And his mind, as soon as it was created, was so full of living virtue that in his mother's womb he made her a prophetess. When the espousals were completed at the sacred font between him and the faith, where they dowered each other with mutual salvation, the lady who gave the assent for him saw in a dream the marvelous fruit destined to issue from him and from his heirs."[9] Here is the marriage ceremony that counters the previous marriage ceremony of Canto 11. I want to draw your attention to the use of these playful images, Dominic as an athlete of faith, a liegeman. Both Francis and Dominic were called the "clowns of the lord," *ioculatores domini* in Latin, for a reason. They bring in a perspective of play in the world. They make fun of the world. They challenge the values of the world, and in this sense they arrive at the most impressive aspect of their theology, ultimately a playful one: the notion that God plays, that creation itself is a spectacle. I call it a "theodrama," a conceptualization that doesn't deprive the Divinity of its seriousness but makes that seriousness part of the world of joy.

In the canto of Dominic, much more than in the canto of Francis, this is a unique moment insomuch as it is a representation in terms of language.

The Dominicans were the intellectual arm of the Church, the Aristotelians, the poets, the philosophers and teachers. There was an idea of orthodoxy strongly associated with Dominic, and yet here the whole representation takes place in terms of language. One example: "Oftentimes his nurse found him silent and awake upon the ground, as though he would say, 'I am come for this.' Oh father of him, Felice indeed! Oh mother of him, Giovanna indeed, if this, being interpreted, means as is said!"[10] Dante is playing with etymologies here: the father is really happy ("felice"), so there is a relationship between his name and his state of mind, and the mother is as full of grace as her name Giovanna would suggest. Orthodoxy and heresy are simply two sides of one coin, for heresy here appears as a question of language, of an order that is above all grammatical. It has a kind of ambiguity that you always presume to be present within the order of language. Even the schisms of *Inferno,* the horrifying picture of a poet who holds his own head like a lamp as he talks to Virgil and Dante, involve questions of language. They are part of the imponderable quality of language, the ambiguities of language, the force of language, and the power of language. But for Dominic in particular, language is at the forefront, and language is play.

The new aesthetics that Dominic manages to release, and Francis too, is a kind of playful idea of the world, a comedy. I tried to explain to you from the first chapters onward how complicated it is to explain why Dante calls his text a comedy. He's talking about how an ordinary man of the year 1300 manages to have the most sublime of experiences. And of course it has a happy ending, and comedies are always the genre of happy endings. And it is about the low level of experiences. And Dante writes it in vernacular Italian. The explanations are numerous, but the real and substantial reason for Dante calling his poem a comedy is exactly that: the poem is a way of responding to this sense of the joyful quality of creation. For all the horror that we have been witnessing through Hell and Purgatory, joy seems to be what Dante is moving toward now. Once you think of play, you can no longer have the tragic vision because you understand that the tragic vision is part of something larger. Comedies, tragedies, and elegies are all linked to the Wheel of Fortune in medieval iconography, so you keep going around and around, but they're all part of something much larger, which is this ludic theology that Dante has been preparing for us all along.

CHAPTER 19

Paradiso 15–17

As we reach the midpoint of *Paradiso,* Cantos 15–17, we move into the heaven of Mars, which is, as you likely know, named for the god of war, and it is also the heaven of music. Dante links Mars and music out of the belief that harmony is the meeting point of discordant elements, a concord reached through discord. The discordant elements can be different sounds, or they can be the passions within us that need tempering. Canto 15 can be read in conjunction with Canto 15 of *Inferno.* Here Dante encounters his ancestor, Cacciaguida, and so inevitably the reference to Brunetto Latini imposes itself on us. We are compelled to draw parallels and see differences between the two forerunners who make different claims on their intellectual or dynastic descendant, Dante.

You could also look at this canto from many other points of view. For instance, the strongest questions that Dante raises here involve the self and history, a relationship that may be new to us, though history has often come up in our discussion. The last time we discussed it was in Canto 6 of *Paradiso,* where Dante gives a history of Rome, its humble beginnings and the deconstruction and crisis of the empire. And the issue of self is also something we have been discussing for a while, ever since we started the *Vita nuova,* with the idea of a lyrical self, a self who removes himself from the world of history, the contingencies of time, and the viscous realities of the city, and takes shelter in the chamber of his imagination, in the world of his ideas, dreams, and memories. There he constructs his own true self. Then when we began reading the *Divine Comedy,* I insisted on an autobiographical focus. This is *his* story, his unique experience. But now, we are talking about self and history in a new way since Dante's never quite coupled the two terms before. They become the double focus around which everything moves in these three cantos.

I draw your attention first to the presence of some mythic references and mythological figures whom Dante is evoking. They are very different among themselves, but they're all a way of reflecting on Dante's own idea of selfhood, his own relationship to his ancestors, his own private history. Canto 15 begins with musical metaphors, which is not surprising, since we are in the heaven of music: "Gracious will, wherein right-breathing love always resolves itself, as cupidity does into grudging will, imposed silence on that sweet lyre and quieted the holy strings which the right hand of Heaven slackens and draws tight." But beyond the music, Dante offers up the first mythological reference of the canto: "Nor did the gem depart from its ribbon, but coursed along the radial strip, and seemed like fire behind alabaster. With like affection did the shade of Anchises stretch forward (if our greatest Muse merits belief), when in Elysium he perceived his son."[1] At the very beginning of *Inferno* Dante made a reference to Paul and Aeneas, disavowing any strict connection with them. Aeneas's father, Anchises, mentioned then, is now recalled here. The encounter between Anchises and Aeneas stands for a relationship that Aeneas has with history; Aeneas goes to Hades in order to find out what the purposes are for his journeying from Troy toward an unknown land, and from his father he receives the prophetic announcement that he is to be a part of history. One belongs in history as part of a providential pattern, which for Aeneas was a destined empire that he has to found as the point of beginning for a new history. This is the epic account, a myth of one's own self belonging in the world of history.

As we move on, though, we get a reversal of this conception of the self in history. Dante problematizes the idea of what the self even is. After all, in the *Vita nuova* the self is a nexus of memories, fantasies, and a will to write poetry. In that sense the text constitutes the subject into a self: I am the author of this text. The text becomes a point of reference, and the poetic image that I give of myself gives you an idea of who I am. It doubles me, it perpetuates me, it's a poetic version of myself. So, as we read the autobiographical account we don't know yet what we are to take as a self.

And Dante also questions what history is. In Canto 16, Dante will consider writing a chronicle of the city of Florence, fitting since Florence is famous for its medieval chroniclers. So is history then to be understood as events? Or is to be understood the way Anchises understands it, as a myth that somehow has a paradigmatic value that can regulate and also arrange? Dante will not answer this question directly in Canto 16, but he does talk about all the Florentine families in an elegiac manner. They're all decayed, finished, and extinct, so whatever value this history may have is an elegiac commemoration of the past. And yet Cacciaguida proves to be elated at the idea that the grandson, the descendant, wants to find out about the past. Questions of history and how to conceive of it linger on.

I think Canto 17 is where we begin to unravel this whole issue of history and the self. It begins in a peculiar manner, with a long periphrastic construction, a long turn of phrase, for the pilgrim to describe himself in terms of Phaethon, the famous figure from classical myth who challenges Apollo. We saw him before, in the corresponding Canto 17 of *Inferno.* Phaethon was uncertain of his ancestry, unsure that his father was Apollo, so he had to reassure himself. This allusion is in the canto of Cacciaguida for a reason. Dante is asking what is the real relationship that joins him to this noble heroic figure of whom he is very proud. He's happy to reaffirm this genealogical line, so history now becomes no longer a chronicle, but a genealogy: "Such was I, and such I was perceived to be both by Beatrice and by the holy lamp which already, for my sake, had changed its place."[2] And yet the figure of Phaethon is a tragic figure because he introduces the possibility of what makes fathers wary of their sons all the time, the idea that the son wants to outdo the father, and the idea of tragic transgression that can breach that line of continuity across the generations. That's what this second myth tells us of history and the self.

Canto 17 goes on discussing, among other things, yet another way of understanding history. I think Dante says it much more sparingly and simply better than anybody else can: "Contingency, which does not extend beyond the volume of your material world, is all depicted in the Eternal Vision." The world of contingency can be subsumed within a larger transcendent paradigm, and that seems to be the order of necessity; the contingent world is linked to the volume where all things are present in the eternal vision. But is there some autonomy to this contingency, or are things determined by an order of necessity downstream from the point where our little ships are set afloat? The musical lexicon appears once more as Dante explains, "Therefrom, even as sweet harmony comes from an organ to the ear, comes to my sight the time that is in store for you."[3] I enjoy very much the implicit connection between time and music, music becoming the metaphor that makes time itself audible. Time is constitutive of music, of course, but it's really an acoustic translation of the silent arrow of time here.

And then we get a third mythological reference. This time Cacciaguida announces exile as the fatality that is hovering over Dante and for which he has to prepare himself: "As Hippolytus departed from Athens, by reason of his pitiless and perfidious stepmother"—Phaedra—"so from Florence must you depart." Dante is not quite Aeneas, since he's not out to establish an empire; he's not quite Phaethon, since he does not want to outdo, at least literally, his father; so perhaps Hippolytus is a closer match. Exile implies a necessary detachment from one's family, one's country, all the possible lines that tend to join us and to limit us. Cacciaguida continues, "So is it willed, so already plotted, and so shall be accomplished soon by him who ponders upon it in the place where every day Christ is bought and sold." Note the difference between "willed" and "plotted," the order of eternal destinies vs. the order of contingency and the infernal maneuvers against the pilgrim. And to really spell it out, Cacciaguida describes exile in all its painful reality, "You shall leave everything beloved most dearly, and this is the arrow which the bow of exile shoots first. You shall come to know how salt is the taste of another's bread, and how hard the path to descend and mount by another man's stairs."[4] Here the translator makes a mistake because Dante is very careful about the word order: down and up, not up and down, following a naturalistic logic. For him to go up is really a descent, lowering and degrading himself. It's a very interesting line, acknowledging a sense of gratitude, a sense of the spiritual ascent being inevitably at first a descent into the self.

To go back to this idea of self, the story of Hippolytus is the story of a stepmother who is trying to seduce her stepson, Theseus's child Hippolytus, who is forced to run away. The destructive desires within that family force him to leave, and he dies away from home. You have to wonder why Dante is thinking of this tragic figure to compare to himself as an exile. The potentially devastating and tragic consequences that befall Hippolytus could also be Dante's fate, or so he suggests. At any rate, this is the last of the three great mythological images through which Dante is contemplating what the self is and how the self can be determined in the world of history.

This series of comparisons is really the same extraordinary burden of a text that I have mentioned many times in this book: *The Confessions* of St. Augustine. That text is also about the question of how the self is related to history, but here Dante disagrees with Augustine. For Augustine, the self is one that takes refuge in its own interiority. Only at the time of the conversion can he rejoin history, and while that is one way Dante sees of entering history, his own stance is far from identical. The idea of self that he is going to have is not really Augustine's; it's that of a man who can belong to the history of the world by writing a poem, this poem. Dante understands the fundamental quality of the exilic experience of human beings, and that's simply not Augustine's stance. No disrespect is meant to Augustine with this contrast; it's just a different experience.

The prophecy of exile with which Canto 17 ends gives an entirely different twist to the self's relationship to history. The other model Dante has is Cacciaguida, who goes on to sacrifice himself for the benefit of a larger cause, the cause of the Christian Crusade in Jerusalem. But this model, like *The Aeneid* and all the others, is rejected. Dante says we all inevitably belong in history. There is no other way for the self to exist if not by measuring oneself with the pressures of historical realities. The political world is going to be his way out of the maze. It's the exilic self, an idea of the self as an art of dislocation from the world of history.

But how are we to understand this dislocation? Is dislocation a way of actually removing oneself altogether? Or is it just saying that one is out of place and out of time, that somehow one has a relationship to history that is perhaps polemical? With other details from the same three cantos, we can come up with an answer. Let's start with Canto 15, where this relationship to Cacciaguida is also played out etymologically. Dante is constantly punning with the metaphor of wings, *ali* in Italian, as in Alighieri, the "bearers of wings." For example, "I speak to you, thanks to her who clothed you with plumes for the lofty flight," or a little later, "I turned to Beatrice, and she heard before I spoke, and smiled to me a sign that made the wings of my desire increase," and a third time, "Will and faculty in mortals, for the reason that is plain to you, are not equally feathered in their wings."[5] He clearly aims to emphasize the etymology of his genealogy.

The main element of his actual exchange with Cacciaguida, though, is a focus on the Florence of old, an invocation of the golden age of the city, a kind of utopian construction. Dante writes, "Florence, within her ancient circle from which she still takes tierce and nones"—these are the times of the day rung by the bells of the nearby church—"abode in peace, sober and chaste. There was no necklace, no coronal, no embroidered gowns, no girdle that was more to be looked at than the person. Nor yet did the daughter at her birth cause fear to the father, for the time and the dowry did not outrun due measure on this side and that. Houses empty of family there were none, nor had Sardanapalus arrived yet to show what could be done in the chamber."[6] First of all, Florence is evoked within a closed circle of self-sufficiency called "her ancient circle." The circularity of the city implies both plentitude and a boundary. Dante does not have an idea of an expanding city; he projects a city held within its own perimeter, "from which she still takes tierce and nones," so that the language of space and time follows, as if everything could be both measured and interrelated. Then Florence is metaphorically linked to a sober, chaste woman, suggesting that here at least he believes in the famous image of the so-called body politic. We've discussed it before, the notion of the organic structure of the city as made up of interdependent parts, just as space and time indicate the interdependent coordinates within which the life of the city can be recalled. This is followed in turn by a sequence of anaphoras, all negatives, "no necklace, no coronal," and so on. People in the Middle Ages sometimes thought of cosmetics as bad rhetoric, perverse forms of seduction by means of which one could disfigure the natural continence and beauty of the human form. So Dante, by repeating these negatives, literally strips the woman of all the superfluities, all these complications, and brings the city back to the simplicity of its original chastity. This is clearly the golden age of Florence.

But does Dante really believe in this myth of the golden age? There is a rhetorical phrase for this sort of move, praising the bygone times: *laudatio,* which means "praise of the past," and is more of a rhetorical strategy to denounce the imperfections of today. In effect, Dante has a radically polemical view of the utopian spirit. He maintains this idea of a perfection that we push back into the past because it's no longer with us, though we want to fantasize about it nonetheless. He preserves it because utopia can become a normative idea by means of which we can alter the configuration of our own contingencies, our own history. Utopias don't exist, and many interesting figures in the history of ideas claim that they are dangerous constructions because they foment illusions about who we are, and yet they become necessary for Dante because in the light of those ideas, we can then alter what we perceive as the degradations of our own times.

Of course, this myth of a Florence of the past literally disintegrates when seen in contrast with the reality of Dante's life as an exile, which is going to await him in the future. So, it's exile that offers a realistic perspective of his being in history. It's not a punishment, though it induces suffering. It becomes a virtue. Furthermore, in effect, it will become a paradigm in which we can all recognize ourselves.

In Canto 16 this myth is extended, with an allusion to the idea that they lived in peace. Whenever I hear the language of peace, I hear an echo of Jerusalem, the city of peace, and that's what makes this reference so interesting. It's a typology of another city, another golden age of the past. Many prophets would recall the peacetime of Jerusalem as what the Jews had lost, hence their need to continue commemorating it in their history.

What makes this conjunction particularly strong in Canto 16 is that Dante also repeatedly refers to chronicles, which are a different mode of historiography. One place where you can find modalities of history is in Boethius, who writes *The Consolation of Philosophy,* at the center of which he figures the Wheel of Fortune. A kind of historiography that derives from this Boethian insight is that of writing the lives of families that ascend and descend, as opposed to the historiography of the fall of empires witnessed, for instance, in Augustine. With the chronicle genre, Dante goes to yet another historiographic model, the idea that history is reducible to the local events and circumstances of one's own life. He recalls all the families to the joy of his grandfather, who is experiencing the pleasure of memory. He shuttles back and forth in memory, between one item and another, recalling everything, but Dante soon discovers that he does not quite belong, that that kind of history does not really account for who he is and who he wants to be above all. Somehow, therefore, his definition of the self will depend on a certain idea of the future rather than the past.

Dante then turns to a mythological history of Florence, speaking of those "who at that time were there, between Mars and the Baptist."[7] Not only does one recount stories of families, one also has to recount stories of the predominant sovereignty of the mythologies that control one's own self-understanding. We tend to understand ourselves in the light of presiding imaginative myths, so here we get Mars, who was the god of Florence before John the Baptist replaced him. This is an account of the shifting mythology of the city, told with a chronicler's precision.

The language then shifts from myth to mixture—"the citizenship, which is now mixed with Campi, with Certaldo, and with Figline"—which later becomes confusion. When Dante has to give a diagnosis of the crisis of the city, he points to the confusion caused by this amalgamation: "The intermingling of people was ever the beginning of harm to the city, as to you the food which is loaded on is to the body."[8] Once again he's talking about the malaise of the city through the connection between bodies and cities. Cities grow and decay and get sick like bodies do. Also, he called the mixture *confusion,* which is another name for Babylon. So the two myths of the city that Dante has in mind for Florence in this scene are those of Jerusalem and Babylon. The two model cities are not antithetical; they are both possible within the same body politic. Florence can look like Jerusalem or like Babylon, according to the way in which the moral life of the city is lived out.

Dante preserves this ambiguity as a sign that the political world is reshaped all the time. There is no definite metaphor or emblem to define a

particular city. A city can constantly change its identity. And we are involved in the city's history because we describe it according to our own as-
pirations and ideas; we share in the shaping and construction of the city.
This perspective is no longer that of the chronicler, but that of a poet. It's a
critique of the inadequacy of the chronicle's view of what history could be.

Then, in Canto 17, with the image of Phaethon Dante questions his
true relationship with Cacciaguida, who is directing him and unveiling for
him what he can expect from the future. Here we get the famous description of Dante's exile, which has already been cited in this chapter: "You
shall leave everything beloved most dearly, and this is the arrow which the
bow of exile shoots first." The harshness of exile could not be crystallized in
sharper terms than these. The severance of the self from the family is apparent as a punishment at this point. He continues, "You shall come to
know how salt is the taste of another's bread." Some feel that Dante is providing mild comic relief here by mentioning the fact that in Florence they
do not use salt in their bread, but I don't think it's all that comical. Bread is
the most sacramental of foods. It's not just a metaphor, and in one of the
next lines Dante makes a further etymological reference to it: "That which
shall most weigh your shoulders down will be the evil and senseless company."[9] The word *company* maintains the reference to bread because it
means a "sharing of bread with others," so bread truly adjoins and brings
about the unity of the body politic.

This "prophecy" is, obviously, a genuine reflection of Dante's own life.
He went into exile in the year 1302, and for a number of years he was plot-
ting along with his fellow exiles to return to Florence and vanquish the enemies who had banished them. It was a revenge plot in order to restore what
they saw as justice. Dante came to understand, however, that this path was
only a route to absolute destruction, so from then on he moves like a shabby
derelict. He represents himself limping at the beginning of *Inferno,* and
that is really the way we are asked to imagine him as he goes through life in
exile. It was not a matter of living in isolated splendor in some court or
other. Exile entails going from place to place begging, so this is absolutely
intended as a form of punishment for him.

Sadly, he is an exile even to other exiles. Both the Guelphs and Ghibellines distrust him and take their distance from him, "but, soon after,
their brows, not yours, shall redden for it. Of their brutish folly their own
conduct shall afford the proof, so that it will be for your fair fame to have
made you a party by yourself."[10] How astonishing, to be absolutely on your
own, "a party by yourself." This is mildly perplexing, to say the least, seeing

as the *Divine Comedy* begins with the representation of the neutral angels, those angels who wanted to be neither for God nor against Him, but rather by themselves. I have pointed out that for Dante this was the most despicable of conditions and choices, though it seems to be a nonchoice. One is really choosing anyway, even when one is choosing "not to choose," and to Dante's thinking it's despicable not to take sides, to sit on the fence. And yet here he seems to attribute that very condition to himself. He has to be by himself, but is that really a kind of neutrality he's imagining? I think that he's actually describing the destitution and loneliness involved in his separation from others.

But in a certain sense the exile is still part of the community. Dante brings about a transformation of the idea of exile from what seemed to be a punishment into a virtue. The language with which Dante presents the world to come for him, his future, suggests that history is understood as, above all, futurity. We are oriented to the future, the only real time that we have. We don't have it yet, but it's the time of one's projects, the time in which one can really define oneself. I have some contact with the past, through my memories, but sometimes a catastrophe occurs, and only the future can define me then.

Dante's prophecy doesn't end simply with mention of exile, though:

> "Your first refuge and first inn shall be the courtesy of the great Lombard [a gentleman of Verona who hosted him for a while, and who was the older brother of Cangrande, whom we encountered earlier and is mentioned below] who bears the holy bird upon the ladder, and he will have for you such benign regard that, in doing and in asking, between you two, that will be first which between others is the slowest. With him you shall see one [Cangrande] who, at his birth, was so stamped by this strong star, that notable shall be his deeds. Not yet have folk taken due note of him, because of his young age, for these wheels have revolved around him only nine years; but before the Gascon deceives the lofty Henry, some sparks of his virtue shall appear, in his caring naught for money or for toils. His magnificence shall hereafter be so known, that his very foes will not be able to keep silent tongues about him. Look you to him and to his benefits. By him shall many folk be changed, the rich and the beggarly altering their condition. And you shall bear hence written of him in your mind, but you shall not tell it"; —and he told things

past the belief even of those who shall see them. Then he added,
"Son, these are the glosses on what was said to you; behold the
snares which are hidden behind but a few circlings. Yet I would
not have you envious of your neighbors, since your life shall be
prolonged far beyond the punishment of their perfidies."[11]

The glosses mentioned here come from *Inferno* 15, of course, when Brunetto
told Dante that his future exile would be glossed by another person, whom
Dante has been thinking would be Beatrice, though it turns out to be his
forefather. The language that accompanies this prediction is the language
of the ethics of exile. Exile brings about and needs hospitality in order to be
bearable and tolerable. Courtesy, gratitude, and giving—it's a new ethics
from the perspective of Dante's exilic experience.

Then Dante concludes with a passage that I think seals what I have
been saying. It begins: "I see well, my father, how time spurs toward me to
give me such a blow as is heaviest to whosoever is most heedless; wherefore
it is good that I arm myself with foresight,'" which is another virtue of exile. Foresight is another way of saying prudence, which is the human counterpart of providence. They have the same etymology, a seeing in advance,
trying not to predict but to forestall the slings and arrows that come our
way, "so that if the dearest place be taken from me, I lose not all the rest by
reason of my songs." He continues:

> "Down in the world endlessly bitter, and upon the mountain
> from whose fair summit my lady's eyes uplifted me, and after,
> through the heavens from light to light, I have learned that
> which, if I tell again, will have for many a savor of great bitter-
> ness; and if I am a timid friend to the truth, I fear to lose life
> among those who shall call this time ancient." The light wherein
> was smiling the treasure I had found there first became flashing
> as a golden mirror in the sun, then it replied, "A conscience
> dark, either with its own or with another's shame, will indeed
> feel your speech to be harsh. But none the less, all falsehood set
> aside, make manifest all that you have seen; and then let them
> scratch where the itch is. For if at first taste your voice be griev-
> ous, yet shall it leave thereafter vital nourishment when di-
> gested. This cry of yours shall do as does the wind, which smites
> most upon the loftiest summits; and this shall be no little cause
> of honor. Therefore only the souls known of fame have been

shown to you within these wheels, upon the mountain, and in the woeful valley; for the mind of him who hears rests not nor confirms its faith by an example that has its roots unknown or hidden, nor for other proof that is not manifest."[12]

What Dante will take as a palliative, at least, or a remedy to his exile, is writing. The writing of the poem becomes the act by which he, an exile, can survive his utter dislocation from his city, from his family, from his habits. The work is the way in which the self enters and shapes history. It's not Aeneas, it's not Phaethon, it's not Hippolytus, it's not even Cacciaguida's account of his own grandiloquent connection with the world of history. The way in which Dante's self enters history is through the power of poetry.

Dante goes beyond the misconception about poetic language that it's but a faint symbol divorced from reality. What Dante is saying is that words are things in themselves, that words are food for thought. Being things, they have a kind of solidity and a truth-value in and of themselves. Dante bends the language to define himself in a relationship to his future project of writing the poem, and that project of writing the poem is his way of establishing his place in a utopian history. I say "utopian" because it doesn't have to be understood in any local sense. Dante corrects the classical idea, which survived in medieval times, that the value of the self is decided by the place one occupies within the economy of the city. Dante says that's not the way it works, that he is the project of writing his poetry, and even through poetry written in exile, outside of the city, he can reenter the world of history. Talking as a man who has been touched by a vision of what justice ought to be, Dante sets a unique path for himself: writing of writing as his own way to join the self and history.

CHAPTER 20

Paradiso 18–22

In Canto 18 Dante is initially still in the heaven of Mars. There he lists a number of warriors, souls who are heroic figures like Cacciaguida. He mentions the biblical figures Joshua and Judas Maccabeus and then he names several medieval figures. First in line is Charlemagne, as Dante is clearly retrospectively justifying the whole issue of the Crusades in which Cacciaguida took part. It can really be brought back to Charlemagne's experience in France and Spain against the Muslims. Of course he also names Charlemagne's paladin, the great, Achilles-like, seemingly invulnerable Roland, who died at Roncevaux because of the hubris that characterized his life, in that case the hubris of not wanting to blow the horn that would have been heard by Charlemagne so that his leader could have come to his rescue. That scene became in the Western imagination a most traumatic experience because it showed that the myth of invincibility of Christian Europe was simply that, an illusion to be turned to rubble by the victorious invading armies. Then Dante refers to a few figures of the Second Crusade, like Godfrey of Bouillon and Robert Guiscard.

With all these names Dante develops a clear thematic thread between the previous cantos and this canto, involving the question of what a heroic life is. The heroic life can even involve a defeat, as in the case of Roland. Still, there is a typology that runs from the epic biblical stories to contemporary history. For Dante a heroic figure is not necessarily a figure who would unify and cut across barriers and divisions. On the contrary, Dante is indicating that there's a possible heroic life in giving of oneself to a cause much larger than oneself.

What I would stress, though, about this particular scene is that Dante is really aware of divisions, of the need to separate what is his from what is not his, what is ours from what is not ours, and so on. He seems to be perpetuating an idea that some might find objectionable, that this separation is dangerous and in itself both caused by war and a cause of wars. And this is not the only time that Dante has established such divisions. For just one example, over the past few chapters, for instance, Dante has also drawn lines on the map, between countries and continents. He always goes out of his way to mention this idea of separation, so there are many divisions in the *Comedy*.

And yet, he seems to believe that Rome and the history of Rome really escape this logic of separation. In effect, as previously mentioned, in the *Monarchia,* the political tract that Dante writes, he does stress the fact that Aeneas is a true Roman. He cannot be thought of as an Asian, which he was, nor can he be thought of as a European, even though there is a sort of universalizing impulse in him, in the measure in which he married three women from three different continents. Dante has to distinguish between two kinds of history, one that transcends barriers and another that maintains them, like that of the people who fought in the Crusades.

An underlying problem in Cantos 15–17 that becomes more central in the heaven of Jupiter in Cantos 18–20 is a very abstract question: namely, what is a place? In Canto 15 Dante had tried to determine whether his history could be reduced to the boundaries of his native town and decided that it was no longer possible because he is an exile. In Latin, *exile* means "being out of one's own soil," so in the Middle Ages they never really thought of exile as more than a physical condition. Dante changes this meaning of exile by making it into a spiritual condition, the precondition for his writing poetry in the first place. But in these later cantos the question becomes broader: what is one's own soil, one's own place? What are the terms in which we can define place?

In Canto 18, he moves into the heaven of Jupiter, a heaven of white light that he links with geometry. Geometry is a very complex science that allows for the measurement of the whole earth, according to its etymology. And it implies the presence of perspective within it, since geometry is what regulates the arrangement of space and permits the measurement of depth. It has a profoundly intimate linkage with ethics, as seen in the rule of the counterpart or *contrapasso* in *Inferno* 28, when Dante has to establish the relationship between crime and punishment. It could not be an even, one-to-one relationship. You cannot simply pluck out someone's eye because someone has plucked out your eye—that's not necessarily justice. There should be some kind of proportionality. The idea is that geometry is related to ethics because its extension always implies a point that is the beginning of a geometric reflection, that always indicates the existence of other points. Geometry and ethics allow for the establishment of a just system of relations.

Dante repeatedly deploys the language of geometry in these cantos. For instance, he introduces the notion of God the geometer in Canto 19: "The primal Will, which of itself is good, has never moved from itself, which is the Supreme Good. All is just that accords with It; no created good draws It to itself, but It, raying forth"—*ray*, which in Italian is a ray of sunlight but also the radius of a circle—"is the cause of it. As the stork circles"—shapes—"over her nest."[1] Or as soon Dante enters the heaven of geometry in Canto 18, we come across a plane, a divine spectacle, a sacred theater where God speaks to human beings by using the souls of the blessed. He writes, "I saw in that torch of Jove the sparkling of the love that was there, trace out our speech to my eyes; and as birds, risen from the shore, as if rejoicing together at their pasture, make of themselves now a round flock"—another geometric image—"now some other shape, so within the lights holy creatures were singing as they flew, and in their figures made of themselves, now *D*, now *I*, now *L*."[2] Within the heaven of geometry, even the letters of the alphabet are considered to be drawings of geometrical lines, the semicircle of the D, the two perpendicular lines of the L, and the vertical line of the I. We discover that the beauty of geometry underlies the rigor of the alphabet.

But more importantly, we discover that these souls that dispose themselves in letters are really God's way of speaking to us. The language that God uses is the language of human beings. We are the syllables, we are the letters disposed in order to convey whatever God's message may be. Dante continues, "They displayed themselves then, in five times seven vowels and consonants; and I took note of the parts as they appeared in utterance to me. *DILIGITE IUSTITIAM . . . QUI IUDICATIS TERRAM.*"[3] They spell out a verse from the Book of Wisdom: love justice, you who judge the Earth. That's another reference to the actual ultimate measurement of geometry, the earth itself. Geography, in a certain sense, is geometry.

But the other crucial concern in these cantos has to do with justice. How will Dante bring justice and geometry together? In Canto 19, he's hungry to know what divine justice is: "Well do I know that if the Divine Justice makes another realm in heaven Its mirror, yours does not apprehend It through a veil. You know how eagerly I prepare myself to listen; you know what is that question which is so old a fast to me." An eagle responds, "He that turned His compass round the limit of the world, and within it marked out so much both hidden and revealed, could not so imprint His power on all the universe that His Word should not remain in infinite excess."[4] This image of God the geometer clearly echoes two biblical texts. One is Job 38, a famous passage, "Where were you when I drew the boundaries of the Earth?" That's the geometrical matrix of this metaphor of God the geometer. And the other one is in the Book of Wisdom: "I was there with him and I was His delight when He was drawing the circle around the deep." Those are two biblical passages that insist on the idea that the shapes of the world are really representations of the perfection of God's geometry. And then Dante refers to "infinite excess," two words that are slightly redundant together because excess means something that is measureless. The language of measure, of accounting, and of limits is set against this idea of something not finite, something that escapes the logic of geometry altogether. In fact, I find the phrase deliberately redundant; it's an excessive idea of the infinite, just to drive the point home. Even the word *universe* is geometrical because it implies a turning. You come to the end of the line, and you turn, drawing a geometrical figure. It's one turning of the sphere, and the two hemispheres make the universe. Dante's quest for justice has been answered with a number of geometrical references.

But it is in the proofs of this mathematical passage that justice really comes to light. The eagle continues, "This is certified by that first proud one"—Lucifer—"who was the highest of all creatures and who, through not awaiting light, fell unripe; from which it is plain that every lesser nature is too scant a vessel for that Good which has no limit and measures Itself by Itself. Thus your vision, which must needs be one of the rays of the Mind with which all things are replete, cannot of its own nature be of such power that it should not perceive its origin to be far beyond all that is apparent to it. Therefore the sight that is granted to your world penetrates within the Eternal Justice as the eye into the sea; which, though from the shore it can see the bottom, in the open sea it sees it not, and none the less it is there, but the depth conceals it."[5] The idea here is that we can see justice only when we have a very superficial understanding of it, just as we see the bottom of the sea when we are near the shore, but otherwise we don't. God's justice is as imponderable and unfathomable as the sea floor can be out in open waters. Dante gets his answer at last.

But then Dante complicates the issue a little bit by asking where this justice can be found. Is justice limited to a place, to a continent, to the economy of Christian Europe? And how is it related to other places? These days we have a notion of what we call alterity, of "the Other," but this notion was certainly not alien in the Middle Ages. People then had an idea of otherness, and it always involved acknowledging the particular difference between oneself and the Other. Up to this point, there has not been any substantial deviation on the part of Dante from the myth and examples of the heroic life, the lives of those who established boundaries and within those boundaries managed to live according to the fullness of their virtues. But now Dante asks what that boundary is. He understands that divine justice is impenetrable but then he asks the extraordinary question of where it can even be found, what its border is. In sum, he asks once more, what is a place?

To answer this complex question, Dante offers up a world tour in the rest of Canto 19. First, he says, "A man is born on the bank of Indus"—in Asia—"and none is there to speak, or read, or write, of Christ, and all his wishes and acts are good, so far as human reason sees, without sin in life or in speech. He dies unbaptized, and without faith. Where is this justice which condemns him? Where is his sin if he does not believe?" Then he continues circling these issues, and we have a return to Europe. The eagle, the symbol of Rome, is mentioned in that particular context: "After those glowing flames of the Holy Spirit became quiet, still in the sign which made the Romans reverend to the world," with allusions to the Romans as if Rome to Dante has become an idea of universality. The eagle also notes: "To this realm none ever rose who believed not in Christ, either before or after he was nailed to the tree. But behold, many cry Christ, Christ, who, at the Judgment, shall be far less near to Him than he who knows not Christ."[6] The Ethiopians in Africa are mentioned, as are the Persians in Asia. The three continents demonstrate divisions of belief that will soon seem to lose all consistency, however, because you may be a European, but there is also moral alterity within Europe. Alterity is not just a question of geographic disposition. Someone who is a Persian is clearly Other to me, but in terms of the moral life, the same kind of otherness exists within Europe. Europe is not uniform.

To illustrate such local diversity, Dante starts with a kingdom of Prague, which "shall be made a desert," and then moves to France, where "shall be seen the woe which he who shall die by a boarskin blow is bringing upon the Seine." One could make a game out of counting all the countries in this canto. He continues, "There shall be seen the pride that quickens thirst, which makes the Scot and the Englishman mad, so that neither can keep within his own bounds." There is a history of violence that transgresses boundaries:

> It will show the lechery and effeminate life of him of Spain, and him of Bohemia, who never knew valor nor wished it. It will show the Cripple of Jerusalem, his goodness marked with an *I*, while an *M* will mark the opposite. It will show the avarice and cowardice of him who has in ward the Isle of Fire [Sicily] where Anchises ended his long life; and to give to understand how paltry he is, the writing for him shall be in contractions that will note much in little space. And plain to all shall be revealed the foul deeds of his uncle and his brother, which have dishonored so eminent a lineage and two crowns. And he of Portugal and he of Norway shall be known there, and he of Rascia, who, to his harm, has seen the coin of Venice. Oh happy Hungary, if she no longer allow herself to be mistreated! and happy Navarre, if she arm herself with the mountains which bind her round! And all should believe that, for earnest of this, Nicosia and Famagosta are now lamenting and complaining because of their beast who departs not from the side of the others.[7]

This is now the history of the whole of Europe, in the same way that Dante gave the history of the Roman Empire earlier. But this is a history of desolation and moral dereliction. The terms become questions of what is "here" and what is "there"? What is within and outside of an economy of redemption? The answer is that we do not know. We do not know how salvation is going to work out. No one can claim, therefore, to decide what exact moral boundaries exist between one place and another. Dante tempers, therefore, both the notion of political boundaries and that of moral boundaries. He distinguishes the two issues and thereby emphasizes cultural divides rather than geographical or religious ones.

One way of understanding what Dante is doing here is to turn to a little story from the *Histories* of Herodotus, a great Greek historian. He writes the story as a warning to the Greeks about to invade Egypt of the dangers they may face as they violate their boundaries. It makes a strong argument in favor of such boundaries.

Once upon a time the king of Egypt, Candaules, who was not a very bright man, had a beautiful wife, and was so taken with the beauty of his wife that he wanted everybody to know about it. But he can't just tell everybody, so he tells his advisor, a prudent man, who responds, "Sire, your majesty, I don't want to know. I believe you, but please don't tell me anymore about this."

But the king was insistent, "You've got to know. In fact, not only do you have to hear it, I also want you to see the naked beauty of my wife. It's beyond belief, and I want you to see it because human beings tend to trust their eyes more than their ears."

The counselor, ever prudent, says, "No, sire, this is really too much trouble. I cannot disobey you, but you are forcing me to insist that this is not a good idea. I believe you completely. You can go right on telling me all about her beauty. But I don't want to see it."

The king ignores him. "Nonsense," he says, "I'm arranging this." And he contrives a little plot. Every night the wife bathes in a room next to the bedroom. And the king leaves the door ajar to allow her to come into the bedroom when she's done. That night, while she's out of the room, he allows the counselor to hide in the shadows, in a little corner. The queen comes in and undresses, so the counselor sees her naked. Then, very quickly and stealthily, he walks out, hoping not to have been seen.

But the next morning the queen, a sharp woman, calls him into her office and says, "I saw you. Tell me what you were doing there." The counselor has no choice but to admit that the king asked him to come and pay witness to her naked beauty.

The queen says, "I imagined that was what happened, but at this point two of you is one too many. The idea that I have been seen naked by two men is unbearably shameful to me. So you must either kill the king or kill yourself."

The counselor does what I'm sure all of you would do, and thus he becomes the new king. The king was a fool. He had no prudence. He had no sense of the difference between the private life and the public need. He had no idea that there are things that you keep to yourself and don't share with others. In other words, he didn't know his limits. He violated crucial boundaries and as a result, he lost his crown, his wife, and his life.

Herodotus is clearly warning us to understand that there is always a limit that we have to set up and protect between what is mine and what is yours. I do not know that Dante would completely agree with Herodotus in these cantos, but what he has been doing is setting up cultural difference as equally necessary. Cultural differences allow for a moral circulation of ideas. What he is taking on there would seem to be what we call, in medieval terms, a Pelagian stance. Pelagian is an adjective that comes from the name of a British monk of roughly the time of St. Augustine, the fifth century, who maintained that through good works and living according to principles of nature alone, human beings can be saved. There seems to be such an emphasis on the ability of human beings to live rationally in this idea that the demands of grace and the demands of faith are somewhat bracketed and a little dim. Nonetheless, I believe that they are present; it's just that Dante is talking as a philosopher in these cantos.

In fact, Dante is really asking for a conversation between philosophy and theology, within reason and faith. He understands that philosophy without theology ends up in a sort of labyrinth of its own constructions and may lose its way. Theology, without philosophy, may end up in mere opinion, which has no validity at all for people who believe in the power of reason. And this potential combination is an extension of the problem of exile. An exile, which requires a sense of the problematical qualities of a place in the world and the relationship that we have with ourselves and with our own ideas, has allowed Dante to see both the theologian and the philosopher within himself.

The philosopher-theologian continues his journey in Cantos 21 and 22, moving to the heaven of Saturn, which is the heaven of contemplation. The myth of Saturn is the myth of time devouring everything that it engenders. Time is the first cannibal in history, eating what it produces, the minutes that are absorbed and wasted. This last planet is also the heaven of astronomy, so Dante is forcing on us the idea of contemplation. Here he finds the contemplatives, and among them there is the soul of a founder of monasticism by the name of Benedict.

Canto 21 begins with another mythological reference as Dante contemplates contemplation: "Already my eyes were fixed again on the face of my lady, and with them my mind, and from every other intent it was withdrawn; and she did not smile, but, 'Were I to smile' she began to me, 'you would become such as was Semele when she was turned to ashes; for my beauty which, along the steps of the eternal palace, is kindled the more, as you have seen, the higher the ascent, were it not tempered, is so resplendent that your mortal powers at its flash would be like the bough shattered by a thunderbolt. We have risen to the seventh splendor which beneath the breast of the burning Lion rays down now mingled with its power. Fix your mind after your eyes, and make of them mirrors to the figure which in this mirror shall be shown to you.' "[8] This is the myth of Semele, the young woman who fell in love with God. It could be an extraordinary spiritual story, but Ovid tells it as a very carnal tale. Semele wants to love Jupiter, and Jupiter agrees to love Semele back on one condition, that she never ask the god to show himself forth for what he is. She has to accept the god's disguises. Love does not want to be seen for what it is and demands simulacra and deceptive figures to cover its essence. Of course, Semele is in love, and love impels curiosity, so she wants Jupiter to reveal himself for what he is, mindless of the danger of death that Jupiter had predicted. In the end, he reveals himself, and Semele, unable to bear the astonishing beauty of the god, is reduced to ashes.

Why would Dante recall this story here? Dante does so because he's aware of the dangers of visionary claims. Beatrice is telling him that he has to endure the limitations of his human nature, and that this trait of his mortality, seeing through images, cannot yet be given up. He does this as he enters the heaven of the contemplatives, who themselves were longing to see God, but accepted this longing as the sign of God's presence and gift to them. Dante indicates the risk of thinking of contemplation as the condition that could bring about the vision of God. Such a vision, Dante is saying, is not going to be possible while we are here on earth.

Dante may or may not be a mystic, but I think that he is definitely a contemplative in the true sense of the word. The word *contemplation* translates a Greek theory of turning the mind toward essentials. The word comes from *templum,* the Latin word for "temple," but also from *tempus,* or "time." These words have the same origin; they both come from the Greek word *temno,* which means "to cut." Saturn, time, cuts with a scythe. The contemplatives cut a piece of time and space and privilege it, cut it off from the flow of history and the flow of profane place, and make it the ground for turning minds to the consideration of higher things.

One such space may be found at the end of Canto 22, where Dante has reached the periphery of the planetary system. Now he will go into the stars, into the heaven of the fixed stars. Beatrice speaks of his position, "You are so near to the final blessedness . . . that you must have your eyes clear and keen." Here Dante will deploy the language of visionariness, which will start with an emphasis on purifying and refining one's eyes and one's eyesight. Beatrice continues, "Therefore, before you enter farther into it, look back downward and behold how great a world I have already set beneath your feet, in order that your heart may present itself, joyous to its utmost, to the triumphal throng which comes glad through this round ether."⁹ It's one of two invitations from Beatrice for Dante to turn his eyes back and have a moment of contemplation.

"With my sight"—Dante is now engaged in this retrospective glance down to the earth—"I returned through all and each of the seven spheres, and saw this globe such that I smiled at its paltry semblance." This perspective comes from outer space. I wouldn't call it infinite space, but certainly a vast distance of space stands between Dante and his home planet. Dante's notion of the universe is not that it's infinite; rather, it is a bounded but vast enclave. From this distance, Dante is able to give us a brief astronomy lesson: "I saw the daughter of Latona"—the moon—"glowing without that shade for which I once believed her rare and dense. The aspect of your son, Hyperion, I there endured, and saw how Maia and Dione move around and near him"—meaning Mercury. "Then appeared to me the tempering of Jove between his father and his son, and then was clear to me the varying they make in their position. And all the seven were displayed to me, how great they are and swift, and how distant each from other in location."¹⁰ So, we are presented with astronomy here in the heaven of astronomy, but it's intriguingly an astronomy indicated mythically and through a process of affiliation. It's the *daughter* of Latona, the *son* of Hyperion, and so on, a sequence of connections as if the universe has followed the logic of generation and production, producing and reproducing itself.

And then Dante turns from astronomy to astrology: "The little threshing-floor which makes us so fierce was all revealed to me from hills to river-mouths, as I circled with the eternal Twins."¹¹ Dante is giving his horoscope indirectly here, for the Twins are the sign under which he was born. It doesn't really imply any astrological lapse on his part; it's just an allusion to his birth sign. He abolishes the differences between astronomy and astrology, but in doing so he belongs fully to his time, when there was no intrinsic conception of astrologists as practicing mere superstition versus the inarguable science of astronomy.

What I truly want to draw your attention to in this passage is the pronoun *us*. For all the distance implied by this poetic fiction, Dante ought to be as distant from the earth as he ever was. But the pronoun strains to have it both ways. On the one hand, Dante asserts the claim of a perspective of eternity on the world, but on the other hand, he does not want to surrender his place in time and history. He is part of humanity, part of "us," so at the end of this great gyration through the universe, Dante claims and reclaims for himself a place within our ranks. The synthesis of the two, the claim of eternity and the sense of contingency of the self in time, is the ultimate goal of the poem and the ultimate goal of the pilgrim's journey. That synthesis will be, as we shall see in upcoming chapters, the very vision of the Incarnation: the immutable structure of history and the process of time will come together.

CHAPTER 21

Paradiso 24–26

Now we are going to look at the three cantos in the eighth sphere of Dante's cosmos, the heaven of the fixed stars. We are beyond the planets, in a sphere where Dante discusses the three theological virtues—so called to distinguish them from the four cardinal virtues that Christians share with the classical tradition, fortitude, prudence, temperance, and justice—of faith, hope, and love (or charity). These are the virtues that deal with the understanding of the divine; they open up this horizon of speculations about the language of God, the way God speaks to us, and the way in which we speak about God. This is the place in Paradise where Dante will focus on the meaning of "basic words," the words that are foundations of the way in which we come to discover who we are. They are words that we use when we may not even know exactly what they mean, though Dante will try to define them for us here.

The three virtues that Dante will describe are terms that always implicate each other. You cannot explain faith without talking about hope. You cannot talk about hope without explaining faith, and both of them are recapitulated and come together within the virtue of love. They are words that are very mysterious in many ways, but there are degrees of understanding to all of them.

Dante will go through the equivalent of a university examination, a medieval bachelor's degree. He presents himself to the teacher who is testing him, and he gives an answer to the teacher's questions according to textbooks. The three teachers here are going to be three of the Apostles. The first is St. Peter, for faith, and that makes sense because his very name stands for the cornerstone on which the edifice of Christian belief is built.

The second one is James, for hope. The connection is less obvious, but he among all the Apostles is the one whose death was recorded in the Acts of the Apostles, a true figure of hopefulness in his yearning for a future and the life of eternity. Finally, John the Apostle, who is the beloved of Jesus, tests Dante on love or charity.

Before we delve into the specifics of these examinations, though, I would like to give you some summary ways of trying to understand these virtues. One subtext running through these three cantos, sometimes but not always visible, is the question of exile. Dante is retrieving the language of exile as if these virtues don't concern the blessed in heaven, as if they only concern us here in time. The blessed in heaven certainly do not need faith or hope, and they don't really need to know about what love may be. Either they have these virtues or they wouldn't be in Paradise. So, the language of exile is a constant presence here, in association with the language of time. We are in time, we are fallen, and it's only through the language of the fall that we can understand exile.

Another element running through this segment of the *Comedy,* especially in Canto 26, is the matter of language itself. What is the language of God? Are we talking about an entity with a name? And if so, where does Dante fall in the whole debate about the tetragrammaton, the four Hebrew letters that are supposedly the name of God? Is God some kind of reality we can never even hope to name, or are we going to be related and connected to this idea, this knowledge of God by analogical discourse? Dante makes these inquiries and presents various positions on them: the mystical position that denies even our knowledge of the name of God, or the analogical position put forth by Aquinas, that we talk about God analogically and the qualities we attribute to God are not real but represented by what we know in our own lives. In short, Dante asks the difficult question: how do we get to know God?

And with these issues in mind, we can turn to the virtues themselves, the first of which is the virtue of faith. It seems that faith, for Dante, has to be placed within a communal context. Canto 24 begins with a telling apostrophe: "O fellowship elect to the great supper of the blessed Lamb, who feeds you so that your desire is ever satisfied, since by God's grace this man has foretaste of that which falls from your table, before death appoints his time, give heed to his measureless craving and bedew him with some drops; you drink always from the fountain whence comes that on which his mind is set."[1] He wants to stress the metaphor of a banquet. We're really dealing with two metaphors here: one is exilic, referencing the manna in the desert,

the falling of dew on the Jewish wanderers; and the other is the eschatological banquet. In both cases, food is part of the experience of a community.

This discussion is not going to address the profession of faith. It's really more a prefiguration of the great debate between two figures of the Renaissance called Erasmus and Luther. They argued at length about the
meaning of a text written about a century earlier, around 1440, by Valla, a
great humanist: *On Free Will*. Erasmus maintains that Valla had defended
the existence of free will. Free will, a gift of God, is something that has been
given to us, and therefore we have to come to know God through the acknowledgment of his authority because the freedom that Valla is talking
about actually comes from Him. It is by free will that we come to know the
existence of the divinity. Luther instead had very radical ideas about the
question of freedom. He claims that there is no such thing. Rather, the universe is a world of absolute faith, and faith is freedom because it releases us
from all obligations, frees us from all constraints, and makes us understand that our own relationship to the Creator is without any intermediary
forces. It's a radical, theological claim of freedom and faith together.

Dante's position in this debate is to remove the question from stances
of either radical subjectivity or radical faith, aware that there may a flip side
to it. Dante focuses on the communal experience, as previously discussed
with the banquet. And then Dante emphasizes the individuality of the private faith. At the end, it's really about his own self

One interesting thing that I want to point out at the outset are Beatrice's words to Peter. She appeals to him to examine Dante, but she does so
in a peculiar way: "O eternal light of the great man with whom our Lord left
the keys"—this is canonical, part of the iconographic representation of Peter with the two keys—"which He bore below, of this marvelous joy, test
this man on points light and grave, as pleases you, concerning the faith by
which you did walk upon the sea."[2] This is an allusion to a passage in the
Gospels when Peter walks on water out of an act of faith, because Jesus asks
him to do so. A key thing about this reference is that Peter did not want to
walk on water. It is a moment of a crisis of faith. He was teetering on the
brink of the abyss, struggling, but he does finally manage to go on. This is a
poignant moment, and Dante is clearly stressing that there are degrees of
faith, and that a crisis of faith must not be seen as a denial of faith. On the
contrary, there is a sort of dialectical movement between a profession of
faith and doubts about owning that gift of faith.

Beatrice's request is swiftly met. Dante uses the language of the university and academic life, as if this were really an academic test. The bachelor

of arts, *baccalaureatus,* arms himself with the weapon of knowledge. And the master, *magister,* "propounds the question—in order to adduce the proof, not to decide it." These issues always require the open-endedness of argumentation and a settling of a point. So, Dante prepares himself: "while she was speaking, I was arming myself with every reason, to be ready for such a questioner and for such a profession."[3]

And the exam begins: "Speak, good Christian, and declare yourself." This is a knowledge that will make him visible, a knowledge that does not keep him hidden. It brings him into existence. What is faith? That's the question that Peter asks. And the answer is: "'May the grace that grants me to confess to the Chief Centurion,' I began, 'cause my conceptions to be well expressed.' And I went on, 'As the veracious pen of your dear brother'"—an allusion to Paul—"'wrote of it, who with you, father, put Rome on the good path, Faith is the substance of things hoped for and the evidence of things not seen.'"[4] Here Dante is questioning an authority, and authority is attained only by those who are worthy of faith. The teacher is not inherently worthy of faith. You can question the opinions of the teacher and reject the questions asked by him or her. There's a distinction between the master and the author, so Dante quotes Paul in order to provide a canonical answer. For Dante, as for Paul, faith is literally the foundation, that which underlies all things.

The most famous formulation of faith in the Middle Ages comes from Tertullian, who says he believes because it is absurd, so that faith becomes a consequence and extension of the absurdity of all things. What one believes has in itself an idea of going beyond reason, and therefore it is absurd. Faith exceeds the law of reason and thus can never quite be an object of knowledge.

Dante does not pursue that line of thought because he tries to show that faith and reason belong together. This is the true sense of the whole metaphorical pattern of the university context, to illustrate that knowledge and faith implicate each other. They are not the same thing because if you could know everything of what you believe, then there would be no reason for belief; faith becomes necessary as a way of acknowledging the limitations of what one knows. But linking knowledge and faith is not simply a way of saying that reason can know some of the content of what Dante believes. At a deeper level, Dante is saying that faith itself is a mode of knowledge. Its modalities are going to be different, because with philosophy, for instance, that knowledge submits to the rules of the rationality, but faith opens your eyes and shows you something about the world that reason alone cannot.

Then the examination continues: "I heard, 'Rightly do you deem, if you understand well why he placed it among the substances and then among the evidences.' And I thereon, 'The deep things which grant to me here the sight of themselves are so hidden to eyes below that there their existence is in belief alone, upon which the lofty hope is founded; and therefore it takes the designation of substance. And from this belief needs must we reason, without seeing more: therefore it receives the designation of evidence.'"[5] Now there is a caesura between belief and what we are—the evidence of things not seen. The paradox remains, so there are things visible here in the heaven of the fixed stars and not available to those of us who are in time and in the fallen world. This passage is a gloss on the medieval theological lexicon that Dante has been deploying.

Peter accepts this answer but replies, "Now the alloy and the weight of this coin have been well enough examined; but tell me if you have it in your purse?" All of a sudden, the question of faith is placed in the realm of money. Dante responds, "'Yes, I have it so shining and so round that in its stamp nothing is doubtful to me.' Then issued from the deep light that was shining there, 'This precious jewel whereon every virtue is founded, whence did it come to you?'"[6] The language is from the plenteous reign of the Holy Spirit, and that metaphor of money as faith has a way of lingering in our minds. What is the connection? One connection is to indicate the preciousness of the faith one holds. It is really as rare and valuable as beautiful jewels can be. That's one thing, but clearly there is more, because the word for money that Dante uses in Italian, *moneta,* comes from the Latin form *meneo,* meaning a warning. It admonishes that the coin is not a counterfeit, that it is really pure, so that's a subtler way of referring to the purity of this faith, its authenticity, so to speak. Another trait of money is that money circulates. Faith has that same power, that virtue that puts everything into motion, and therefore questions and establishes the values of everything around us. Fourth, Dante wants us to think about the resonance of profanation that is in the language of money and to link it with the purity of faith. Faith belongs to the world of time and can be profane, and yet it still manages to put things into circulation. The ambiguity of this metaphor of money is the strongest sign that while Dante is being examined regarding these virtues, he is also examining them in all their complexity for us.

Let us turn now to the question of hope that comes to light in the next canto, with the examination by St. James. The Greeks never thought of hope as a virtue. Hope is one of the entities in Pandora's Box, which was opened, allowing all of the evils of the world to come out, save for one, hope. It's a view that casts hope as a form of evil or a delusion, and in fact, for the Greeks the idea of hope is always a term that indicates the delusion of exiles, those who lose their land and are left with nothing but hope. It's a radical illusion.

Dante does not follow that route for hope. He finds in the Bible a different horizon for rethinking the way in which hope can be viewed. Hope, first of all, is a virtue of time. It's a virtue specifically of the future. If I have hope, I can't really hope about the past; that would fly in the face of all logic. Hope then is linked to temporality.

But it's not only a virtue of time. It's the most realistic of virtues. The Greeks would have argued that if you hope, it's because you are really desperate. You hope because you have no rational, realistic reason to believe that things are going to go the way that you wish they will go. Dante disagrees, arguing that hope is the most realistic of virtues because it tells us that nothing is ever really over. The negation of hope, its opposite, would be despair, as embodied in Cantos 8 and 9 of *Inferno,* with the encounter with the Furies and Medusa. Medusa can turn you into stone, so that you remain caught either in the particular reality that you have at that moment, or an idea of yourself as you think you have been, in an idea of the past. Hope, instead, is a virtue of the future that can change the past.

In that sense, it affects the past. It tells us that the past may not be what we thought it was. Whatever disaster you may have had, whatever disappointment you may have suffered in the past, that disappointment or disaster may contain seeds that will reappear in the future. They may be preparing a future that will surprise you. This is a different understanding of time that Dante presents, and it's an understanding of time that fulfills the previous virtue of faith. You cannot go on hoping for something unless you have an act of faith. Dante explains it all in existential terms and ties it to his own hope of returning to his homeland.

Canto 25 begins with what we call an optative, a statement that "I wish" that things were going a certain way: "If ever it come to pass that the sacred poem"—remember that Dante always uses the word *sacred* in a double sense, never reducible or localizable in one object only or in one particular place—"to which heaven and earth have so set their hand"—an incredible moment of prophetic self-awareness, with Dante saying that he is writing but knows that without God he would not be able to do so—"that it has made me lean for many years should overcome the cruelty which bars me from the fair sheepfold where I slept as a lamb, an enemy to the wolves which war on it, with changed voice now and with changed fleece a poet will I return, and at the font of my baptism will I take the crown; because there I entered into the Faith that makes souls known to God; and afterward Peter, for its sake, thus encircled my brow."[7] Writing is an ascetic labor of the soul. It makes Dante lean as if he were fasting, undergoing the rituals of the commitment to a particular labor, the ascetic labor of the soul. He labors away, as the metaphor of the city as a sheepfold reveals in the language you expect to find in *The Eclogues* of Virgil, the language of the pastoral tradition. Dante is in an idyllic world, the heaven of hope, and now he's thinking about the last ceremony of Peter, who blesses him three times. It is as if faith and hope are converging. The two virtues are brought together.

What is Dante saying about his hometown at the beginning of this canto? He's casting Florence in pastoral language, as a sheepfold. And he's alluding to a Messianic time when the peace would be restored, when the factions, the wolves—the Guelphs, in an etymological pun—and the lambs, will lie together. It's an impossible time. Then Dante adds as part of his hope that he would be acknowledged as a poet on the font of his baptism, referring to the Baptistery in Florence, where he actually was christened, according to records that we have. Why would he use this particular metaphor? The baptism is the time when a community is constituted, and the baptismal font is clearly a space that has that same value. It also has a textual and historical element related to the sacrament that takes place there, which is a ceremony that reenacts Exodus. When a child is baptized, he is told that he is re-creating the crossing of the Red Sea in Exodus.

So Dante is asking: how does a poet come home? The answer, initially, is one of hope, hope for a homecoming where everybody will be at peace. There will be a feast and a festive mood. It is his great fantasy of the winner's return. Yet, he's also using this language of a baptismal font, as if he were saying that the poet could only come home in order to tell his community that he has to get out again. He has been punished, and exile itself is the only message that his poetry can convey to the community from which he has been exiled. He is convoking the whole community around the baptismal font to tell them that this is where they belong—in exile, or at least in the language of spiritual exile, a language that implies a kind of remaking and rethinking of oneself.

Beatrice's presentation of Dante to St. James reveals that Exodus is a predominant influence on this canto: "And that compassionate one, who had guided the feathers of my wings to such lofty flight, anticipated my reply thus, 'The Church Militant has not any child possessed of more hope, as is written in the Sun which irradiates all our host; therefore is it granted him to come from Egypt to Jerusalem, that he may see, before his term of warfare is completed. The other two points which are asked, not for sake of knowing, but that he may report how greatly this virtue is pleasing to you, I leave to him, for they will not be difficult to him, nor of vainglory.'" This statement from Beatrice demonstrates that Dante's whole journey can be glossed through one biblical referent, namely Exodus. Dante's journey is described here as a voyage from Egypt to Jerusalem, which is the master plot of the Hebrews' exile from bondage to freedom, with exile, of course, as the master figure of the poem. Dante is therefore linking exile and hope, and I think I have already indicated to you that this idea of writing in the mode of exile involves the whole of history. History has to be seen from the standpoint of exile. Near the end of the canto, Dante says that hope "is a sure expectation of future glory, which divine grace produces, and preceding merit. From many stars this light comes to me, but he first instilled it into my heart who was the supreme singer of the Supreme Leader."[8] With this allusion to David, who, to Dante, is the greatest of poets, Dante brings together past and future, history and hope.

And now we can move on to the last virtue, love or charity. There is a progression: faith, hope, and then charity, and you have to know all of these virtues before the beatific vision can even be a possibility for you. You have to understand what it is that these virtues do to you and produce in you. Aiming to understand, we come to love, but if we are looking for a definition of it as a kind of formula, like those given in Cantos 24 and 25, we are seeking it in vain. There's no definition of love, and it's clear that Dante really thinks that love is *the* word. Love is the key word that seems to escape all possible definitions. In a variety of ways, we understand it, and yet we cannot quite confine it and define it, and to define it would really just be a way of reducing its impact and its value. It's such a basic word that Dante says in his treatise on language, the *De vulgari eloquentia*, that the word *love* is the only residual term from the past that shows that language is a way of bringing us together. So, love escapes any particular definition, and yet it's the culmination of the theological virtues.

Love's meaning for Dante, as a linguistic unifier, becomes clearer at the end of Canto 26, when Dante meets Adam. This scene is a confrontation with the beginning, with the arch poet, because Adam is the one who names the world and thereby brings it into existence. That's really what we mean by poet, "maker." That's what we're expecting poets to do. To begin, Dante addresses Adam: "O fruit that were alone produced mature."[9] What a strange way of addressing someone! There were many theological debates as to whether ripeness is an element of grace or a description of grace for Dante. According to this metaphor, you are ripe when you have received and been touched by grace. But was Adam created in a natural state, or was he already created in a state of grace? How long was he in the earthly paradise before he fell? If he was in a state of grace, why did he fall? If he was in a state of grace, why could he commit this sin of transgression? Is it a transgression that he commits by eating of the fruit of the tree? Dante, when he calls him ripe, implies that Adam was, in fact, in a state of grace.

Dante asks Adam to help him to resolve some of these questions, and Adam responds at length. First he says, "Now now, my son, that the tasting of the tree was not in itself the cause of so long an exile"—even the Fall was a state of exile, exile from the garden, a fall into the wilderness where Adam had to transform the wild landscape into a garden, with work as the means to regain that which he had lost—"but solely the overpassing of the bound."[10] This is Canto 26 of *Paradiso,* and this Canto 26 is symmetrically connected with the other two Cantos 26, including the canto in *Inferno* of Ulysses, who also trespasses boundaries, who is a metaphysician of sorts, who is dealing with space and who doesn't know where on earth he is going. There seems to be a contrast between Ulysses' form of knowledge and Adam's form of knowledge, though both involve an overstepping of boundaries. As Dante elucidates here, it's not the tasting of the tree that was the sin; the sin was that he abolished all boundaries. It's clear that Dante thinks that Adam's act of eating of the tree was good—it was a *felix culpa*—for that act was actually the discovery of a knowledge that managed to elevate Adam and all who followed him. Ulysses' problem is that he doesn't even know where he is going, even in purely metaphysical terms. He had no directions; it was a gratuitous quest. In the case of Adam, this is not an issue. In fact, Dante says, maybe real knowledge is always going to be tied to an act of making discoveries, maybe even transgressions.

How are we to understand the loss of boundaries, then? It was the kind of knowledge that made Adam see that he could be divine; that was his problem. God's imposition of the boundary between the human and the divine was a way of letting Adam know that he had to be aware of his limitations. But Adam wanted to grow in knowledge, and in so doing he discovered that he could also be divine, defying God's imposed limits. For him to fall, then, would be a way of reestablishing that boundary, which is actually a growth in self-knowledge. If you really know who you are, you have grown. It's that simple. Dante's changing the sense of what the fall of man is, limiting it to the problematic belief that humans can, through knowledge, become divine. The whole poem is trying to convey to us that this notion is a steady temptation that human beings seem to have, so we need to be reminded, especially when we hear it from God himself and still don't quite believe it, that we have to grow into a recognition of boundaries between ourselves and something that we aspire to but have not yet attained.

Then Dante turns to the central topic of his discourse, language: "The tongue which I spoke was all extinct before the people of Nimrod attempted their unaccomplishable work"—the building of the Tower of Babel that would not be finished—"for never was any product of reason durable forever, because of human liking, which alters, following the heavens. That man should speak is nature's doing, but whether thus or thus, nature then leaves you to follow your own pleasure."[11] Language is the key now, and retrospectively we come to understand the language of theology. We get answers to the questions: What are the properties of theological language? What are the properties, beyond that, of all words?

Adam continues, "Before I descended to the anguish of Hell the Supreme Good from whom comes the joy that swathes me was named *I* on earth"—the letter, not "I" in the sense of the subject—"and later He was called *El*."[12] Dante is using two Hebrew words, or at least what he takes to be Hebrew words, for the name of God. One of my students once pointed out to me that if you read these names backwards, they spell out the word Eli, which is a word that we could acknowledge nowadays as a word for an appeal to God. Adam is changing the account that Dante had given in the *De vulgari eloquentia,* which is a story about the origin of words, where he had claimed that Hebrew, Adam's language, remained unchanged throughout history because it was inconceivable that Jesus would be using a language other than the primal language, certainly not the corrupt language of human beings. Here, instead, Adam's language had suffered alterations in the Garden, where the names of God keep changing. This, I think, is key. This is the whole question of theology, then, the idea that there is no proper name for God. We only have words or languages that keep changing according to our own historical circumstances, and Dante even continues changing his paradigmatic account about the status of the sacred language. He says there is no such a thing as a persistent sacred language in history. What comes out is that language is the mark of our own distance from the divine, that language is a part of our own exilic predicament, and therefore all the language of theology that Dante has been describing is part of this exilic longing of human beings.

And so we conclude the story of the virtues found in Cantos 24, 25, and 26. Dante uses theology and examination of theology only to place us back in this world, where we go on believing, hoping, and loving. We come to realize that these are all mysterious terms, which can only function together, and each is understood in terms of the other, for there is no love without faith in an ongoing circulation. Where we have hope as the realization of faith, and love as the realization of hope, the meaning that mysteriously escapes us no longer matters.

CHAPTER 22

Paradiso 27–29

In Cantos 27, 28, and 29 of *Paradiso,* Dante constructs and puts forth a theory of creation and cosmology, which are not quite the same thing. Beatrice explains the shape of the cosmos, a very difficult task, and Dante's dealing with two forms of the universe, a spiritual one and a physical one. Though they are not identical, they are not really all that distinct. There is a very tenuous, thin line separating the two of them.

Where are we, first of all? We are somewhere in the celestial spheres. Dante has now gone past the heaven of the fixed stars. Here in Canto 27 Dante continues in their afterglow, but the focus is still on St. Peter, who had been examining Dante. But now Peter launches into a prophetic denunciation, lambasting the collusion between the papacy, instituted because of him, and his successors. In his great attack, he says, "It was not our purpose that one part of the Christian people should sit on the right of our successors, and one part on the left; nor that the keys which were committed to me should become the ensign on a banner for warfare on the baptized; nor that I should be made a figure on a seal to sold and lying privileges, whereat I often blush and flash."[1] This declaration is imbued with the fire of prophecy, without a doubt, but it's also, retrospectively, a reference to the attack against Boniface, who in the parallel Canto 27 of *Inferno* is shown to be colluding with Guido da Montefeltro. There is a clear symmetry between the two cantos.

After this outburst by Peter, Beatrice and the pilgrim move on to the next heaven, the so-called crystalline heaven, the so-called Prime Mover, which is still material, at least according to Beatrice's cosmological description of the universe. They are at the boundary of the material universe; it's a very thin materiality, almost but not quite purely spiritual. It's called the Prime Mover (or Primum Mobile) because it's here in this heaven that we discover origins, the origin of time, the origin of space. Dante is at the edge of the cosmos (not an actual edge, since the universe here is a sphere, but the boundary, the end of the world), and Beatrice tells him to look back and measure the distance he has traveled from the earth. He does what she asks and says, "From the time when I had looked before, I saw that I had moved through the whole arc"—the language of the sphere: an arc, part of a circle—"which the first climate makes from its middle to its end; so that on the one hand, beyond Cadiz, I saw the mad track of Ulysses."[2] From the edge of the universe, Dante pinpoints that little place where Ulysses trespassed the boundaries of the world, an act for which he has been damned in Canto 26 of *Inferno*.

Why does Dante focus on Ulysses once again? Ulysses is clearly still part of this fascination that exerts an incredible power on the imagination of the poet and the pilgrim. Am I—he asks—like Ulysses? Am I going to be lost now like Ulysses? At the same time, it's a way of hinting at how much he has exceeded Ulysses' adventure. Ulysses only went past the Pillars of Hercules; he, Dante, is now at the outermost boundary of the universe, so there's a way in which a bit of detachment is attached to this constant interest.

At the other end Dante also sees "nearly to the shore where Europa made herself a sweet burden."[3] This line refers to the eastern part of the known world, Europe, via the rape of Europa by Jupiter. With it, we can thus add an erotic transgression to Ulysses' intellectual transgression, as if the two are once again intertwined. In Dante's vision, knowledge and desire really have to coincide. He's coming to the point where the beautiful and the good are one, the point where all of the great distinctions that we have been pursuing have to converge.

Dante then moves farther into the Prime Mover, "the swiftest part of heaven," the place where all motion begins. Dante is moving from what would seem to be an ethical scene, Peter's denunciation of the abuses within the Church into the heaven of metaphysics. Dante refers to it, as many did, as Aristotle referred to it, as the "first philosophy." They called it first because it reigns supreme among all the arts and all the sciences. It's the most important of their number. It's the point of arrival of all knowledge. It's also called first philosophy because it explains questions of origins, and thus the language of origins abounds here: the origin of time, the origin of space, creation itself, the beginning of the world, causes, foundations. The interesting thing is that Dante has to connect metaphysics with physics. They really go hand in hand, since one tries to explain the physical world, while the other addresses the theoretical. They aren't so different, but the point is that there is a science for Dante that deals with causes and beginnings.

And it is in the heart of a realm of beginnings that Beatrice starts discussing cosmology, commencing with the sphericity of this space: "The nature of the universe which holds the center quiet and moves all the rest around it, begins here as from its starting-point"—the language of beginnings—"and this heaven has no other *Where* than the divine mind."[4] The real beginning, the real universe for that matter, is in God's mind. Dante distinguishes two worlds, the physical world we see and the spiritual world in God's mind. In a way, then, Dante is journeying into the mind of God. Bonaventure, whom you have met before in this text, wrote a book called *The Journey of the Mind into God,* which offered a way of trying to enter mystically the deity's mind. Dante doesn't do it in a mystical way; he simply tries to understand what's beyond the physical world.

A more complex description of the shape of the universe follows: "Light and love enclose it in a circle, as it does the others, and this engirdment He alone who girds it understands."[5] This Prime Mover is a kind of curve that envelops all the other heavens. It's not only a boundary, since Dante also views it as the threshold for the spiritual universe, but in terms of its physical shape; it is somehow simultaneously convex and concave, a semicircle, perhaps, or the spiral of a shell, or more aptly, since Dante thinks of the cosmos as a book, a parchment rolled up within itself. Ancient parchments were all rolled up around a stick and then held together by a ring— that's really the shape of Dante's cosmos. So, the physical universe consists of spirals, one following the other, and next to it there is a spiritual universe, which we'll discuss later.

Beatrice then explains how time works here: "Its motion is not determined by another's, but the others are measured by this, just as ten by its half and its fifth. And how time should have its roots in such a flower-pot, and in the others its leaves, may now be manifest to you."[6] Even time begins here. Dante sees that there is a sort of tree of time growing from part of eternity. He does not understand time in a linear way, with a beginning and an end, nor as a wheel, like the wheel of becoming, a Platonic idea of time, where all things are contained. Dante thinks of time instead as a tree, the roots of which are in the pot of eternity while its foliage reaches into our own world. We are in the shadow of the tree of time. We only see leaves that will fall, allowing for our idea of the dispersion and passage of time. Beatrice has now made sense of time and space, both for Dante and for the reader.

Canto 28 steps outside the bounds of the universe and deals with the angelic hierarchy. We are still in the Prime Mover, but Dante starts seeing into the other universe, the spiritual one. He sees a realm adjacent to the physical universe inhabited by angels. It corresponds to our world in that there are nine planets—seven planets plus the fixed stars and the crystalline heaven—and there you have the nine orders of angels, arranged in three triads: angels, archangels, and thrones. This language comes from the Bible, the Old Testament, apparently drawing on Persian apocalyptic sources; and Dante's direct sources regarding the angelic hierarchies were Pseudo-Dionysius and Gregory the Great. The two universes are also linked by their shared spherical shape: "And when I turned and my own eyes were met by what appears in that revolving sphere whenever one gazes intently on its circling, I saw a point which radiated a light so keen that the eye on which it blazes needs must close because of its great keenness."[7] Once again, we find a series of revolving spheres. More accurately, though, this universe is not the projection of the other universe; they are separate and adjacent. They are two hemispheres.

Dante takes a moment to acknowledge that his ordering of the angels is very different from that of Pseudo-Dionysius: "These orders all gaze upward and prevail downward, so that toward God all are drawn, and all do draw. And Dionysius with such great desire set himself to contemplate these orders."[8] Pseudo-Dionysius had written about the same angelic hierarchy, but Dante wants us to know that his idea of angels is a little different from Dionysus's and from Pope Gregory's. Dante has Beatrice finish the description of this sacred order of angelic intelligences. According to her, their function is to impart motion to the spheres, to move between the divinity and human beings. They are the messengers. They keep everything in motion. In doing this, Dante makes a clear statement of his intellectual independence, both in terms of the theologian and in terms of an ecclesiastical authority.

With that we move to Canto 29, where the language of cosmology shifts to the language of creation in an extraordinarily interesting way. Beatrice has been talking nonstop, probably with a touch of playfulness, about the angelic orders, and then she moves almost without catching her breath to talking about creation. The canto begins, "When the two children of Latona"—the sun and the moon—"covered by the Ram and by the Scales, make the horizon their belt at one same moment, as long as from the instant when the zenith holds them balanced till the one and the other, changing hemispheres, are unbalanced from that belt, for so long, her face illumined with a smile, was Beatrice silent, looking fixedly at the point which had overcome me."⁹ He starts with a reference to the children of Latona, that is to say Apollo and Diana, which thus incorporates mythical language. But then he also uses scientific language: the constellations the Ram and the Scales, "a belt of the horizon," an Arabic word meaning the boundary of the heavens, "the zenith." The mixture of science and myth requires a balance as fleeting as it could ever be, but that's precisely the point that Dante aims to make, that there was a moment of silence, but he could almost not even tell that there was a break in Beatrice's speech.

When we speak, things seem to be continuous, and just as between every syllable, between one sound and another, there is always an interval, so there was in the language of Beatrice. That interval, to him, is the idea of creation. The opposite of creation would be the eternity of the world, something with no beginning and no identifiable break. If the universe is eternal, it contains no differences inside it, while Dante wants to say that the universe seems to involve continuous extension, but you can identify breaks in it. However minute it may have been, there *is* a break between Beatrice's exposition about the angelic orders and her exposition about creation.

A rare equilibrium of this sort disappears quickly, and sure enough, Beatrice will swiftly continue speaking, this time on the theory of creation. She says, "I tell, not ask, what you wish to hear; for I have seen it there where every *ubi* and every *quando* is centered"—a point where space and time coincide. "Not for gain of good unto Himself, which cannot be, but that His splendor might, in resplendence, say, '*Subsisto*'—in His eternity beyond time, beyond every other bound, as it pleased Him, the Eternal Love opened into new loves."¹⁰ I take this word *opened* to be part of a sexual language, with a new love that engenders by opening itself into further new loves.

Beatrice continues, "Nor before, as if inert, did He lie, for neither before nor after did the moving of God upon these waters proceed." This is an allusion to Aristotle's *Physics,* where Aristotle has to define time and says it's the measure of motion in regard to a before and an after. Dante says that before the time of creation there was no such thing. Before and after could not be distinguished prior to the beginning of the universe in Genesis, which is described with a vaguely sexual metaphor: "Form and matter, conjoined and simple, came into being which had no defect, as three arrows from a three-stringed bow."¹¹ The question of creation is a coming together here, a conjunction. Creation takes place as an act of love, as passion. It's as physical as possible in terms of the language of natural production and re-production. Creation is that which introduces the possibility of distinguishing between a before and an after, a unity that introduces a difference.

Beatrice proceeds with form and matter, united and separate, pure and conjoined. She says, "As in glass, in amber, or in crystal, a ray shines so that there is no interval between its coming and its pervading all, so did the triform effect ray from from its Lord into its being, all at once, without distinction of beginning. Therewith order was created and ordained for the substances; and those in whom pure act was produced were the summit of the universe. Pure potentiality held the lowest place."[12] The idea is that there is a universe of creation that seems to be very much like the physical world. It's described in physical terms, the terms of the moon and sexuality, the cosmological language and scientific terms. And yet, there is a difference. Without creation we would not have differences. We would not even have origins.

But prior to the imparting of all this information on the part of Beatrice, Dante experienced a fleeting moment in the alignment of the stars, and a question lingers: why this metaphor? I think it is an allusion to Francesca, from Canto 5 of *Inferno*. Dante says, "Beatrice [was] silent, looking fixedly at the point which had overcome me." Francesca said that only a point was what overcame her and Paolo. So, cosmology was linked to Ulysses, and now creation is tied to Francesca. Why is Dante alluding to these two infernal figures and framing his discussion of the heavens with them? Why refer to these transgressors, one who wants to trespass the boundaries of the world in order to know, and another who exceeds the norms of what is allowed on love's account. Knowledge and love somehow come into play but in their infernal versions—why? What Dante is doing is allowing us to see the world of *Inferno* in a new light. We previously saw it only as a world of the rejected, as a world of evil and horror, but now, all of a sudden, it is retrieved as the best exemplar of what we may come to know of the spiritual world. It is an imaginative redemption of Hell. Dante is implying that as one goes back to the beginnings of the universe, the journey has to be seen as redemption of order that has been falling away. There can be no such redemption unless the whole of evil is overcome and destroyed, so that even the world of Hell now appears all as part of what we get to know about the ultimate structure of the universe. This seems to me to be the real lesson, the underlying and powerful message that Dante is sending with his references to Francesca and Ulysses in these three cantos in the heaven of metaphysics.

It's especially interesting that Dante should bring up the image of Ulysses in Canto 27. He probably realizes how different he is from Ulysses, but he maintains a kind of retrospective fascination with the traveler from Ithaca. He's looking back and pinpointing the tragic moment of the rise of Ulysses' madness because it implies that this man had violated limits, including the limits of reason, in his pursuit, his philosophical investigation of the world. Dante may be equally mad, but he knows he's at least a little safer because he's in the hands of Beatrice. He trusts Beatrice, and for that reason I could even see an element of relief on the part of Dante. There is also relief in the fact that his own adventure diminishes that of the Greek epic hero, who really did very little in the end, just venturing beyond the Pillars of Hercules.

We could stop there. It happens though, retrospectively, that we can also see the story of Ulysses as the story of a metaphysician. Dante is in the heaven of metaphysics, after all. Metaphysics deals with space and time, and thus we can understand why going from place to place is the metaphor that seems to distinguish Ulysses in these cantos. Ulysses is a failed metaphysician, but we understand that he was trying to go to the absolute, to boldly go where no one other than Dante and Paul before him have gone before.

But metaphysics also deals with time. Dante is attempting to understand eternity and origins, and in so doing he makes the mistake of trying to localize time. Beatrice reminded him of a point of joy that overcame him. Maybe he's alluding, because the language is that of Francesca, of lust, to a kiss they shared that he remembers. The context is very spiritualized, since Dante is never vulgar. But it is certainly possible that he's alluding to a kiss they had exchanged, or perhaps just the will, the desire, the longing to kiss her now. One thing is clear: he's thinking of Francesca as a kind of metaphysician, too. What is her metaphysics? It's a metaphysics of desire, which is metaphysical by its own definition, in the sense that it's always moving beyond the objects it gains because it burns through them. Today I want this book, then I want another book, then I want the whole library, and so on; that's the infinite movement of desire. And not only is she a metaphysician, she lives in time, so she's a complementary figure to Ulysses. Ulysses is all about place: Ceuta, Seville, and so on. Francesca instead says how difficult it is to remember the joys of the past; she is another failed metaphysician, but one of a different stamp. Both Francesca and Ulysses would have liked to arrive where Dante is currently, able to witness a conjunction of space and time, *ubi* and *quando,* to see the point where all things cohere.

Such a stance on these recurring figures makes it possible to think of *Paradiso* as Dante's admission of schadenfreude. His joy, it's possible to argue, is increased by the thought of those who are suffering; seeing someone who wanted what he now has being punished could reveal to him just how lucky he is. I don't think that that's Dante, though. He's talking about cosmology and creation, the order of everything, how this order is an order of love and how he's coming to know this order of love because knowledge is love and love is knowledge. What he's really saying is that he is now able to see how things work, but sinful people on earth, those who live in the shadows of time, were trying to do the same thing and were simply not lucky enough to succeed, to reach the heights he has attained. But they *could* because he has. I could push this line of thought to the point of absurdity, to say that if this is true, Dante is also saying that the suffering sinners in Hell may still get to where he is, after all. They may be taken and placed into the bosom of Abraham where all the blessed dwell. Is this just wishful thinking on my part? I grant you, it probably is, but there is absolutely a theology of redemption in the *Comedy.*

Let me be very clear. Dante never says explicitly that the entire world of creation is redeemable. It becomes part of a conscious articulation on his part; he makes it a clear theme, but he never says it outright. There are really two implications that I'm drawing on in order to be able to make that kind of statement. The first is the very idea of the cosmos as a sphere, which means that wherever you are going as you are going toward God, you are also going back to the beginning. Everything can therefore go back to the start because that's the form our universe takes. The other reason is that there is such a thing as redemption. The whole cosmos can be restored to its original form. In the overt sense of the poem, there is a theology of redemption, which could entail a return to the beginning for everyone and everything.

If we look once more at the famous image of the two children of Latona at the beginning of Canto 29, we can learn a bit more about this theology of redemption. In the Italian, the first word is *quando,* "when," and the last word in line 12 is also *quando.* Going back to the first line, the last word in that line is "Latona," the first two letters of which, *la,* are also the first two letters of line 12. That's a chiasmus. And if were to draw lines to make the cross formed by this poetic structure, they would meet exactly at the word "hemisphere." That's the center of this design. I think Dante's placing us at a cosmic crossroads. He is locating us, he's telling us where we are, but he's also telling us that this universe has very occult and very secret laws that govern it. The poem is regulated by these same secret rules. And one such tacit regulation could involve a radical redemptive theology. Dante is making an allowance for a possible absolute purification of evil. The universe may return to its previous pristine purity.

How would this come about? The Incarnation is the redemptive event that would allow it to occur. A new Adam comes into the world, and that new Adam, through his sacrifice and through the gift God gave, allowed the Incarnation because human beings on their own would not be capable of doing so. That's the root of theology of redemption: human beings on their own would not be able to save and redeem themselves, so an intervention from God, through his Son, was rendered inevitable in order to reconstruct and reproduce the original order of the cosmos. Nonetheless, this should not obscure the fact that there is a paired juxtaposition between the physical description of the world and the spiritual description of the world. There are two hemispheres, and yet they are connected. The spiritual experience of creation is really the way of positing a difference in the universe, dramatically affecting the theory that the physical world is eternal. These were two conceptions of the world's duration, operative in the Middle Ages. One comes from Aquinas, who argues in the *Summa contra gentiles* that the theory of the eternity of the world, held by the Greek philosophers, the idea that there was no moment of creation, could be philosophically demonstrated. It could also be philosophically repudiated. Philosophy can argue one side of it, and he goes on asking the oldest objections in the book, questions like, "Who created the Creator?" However, there is a view of creation made possible on account of faith, which is tied to freedom. Bonaventure picks up some of these ideas, which were hotly debated in Paris in the thirteenth century. Bonaventure says no, this idea of the eternity of the world is untenable. If the world were eternal, then we would have no succession of generations. There would be endless people who had lived before us, and there's no evidence for this. Thus, he upholds the idea of creation.

Dante intervenes in this debate and says that the physical world and the spiritual world are effectively united and continuous. They're complementary to each other. And yet a difference lingers. The difference is the same difference that he finds in Beatrice's speech, that little intrusion of time that distinguishes between one sound and another sound. The spiritual universe originates in the world of nature as a natural production and reproduction, emerging from God's love, and the physical world operates in exactly the same way. There is a kind of symmetry to their origins, and they remain adjacent to each other for this reason, separate but equal and joined at their edges. This is not Plato's inverted universe, though it resonates with Neoplatonic strains of emanationism. It is as if Dante discovers that there are simply more dimensions to the world that we see than cosmologists before him had imagined.

CHAPTER 23

Paradiso 30–33

In the last chapter, we saw the context of Dante's experience, the way he moves in the cosmos, the tale he's telling about this extraordinary experience he has had. He described the materiality and the spirituality of two hemispheres placed in one universe, with the Empyrean as the threshold and limit of the physical cosmos, the way of entering into the spiritual cosmos. Now, Dante moves straight into the Empyrean. This is the end of the road for him. Here there will be a changing of the guard. How is Dante going to say farewell to Beatrice? For the role of Beatrice as a guide will come to a close with Canto 30 of *Paradiso,* which is quite fitting, since she first appeared in Canto 30 of *Purgatorio.*

Dante is forced to move from Beatrice to a historical figure, Bernard of Clairvaux, who was a famous French monk who had written treatises on contemplation and mystical visions. Appropriately, he is the one who will pray to the Virgin Mary that she may in turn pray to her son, causing a chain of mediations that permits the beatific vision to be granted to Dante in Canto 33.

We are going to find out the difficulties that Dante has in seeing and, above all, in recalling and recollecting this experience. The poem will end up registering the unavoidable defeat of memory and the importance of forgetfulness. We are going to discover in Canto 33 a further twist to the metaphor from Canto 33 of *Purgatorio,* when Dante was immersed ritually into the river Lethe and then into the river Eunoe, one the river of forgetfulness, the other the river of memory. Dante emphasized that he was at the point where the two streams were originating from the same source, as if memory and forgetfulness were born from the same material. Dante was already preparing what will now move to center stage in *Paradiso* 33, namely the notion of a forgetful memory, the two forces brought together. It's not a mystical proposition that he advances; it's actually a way of justifying his whole poem, but we'll come back to that defense when we arrive at Canto 33.

To begin with Canto 30, though, Dante is entering into the Heavenly Jerusalem, which is both a garden and a city. It will be described as an amalgam of settings, first of all as a amphitheater, a fixture of urban culture: "So above the light round and round about in more than a thousand tiers I saw all that of us have won return up there. And if the lowest rank"— drawing on the image of the theater as an auditorium, with tiered setting— "encloses within itself so great a light, how vast is the spread of this rose in its outermost leaves!"[1] The second image that is used here to describe the Heavenly Jerusalem is of a mystical rose, a flower plucked from an otherworldly garden. This rose comes straight from a thirteenth-century French poem called *The Romance of the Rose,* which Dante had translated into a sequence of sonnets as a young man, part of his experimentation with various poetic forms.

But this metaphor is also deeply altered because *The Romance of the Rose* was a satirical poem, a compendium of all knowledge that dealt with the connections between nature and reason, but also a story with a sexual theme. Dante takes the language of *The Romance of the Rose* and spiritualizes and reverses it. But the resonances of the original poem are still there, so that you are forced to think of the Heavenly Jerusalem as having some kind of materiality within it. You cannot just take an image, place it in a different context, and hope that the residue of that original image are going to be completely effaced. It's all part of Dante's strategy of intimating that spirituality and materiality are converging here. That's the archeology, let's say, of this image of the rose.

The spectacular display continues: "Into the yellow of the eternal rose, which rises in ranks and expands and breathes forth odors of praise unto the Sun which makes perpetual spring, Beatrice drew me as one who is silent and wishes to speak, and she said, 'Behold how great the assembly of the white robes!'"[2] This is a procession and the whole of Paradise is a theatrical performance. Whenever we think of a theater, we understand that it implies the reduction of the world to a spectacle. The world is something to be seen, an optical phenomenon, a representation. And we become spectators. We can really watch this world and see it in its totality, just as Dante is seeing the whole of the universe, the totality of the blessed. Furthermore, the theater is an image of multiple perspectives, but Dante wants to say that he's enjoying an overall perspective. He can see the whole of reality. He's not seeing something isolated or disconnected from the rest of the world. This is, to him, what legitimizes a claim to be a visionary poet. To be truly a visionary poet, you have to be able to see the whole of reality, not just your own image like Narcissus.

Beatrice then directs Dante's gaze: "See our city, how wide is its circuit!"[3] It has been described in terms of a rose and a garden, but now it's a city. That's an interesting shift for a number of reasons. The whole poem now appears as a journey from the wilderness, not to the garden, but to a city or to a garden that is also a city. It is a way of encompassing the whole movement of the poem within these two images, a firm and total reintegration. It is a way of seeing the world as a whole, of which Dante wants to be a part, and his way of being part of this whole is to write this political poem. The idea of the city always implies some human contact, some involvement with the *polis,* the political reality of the people. We also have a compression of images from the pastoral tradition; in pastoral literature one usually finds a division between the urban and the rustic. There is almost a hint of a schizophrenic existence to the world. What Dante is doing is shattering the distance between the two modes. In an eschatological perspective, a perspective that is at the end, the city and the garden come together. They are not two divergent modes of the *imaginatio;* they cohere within one. No matter what Dante is touching with his imagination, all the oppositions, all systems of contrarieties, he always tries to bring them together in a kind of concordance. Dante aims at harmony.

But then there is another image that complicates the problem: "See our seats so filled that few souls are now wanted there!"[4] This line is really strange because it's implying that for all of us latecomers there is no room, not even standing-room-only seats. The places have all been taken already. Very few individuals are going to be saved. Based on these implications, one could say that Dante is having what we can call an apocalyptic vision. Only a few seats are available because the end of the world is near. But I don't think that Dante really has an apocalyptic vision here, in the sense that he is not proclaiming the imminence of the ending of history. A man who keeps thinking as he does about the renewal or the corruption of institutions, about the hope that some intervention will come from other human beings, from history, or from the world of grace, cannot really have a sense of the imminent consummation of history. He wouldn't be so worried about renewing institutions if he believed the world was at the brink of extinction. This line is meant to suggest, I would argue, that the scene comes from the perspective of eternity. In terms of the totality of time, relatively few seats remain, but only because so much time has already passed by.

A haunting image comes next that sheds further light on whether Dante has an apocalyptic imagination or not: "And in that great chair whereon you fix your eyes because of the crown that already is set above it"—an empty seat where a king is meant to sit, a portrait of royal absence—"before you sup at these nuptials shall sit the soul, which on earth will be imperial, of the lofty Henry."[5] This refers to the emperor, who died in 1313, whom Dante was hoping would come down to Italy from the Holy Roman Empire in order to set Italy straight. Dante believed Henry could placate the violence between the cities and affect the whole history of Italian communes. Sadly, however, he died prematurely, and here he is expected in heaven. There is a way in which the emperor is beatified, his seat in heaven assured, and yet his blessed state allows the violence in history to be, for the time being, continued and prolonged. Once again, therefore, political interests, Dante's fantasies of political renewals, temper all views that Dante may have, of an apocalyptic imagination.

If Canto 30 is a farewell to apocalyptic ideas, Canto 31 is a farewell to a much-beloved figure in Dante's life, his most recent guide, Beatrice. Dante writes,

> I, who to the divine from the human, to the eternal from time had come, and from Florence to a people just and sane, with what amazement must I have been full! Truly, what with it and with the joy, I was content to hear naught and to stand mute. And as a pilgrim who is refreshed within the temple of his vow as he looks around, and already hopes to tell again how it was, so, taking my way upwards through the living light, I led my eyes along the ranks, now up, now down, and now circling about. I saw faces all given to love, adorned by the light of Another, and by their own smile, and movements graced with every dignity. My look had now taken in the general form of Paradise as a whole, and on no part as yet had my sight paused; and I turned with rekindled will to ask my lady about things as to which my mind was in suspense.[6]

We have here a revision of the scene of Virgil's disappearance when Beatrice was just about to appear. Dante was so stricken by tremors at the approaching of Beatrice that he turned around to try to get comfort from Virgil, but Virgil had vanished.

This is a variant of that same vanishing act:

> One thing I purposed, and another answered me: I thought to see Beatrice, and I saw an elder [the aforementioned Bernard of Clairvaux], clad like the folk in glory. His eyes and cheeks were suffused with benign gladness, his mien kindly such as befits a tender father. And, "Where is she?" I said at once; whereon he, "To terminate your desire Beatrice urged me from my place; and if you look up to the circle which is third from the highest tier, you will see her again, in the throne her merits have allotted to her." Without answering I lifted up my eyes and saw her where she made for herself a crown as she reflected the eternal rays. From the region which thunders most high no mortal eye is so far distant, were it plunged most deep within the sea, as there from Beatrice was my sight. But to me it made no difference, for her image came down to me unblurred by aught between. "O lady, in whom my hope is strong, and who for my salvation did endure to leave in Hell your footprints, of all those things which I have seen I acknowledge the grace and the virtue to be from your power and your excellence. It is you who have drawn me from bondage into liberty."[7]

The great theme of liberty in the *Comedy* is sealed here in the presence of Beatrice.

You may remember that Canto 29 ended with Beatrice very worried that Dante has been expounding too much. Beatrice got upset because the whole issue seemed to her to be a way of thinking more about the appearance of things rather than the truth of things. She attacked the human beings on earth who do nothing else but go after false appearances. Dante now goes back to these questions of appearances, and says to Beatrice that her image is exactly what he is going to preserve of her. He's telling her that we are always in a world of images and that the image is somehow the locus of sacredness, though the image also has a fleeting quality. The journey of Dante is thus to go between images and essences. He's preparing for the final leap, for Dante's journey was not a voyage to Beatrice but a voyage to God. Beatrice is simply the stepping stone for the pilgrim's entering the experience of the beatific vision.

In fact, toward the end of Canto 31, Dante writes, "As is he who comes perchance from Croatia to look on our Veronica, and whose old hunger is not sated, but he says in thought so long as it is shown, 'My Lord Jesus Christ, true God, was then your semblance like to this?' such was I, gazing on the living charity of him who, in this world, in contemplation tasted of that peace."[8] Veronica is an allusion to one of the pious women who, during the Calvary ascent of Jesus, is said to have wiped his face. The face of Jesus remained imprinted on her veil, so that the name Veronica was also understood in the whole of the Middle Ages as *vera icona,* a phony but accepted etymology. Dante is here evoking the pilgrims who went to Rome to see the true image on the veil of Veronica. And Dante himself is like one of those pilgrims; he sees the image, but he wants to move beyond images, to see what lies behind them. The journey of the *Divine Comedy* is no more and no less than that very journey betwixt and between appearances and essences, spelled out in tercets.

With that conception of the text in mind, we are ready to enter Canto 33, the final canto and the final vision. There are a number of dramas that are going to unfold in this canto. The first drama is that of the pilgrim who wants to see the face of God, to preserve his wit so that he can be able to come back and retell the story. He wants to be able to write the poem as a witnessing to the vision he has had. It's a way of thinking about the relationship between vision and language, in broad terms. Another drama is: how is Dante going to remember what he sees? And still more dramas are wrapped up in the question of what it is that he really sees. There are clearly a number of problems that he faces.

Canto 33 begins with a prayer to the Virgin Mary, and it's going to be constructed through a series of paradoxes, like calling the Virgin Mother the daughter of her son. A paradox can be about time or about reversals of the natural order, as when Mary is referred to as "humble and exalted more than any creature," challenging the rational understanding of the world as we typically encounter it.[9] In other words, we are intended to see that this account is not going to be a rational representation of what Dante sees.

Dante moves from this paradoxical prayer to that motif of birth that we have discussed since *Inferno* 1. The idea of birth as an image of beginning and an image of nature becoming a historical event is explicitly rendered in *Paradiso* 33: "In thy womb was rekindled the Love under whose warmth this flower"—meaning the whole of the mystical rose that he has just seen—"in the eternal peace has thus unfolded."[10] This image of the womb is another representation of the immense sphere of the mystic realm, within which the finite and the infinite come together. The immense sphere whose center is everywhere, whose circumference is nowhere, is the way that Dante is understanding and explaining this motif of the Incarnation.

What is crucial about this image is, first of all, the humanization of the divine. The divine becomes human because it enters history and experiences all that human beings experience on earth. The other element, I think, that Dante is putting forth is the feminization of the divine, in the sense that here the divine has become the child of a woman, and the woman is therefore part of the divinity. It's a theology of a feminine element in God.

A second stylistic theme here is repetition, the iterative mode. We see, for instance, "In thee is mercy, in thee pity, in thee munificence, in thee is found whatever of goodness is in any creature."[11] What is the point of this iterativeness, of anaphoric style? I think the main reason is that a language that is falling upon itself has a way of giving consistency to itself. The poem at this point is really dealing with vanishing traces, things that cannot quite be pinpointed or placed within logical propositions, and therefore the language becomes incantatory in an effort to create a more solid reality through the mood induced by these iterations.

At any rate, the prayer of Bernard continues, "This man, who from the lowest pit of the universe even to here has seen one by one the spiritual lives, implores thee of thy grace for power such that he may be able with his eyes to rise still higher towards the last salvation. And I"—Dante strays so far from the temptations of mystical writing, which ends up always evoking representable identities by distinguishing very carefully between "I" and "he," allowing for individualities in this Paradise of Dante's imagination— "who never for my own vision burned more than I do for his, proffer to thee all my prayers, and pray that they be not scant, that with thy prayers thou wouldst dispel for him every cloud of his mortality, so that the Supreme Pleasure may be disclosed to him." Then he prays directly to the Virgin: "Further I pray thee, Queen, who canst do whatever thou wilt, that thou preserve sound for him his affections, after so great a vision." The prime danger to the pilgrim is that he may literally lose his mind. The vision of God may obliterate his powers of rational thought. Bernard knows Dante will need divine succor: "Let thy protection vanquish human impulses. Behold Beatrice, with how many saints, for my prayers clasping their hands to thee."[12] The whole of the cosmos is praying for Dante to survive the beatific vision unscathed, and Bernard is merely vocalizing this shared wish.

Up to now the poem has been called so many things: a poem of hope, a poem of peace, a poem of exile, a poem of desire, and a poem of love and longing. The prayer here is the representation of this longing. In prayer, you address someone you don't see, hoping that you can be heard and that your prayer can be answered. Prayer implies a desire for a response, which is really the mode of Dante's theology. At the heart of his theological universe, there is a constant sense of not quite being where he wants to be, and this dislocation coincides with one's own religious consciousness. But very soon the language of Dante will change from desire to enjoyment, as he finally starts to get a sense of sweetness and an idea of the fullness of his pleasures: "I, who was drawing near to the end of all desires, raised to its utmost, even as I ought, the ardor of my longing. Bernard was signing to me with a smile to look upward, but I was already of myself such as he wished; for my sight, becoming pure, was entering more and more through the beam of the lofty Light which in Itself is true."[13] Dante is at long last attaining his hopes and dreams.

And yet, this is also where we find his first major defeat, as Dante starts recording the forgetfulness of this experience: "Thenceforward my vision was greater than speech can show, which fails at such a sight."[14] How is he going to make a failure become a success? The fact that he is not going to be able to see will become a mode of its own, not in the sense of being a form of humility because it would actually be a success in terms of the pilgrim's own humility, but in terms of the writing of the poem. It offers a different way of understanding the poem, not just as a representation of the plenitude of vision, but a statement of a longing for a vision that may or may not come.

The memory too fails in such excess. An excess is an overreaching that provokes outrage in the face of its hyperbolic nature. Dante will not be left with much: "As is he who dreaming sees, and after the dream the passion remains imprinted and the rest returns not to the mind; such am I, for my vision almost wholly fades away, yet does the sweetness that was born of it still drop within my heart."[15] All that remains to him is this sweetness that gathers in the chamber of the heart. This journey to God has truly been a journey of the heart, a journey of the mind as well, but primarily a journey of the heart. You have to come to know God through the heart, or not at all.

Then he continues, "Thus is the snow unsealed by the sun." This image is one of the liquefaction of shapes, the loss of form, water that had been crystallized and now just dissolves. It is followed by another image of dissipation, one that brings us back to the third book of *The Aeneid:* "Thus in the wind, on the light leaves, the Sibyl's oracle was lost."[16] When Aeneas goes to the Sibyl's cave to find out about his future, as the Sibyl opens the gates, the wind comes and scatters all the leaves in the cave. It's the impossibility of reading and deciphering the actual leaves. It's the messiness and confusion. That's exactly the state of mind in which Dante seems to find himself.

"O Light Supreme," Dante now shifts to another mode on his own, a sequence of prayers, "that art so far uplifted above mortal conceiving, relend to my mind a little of what Thou didst appear, and give my tongue such power that it may leave only a single spark of Thy glory for the folk to come."[17] This prayer asks that somehow language may triumph over the threat of forgetfulness. What Dante is saying is that his poem is meant for the future, that, in effect, he's envisioning a future. This is not a poem written for him, or for his contemporaries, but a positing of a time yet to come. For Dante, a work of art invents and prepares a future, more than acting as a remembrance, and the poem will thus be a prolepsis, or a movement forward.

So, why do I insist on discussing memory when Dante seems to be becoming more utopian? Because that's the answer: he talks about retrieving the memory of what he has seen because he can only write his poem, he can only have some authority for his voice, if he remembers what he has seen. In order to ground the poem in the notion of the vision of God that will permit him to say all of the things he has been saying about the living and the dead, the powerful and the not so powerful, the historical figures and the cultural figures of the past, it's crucial for him to remember. Memory becomes the actual foundation of his representation, forward-glancing though it may be.

For this reason, he's forced to go on remembering, and yet he cannot. Where does his authority actually come from, then? "I remember," he says, "that on this account I was the bolder to sustain it, until I united my gaze with the Infinite Goodness." Then, once again breaking the narrative and turning it into a sort of meditative prayer, begging that the divine reveal itself and remain with him, he continues, "O abounding grace whereby I presumed to fix my look through the Eternal Light so far that all my sight was spent therein. In its depth I saw ingathered, bound by love in one single volume, that which is dispersed in leaves throughout the universe: substances and accidents and their relations, as though fused together in such a way that what I tell is but a simple light."[18] The cosmos is once more represented as a book, as a kind of allegory wrapped up in words. *Volume* was the same word that Dante had used for Virgil at the beginning of the poem.

Here, therefore, it serves as a way to give continuity to his quest. Virgil's book becomes a prefiguration of the poem and of the book of the cosmos that Dante now sees bound together.

This is the moment of the recovery of a state of joy that excludes absence: "The universal form of this knot I believe that I saw, because, in telling this, I feel my joy increase."[19] Desire has to be replaced by joy because desire always entails a lack. We long for what we do not have, at least at that moment. Joy is instead tied to an experience of plenitude. And Dante finally has it all, at least for now.

All the dialectics of memory and forgetfulness come together in a mythological metaphor: "A single moment makes for me greater oblivion than five and twenty centuries have wrought upon the enterprise that made Neptune wonder at the shadow of the Argo."[20] Time doesn't exist here. It exists in Dante, since Dante is still human, he still has time, and his life can only be measured by time, but he's in the presence of the eternal instant. That single instance made him forget more than what we have forgotten in the twenty-five centuries since the Argo sailed the seas, an allusion to the Argonauts, another mythological counter to Dante's own journey. Something else in that story of the Argonauts, as Dante retrieves it, is that the god is down below, Neptune is in the depths, and Dante is thus thinking of the divine as being also caught in its own unreachable, unfathomable depths. And yet it is also found at such great heights that there are two different perspectives presented as one. More importantly, Dante sees Neptune wondering at the daring of man, and the implication is that he too has had this kind of daring, and God may be wondering at Dante's own achievement in the same way.

So, language fails him, memory fails him, and now speech fails him, too: "Now will my speech fall more short, even in respect to that which I remember, than that of an infant who still bathes his tongue at the breast." The word *infant*, which we usually take to refer to any child, literally means a child who cannot speak. Dante continues in this vein, emphasizing the failings of his fickle tongue: "Not because more than one simple semblance was in the Living Light wherein I was gazing, which ever is such as it was before; but through my sight, which was growing strong in me as I looked, one sole appearance, even as I changed, was altering itself to me. Within the profound and shining subsistence of the lofty Light appeared to me three circles of three colors and one magnitude; and one seemed reflected by the other, as rainbow by rainbow, and the third seemed fire breathed forth equally from the one and the other. O how scant is speech, and how feeble to my conception!"[21] Speech is unable to contain the abundance of what he sees. Vision exceeds language, for there is more to Dante's experience of the world than what he can put into words. Not everything is reducible to the syllables of our language.

Admitting this inability, Dante still soldiers on in his impossible description, now placing emphasis on the inner closure or circularity of the divine: "This, to what I saw, is such that it is not enough to call it little. O Light Eternal, who alone abidest in Thyself"—a divinity caught within itself and self-contained—"alone knowest Thyself, and, known to Thyself and knowing, lovest and smilest on Thyself!"[22] The words keep repeating and falling back on themselves to convey the idea of the self-enclosed nature of God, the result of which is that there is always something that escapes Dante's grasp here. For all of the diffusiveness of God in the creation there is an element of the divine that is absolutely self-transcendent, that transcends itself completely.

Dante is awed by this image of the divinity, aware of its unknowability, and yet he manages to find a way to relate to it. He says, "That circling which, thus begotten, appeared in Thee as reflected light, when my eyes had dwelt on it for a time, seemed to me depicted with our image within itself and in its own color."[23] It is important to note that he doesn't say "my image." His is a poem, therefore, that seems to want to retrieve the commonality of the human likeness that we all share. What he sees is the Incarnation, the human image within God, because in God there is also the human. We are creations of God, created in His image, so therefore there's also something human within the divine.

And then Dante continues, "As is the geometer who wholly applies himself to measure the circle, and finds not, in pondering, the principle of which he is in need, such was I at that new sight. I wished to see how the image conformed to the circle and how it has its place therein; but my own wings were not sufficient for that, save that my mind was smitten by a flash wherein its wish came to it. Here power failed the lofty phantasy."[24] The first part of this passage references a famous mathematical surd in the Middle Ages, meaning one of the impossible paradoxes involving questions like how one squares a circle, and medieval geometers spent much time reflecting on these concerns. The science of measurement stumbles against this paradox that the geometer posits and it fails. So, from science Dante moves to fantasy. Fantasy here is the highest form of the imagination, with which almost anything is usually possible, and yet it too fails here.

However, the poem ends on a more positive note than all these failings would suggest: "But already my desire and my will were revolved, like a wheel that is evenly moved, by the Love which moves the sun and the other stars."[25] Dante is finally coming to understand the Prime Mover, not the way he did at the beginning of *Paradiso* 1, but as Love. The Aristotelian-Thomistic definition of God as simply the Prime Mover seemed to have a limitation for Dante, since the Prime Mover moves the universe, and that act somehow simultaneously disengages Him from it. Now Dante sees that primal motion as a motion of love, the universe as a universe of love, with God, who transcends and yet is part of the world, holding it together and preventing it from falling apart. His power of love prevents chaos; it moves the sun and the stars and all things, but it is also the only stable thing, the only thing that makes it all cohere.

Of course, *love* is not the only word that matters at the end of the poem. This canticle, like the first two, ends with the word *stars*. Dante uses the same word symmetrically at the end of *Inferno* and at the end of *Purgatorio*. So when Dante says that love moves the sun and the other stars, what he's really doing is placing himself immediately right back on earth, back at the beginning of his quest. He's here with us looking up at the stars. It's the line that allows him to shift away from the moment of this vision that he has, a vision that is ultimately the vision of the Incarnation. All he sees, all he remembers, is our own likeness among the stars, and then he comes back down to earth. And the line also means that Dante places himself back in *Inferno* 1, allowing for the story of the poem to begin again and to be written.

We have been reading an account of the experience of a pilgrim who goes from the dark wood to the beatific vision and then comes back to tell us about it. But we are now also discovering, thanks to the circularity of the poem, that by the end of the poem Dante is telling us that only now is his journey really starting. The real journey was the poem itself we have finished reading and are invited to read again. By that last line, we are caught in the circle of Dante's telling, in the drama of Dante's story. It's a witty way for Dante to say that this poem will hold you, that it's meant to hold you in its spell, the poem endlessly revolving between the story of a journey and a journey in itself, beautifully mirroring the ceaseless movement of the sun and the other stars.

Notes

CHAPTER 2
Vita Nuova

1. Dante Alighieri, *Vita nuova,* trans., with an essay by Mark Musa (Bloomington: Indiana University Press, 1973), 3.
2. Ibid., 86.
3. Ibid., 3–4.
4. Ibid., 6.
5. Ibid., 32.
6. Ibid., 37–38.
7. Ibid., 57.
8. Ibid., 83.
9. Ibid., 85.

CHAPTER 3
Inferno 1–4

1. Dante Alighieri, *The Divine Comedy: Inferno,* trans., with a commentary by Charles S. Singleton (Princeton, N.J.: Princeton University Press, 1989), 3–5.
2. Ibid., 3.
3. Ibid., 5.
4. Ibid.
5. Ibid., 7.
6. Ibid.
7. Ibid., 9.
8. Ibid., 11.
9. Ibid., 13–15.
10. Ibid., 15.
11. Ibid., 27.
12. Ibid., 33.
13. Ibid., 39–41.
14. Ibid., 41.
15. Ibid.
16. Ibid., 43.

CHAPTER 4
Inferno 5–7

1. Dante Alighieri, *The Divine Comedy: Inferno,* trans., with a commentary by Charles S. Singleton (Princeton, N.J.: Princeton University Press, 1989), 49–51.
2. Ibid., 51.

3. Ibid.
4. Ibid.
5. Ibid., 51–53.
6. Ibid., 53.
7. Ibid.
8. Ibid.
9. Dante Alighieri, *Vita nuova,* trans., with an essay by Mark Musa (Bloomington: Indiana University Press, 1973), 37–38.
10. *Inferno,* 55–57.
11. Ibid., 59.
12. Ibid., 61.
13. Ibid., 61–63.
14. Ibid., 63.
15. Ibid., 63–65.
16. Ibid., 73–75.

CHAPTER 5
Inferno 9–11

1. Dante Alighieri, *The Divine Comedy: Inferno,* trans., with a commentary by Charles S. Singleton (Princeton, N.J.: Princeton University Press, 1989), 93.
2. Ibid.
3. Augustine, *The Confessions,* trans. Edward B. Pusey (New York: Collier Books, 1961), 87–88.
4. *Inferno,* 99.
5. Ibid.
6. Ibid., 101.
7. Ibid., 103.
8. Ibid.
9. Ibid., 115–17.

CHAPTER 6
Inferno 12–16

1. Dante Alighieri, *The Divine Comedy: Inferno,* trans., with a commentary by Charles S. Singleton (Princeton, N.J.: Princeton University Press, 1989), 129.
2. Ibid., 129.
3. Ibid., 129–31.
4. Ibid., 131–33.
5. Ibid., 133.
6. Ibid.
7. Ibid.
8. Ibid.
9. Ibid.
10. Ibid., 153.
11. Ibid., 153–55.

12. Ibid., 155.
13. Ibid., 155–57.
14. Ibid., 157.
15. Ibid., 157–59.
16. Ibid., 159–61.
17. Ibid., 171.

CHAPTER 7
Inferno 17–26

1. Dante Alighieri, *The Divine Comedy: Inferno,* trans., with a commentary by Charles S. Singleton (Princeton, N.J.: Princeton University Press, 1989), 193.
2. Ibid., 193–95.
3. Ibid., 195.
4. Ibid., 195–97.
5. Ibid., 197–99.
6. Ibid., 265.
7. Ibid.
8. Ibid., 271.
9. Ibid., 273.
10. Ibid.
11. Ibid., 275.
12. Ibid.
13. Ibid., 277.
14. Ibid., 277–79.
15. Ibid., 279.

CHAPTER 8
Inferno 27–29

1. Dante Alighieri, *The Divine Comedy: Inferno,* trans., with a commentary by Charles S. Singleton (Princeton, N.J.: Princeton University Press, 1989), 283.
2. Ibid., 285.
3. Ibid., 287.
4. Ibid.
5. Ibid., 289.
6. Ibid.
7. Ibid., 289–91.
8. Ibid., 293–95.
9. Ibid., 301.
10. Ibid.
11. Ibid., 303.
12. Ibid., 305.
13. Ibid., 307.

CHAPTER 9
Inferno 30–34

1. Dante Alighieri, *The Divine Comedy: Inferno*, trans., with a commentary by Charles S. Singleton (Princeton, N.J.: Princeton University Press, 1989), 315.
2. Ibid., 331–33.
3. Ibid., 339.
4. Ibid., 347.
5. Ibid., 349.
6. Ibid.
7. Ibid., 351–53.
8. Ibid., 353.
9. Ibid.
10. Ibid., 355.
11. Ibid.
12. Ibid., 369.

CHAPTER 10
Purgatorio 1–2

1. Dante Alighieri, *The Divine Comedy: Purgatorio*, trans., with a commentary by Charles S. Singleton (Princeton, N.J.: Princeton University Press, 1991), 3.
2. Ibid., 3–5.
3. Ibid., 5.
4. Ibid., 7–9.
5. Ibid., 11.
6. Ibid.
7. Ibid., 13.
8. Ibid., 15.
9. Ibid., 17.
10. Ibid., 19–21.
11. Ibid., 21.
12. Ibid.

CHAPTER 11
Purgatorio 5–10

1. Dante Alighieri, *The Divine Comedy: Purgatorio*, trans., with a commentary by Charles S. Singleton (Princeton, N.J.: Princeton University Press, 1991), 51.
2. Ibid.
3. Ibid., 53.
4. Ibid., 55.
5. Ibid., 59–61.
6. Ibid., 63.
7. Ibid., 99.
8. Ibid., 99–101.
9. Ibid., 101.

10. Ibid.
11. Ibid.
12. Ibid., 101–3.
13. Ibid., 103.
14. Ibid., 103–5.
15. Ibid., 105.
16. Ibid., 107.
17. Ibid.
18. Ibid.

CHAPTER 12
Purgatorio 11–17

1. Dante Alighieri, *The Divine Comedy: Purgatorio,* trans., with a commentary by Charles S. Singleton (Princeton, N.J.: Princeton University Press, 1991), 109.
2. Ibid., 115.
3. Ibid., 125.
4. Ibid., 159.
5. Ibid., 167–71.
6. Ibid., 171–73.
7. Ibid., 173.
8. Ibid., 173–75.
9. Ibid., 179.
10. Ibid.
11. Ibid., 185.

CHAPTER 13
Purgatorio 18–22

1. Dante Alighieri, *The Divine Comedy: Purgatorio,* trans., with a commentary by Charles S. Singleton (Princeton, N.J.: Princeton University Press, 1991), 189.
2. Ibid., 191.
3. Ibid., 191–93.
4. Ibid., 199.
5. Ibid., 201–3.
6. Ibid., 229.
7. Ibid., 231.
8. Ibid., 233.
9. Ibid., 237.
10. Ibid.
11. Ibid., 239.
12. Ibid.
13. Ibid.

CHAPTER 14
Purgatorio 24–26

1. Dante Alighieri, *The Divine Comedy: Purgatorio,* trans., with a commentary by Charles S. Singleton (Princeton, N.J.: Princeton University Press, 1991), 261.
2. Ibid., 273.
3. Ibid., 285.
4. Ibid., 288.

CHAPTER 15
Purgatorio 27–33

1. Dante Alighieri, *The Divine Comedy: Purgatorio,* trans., with a commentary by Charles S. Singleton (Princeton, N.J.: Princeton University Press, 1991), 299.
2. Ibid.
3. Ibid.
4. Ibid., 301.
5. Ibid., 303–5.
6. Ibid., 305.
7. Ibid., 307.
8. Ibid., 313.
9. Ibid., 327–29.
10. Ibid., 329.
11. Ibid., 329–31.
12. Ibid., 331.
13. Ibid., 341.
14. Ibid., 365–67.
15. Ibid., 373.

CHAPTER 16
Paradiso 1–2

1. Dante Alighieri, *The Divine Comedy: Paradiso,* trans., with a commentary by Charles S. Singleton (Princeton, N.J.: Princeton University Press, 1991), 3.
2. Ibid.; emphasis mine.
3. Ibid.
4. Ibid.
5. Ibid., 3–5.
6. Ibid., 7.
7. Ibid.
8. Ibid., 9.
9. Ibid.
10. Ibid., 9–11.
11. Ibid., 15.
12. Ibid.

CHAPTER 17
Paradiso 3–10

1. Dante Alighieri, *The Divine Comedy: Paradiso,* trans., with a commentary by Charles S. Singleton (Princeton, N.J.: Princeton University Press, 1991), 37.
2. Ibid., 39.
3. Ibid.
4. Ibid.
5. Ibid.
6. Ibid., 41.
7. Ibid.
8. Ibid., 59.
9. Ibid., 61.
10. Ibid., 65–67.
11. Ibid., 67–69.
12. Ibid., 107.
13. Pseudo-Dionysius, *Pseudo-Dionysius: The Complete Works,* ed. Colm Luibhéid (Mahwah, N.J.: Paulist Press, 1987), 72.
14. *Paradiso,* 113–15.
15. Ibid., 115.
16. Ibid., 117.

CHAPTER 18
Paradiso 11–12

1. Dante Alighieri, *The Divine Comedy: Paradiso,* trans., with a commentary by Charles S. Singleton (Princeton, N.J.: Princeton University Press, 1991), 137–39.
2. Ibid., 119.
3. Ibid., 121.
4. Ibid.
5. Ibid., 123.
6. Ibid., 123–25.
7. Ibid., 125.
8. Ibid., 131–33.
9. Ibid., 133.
10. Ibid., 133–35.

CHAPTER 19
Paradiso 15–17

1. Dante Alighieri, *The Divine Comedy: Paradiso,* trans., with a commentary by Charles S. Singleton (Princeton, N.J.: Princeton University Press, 1991), 163–65.
2. Ibid., 187.
3. Ibid., 189.
4. Ibid., 189–91.
5. Ibid., 167–69.
6. Ibid., 169.

7. Ibid., 177.
8. Ibid., 179.
9. Ibid., 191.
10. Ibid.
11. Ibid., 191–93.
12. Ibid., 193–97.

CHAPTER 20
Paradiso 18–22

1. Dante Alighieri, *The Divine Comedy: Paradiso,* trans., with a commentary by Charles S. Singleton (Princeton, N.J.: Princeton University Press, 1991), 215.
2. Ibid., 203.
3. Ibid., 205.
4. Ibid., 211.
5. Ibid., 211–13.
6. Ibid., 215.
7. Ibid., 217–19.
8. Ibid., 233.
9. Ibid., 253.
10. Ibid., 253–55.
11. Ibid., 255.

CHAPTER 21
Paradiso 24–26

1. Dante Alighieri, *The Divine Comedy: Paradiso,* trans., with a commentary by Charles S. Singleton (Princeton, N.J.: Princeton University Press, 1991), 267.
2. Ibid., 269.
3. Ibid., 269–71.
4. Ibid., 271.
5. Ibid.
6. Ibid., 273.
7. Ibid., 279.
8. Ibid., 281–83.
9. Ibid., 295.
10. Ibid., 297.
11. Ibid.
12. Ibid.

CHAPTER 22
Paradiso 27–29

1. Dante Alighieri, *The Divine Comedy: Paradiso,* trans., with a commentary by Charles S. Singleton (Princeton, N.J.: Princeton University Press, 1991), 303–5.
2. Ibid., 307.

3. Ibid.
4. Ibid., 307–9.
5. Ibid., 309.
6. Ibid.
7. Ibid., 313.
8. Ibid., 321.
9. Ibid., 323.
10. Ibid.
11. Ibid., 325.
12. Ibid.

CHAPTER 23
Paradiso 30–33

1. Dante Alighieri, *The Divine Comedy: Paradiso,* trans., with a commentary by Charles S. Singleton (Princeton, N.J.: Princeton University Press, 1991), 343.
2. Ibid.
3. Ibid.
4. Ibid.
5. Ibid.
6. Ibid., 349–51.
7. Ibid., 351–53.
8. Ibid., 353–55.
9. Ibid., 371.
10. Ibid.
11. Ibid., 373.
12. Ibid.
13. Ibid., 373–75.
14. Ibid., 375.
15. Ibid.
16. Ibid.
17. Ibid.
18. Ibid., 377.
19. Ibid.
20. Ibid.
21. Ibid., 377–79.
22. Ibid., 379.
23. Ibid.
24. Ibid., 379–81.
25. Ibid., 381.

Index